UNCERTAINTY IN ECONOMICS
AND OTHER REFLECTIONS

To
G. PATRICK MEREDITH

UNCERTAINTY IN ECONOMICS
AND OTHER REFLECTIONS

BY

G. L. S. SHACKLE

Brunner Professor of Economic Science in
the University of Liverpool

CAMBRIDGE
AT THE UNIVERSITY PRESS
1955
REPRINTED
1968

CAMBRIDGE UNIVERSITY PRESS
Cambridge, New York, Melbourne, Madrid, Cape Town, Singapore,
São Paulo, Delhi, Dubai, Tokyo, Mexico City

Cambridge University Press
The Edinburgh Building, Cambridge CB2 8RU, UK

Published in the United States of America by Cambridge University Press, New York

www.cambridge.org
Information on this title: www.cambridge.org/9780521153317

First published 1955
Reprinted 1968
First paperback printing 2010

A catalogue record for this publication is available from the British Library

Library of Congress Catalogue Card Number: 55–14744

ISBN 978-0-521-07397-4 Hardback
ISBN 978-0-521-15331-7 Paperback

CONTENTS

PART IV. ON THE PHILOSOPHY OF ECONOMICS

PREFACE

The strand of thought which links these essays is the nature and effects of uncertain expectation. But only the first of the four parts of this book is concerned with the evolution since 1949 of the ideas which I then put forward in *Expectation in Economics*. The first essay of all is an attempt to express those ideas without any technical apparatus of diagrams or mathematical notation. Of the three cardinal ideas which constitute my theory of expectation, the most difficult to explain has proved to be that of potential surprise. This difficulty appeared with especial vividness when I was honoured by an invitation to take part in the Colloquium on the Theory of Risk in Econometrics held at the Sorbonne in May 1952. Amongst the other members of the Colloquium I found only three who seemed able to place themselves at my viewpoint, Professor Kenneth Arrow, M. Pierre Massé and Professor Herman Wold. It was the last-named whose profound and sympathetic examination of my approach mainly inspired me to try to make still clearer its point and purpose, and to express more systematically my objections to the use of probability as a means of analysing and describing a mental state of uncertainty, and my grounds for claiming that the difficulties could be resolved by the concept of potential surprise. The occasion for this attempt was provided by the invitation to deliver a Special University Lecture at the University of London in October 1952, and this lecture is here reprinted as the second essay of Part I. The editor of *Metroeconomica*, Professor Eraldo Fossati (to whom I feel the warmest gratitude for great and repeated kindness), having published what appear here as Essays I and II, then asked me to complete the restatement of my ideas by writing Essay III. Essay IV seeks to push the analysis of the nature of expectation a step further, in one direction, than was done in *Expectation in Economics*. Essays V, VI and VII were written in the effort to get those elements of my theory, which critics found hardest to assimilate, understood and accepted. The last two essays of Part I seek to make the theory a means of stating, if no more, the problem of profit in a form which is not stultified by failure to distinguish between past and future.

I believe that those readers who turn to this Part I as an exegesis and development of the argument of *Expectation in Economics* will be indulgent to some inevitable repetition which arises from the circumstances in which the essays were written.

Part II of this book is concerned with the theory of interest-rates. An easy answer to the question 'Why should interest exist?' is that goods available at different times are different goods no matter how nearly identical they may be in all other respects, and therefore it is natural that they should be able to exchange for one another at prices differing from that of an ounce for an ounce, or a shilling for a shilling. But this answer neglects the fact that in comparing an object A available at date 1 with an object B available at date 2, we do not look at object A at date 1 and then transfer ourselves to date 2 in order to consider object B. The decision between them must be made at a single date, and in fact if it is to merit the name of *decision* it must be made neither later nor earlier than the moment immediately preceding date 1. Thus what is compared is not A and B, but the imagined satisfactions obtainable from A and B, after allowing for the inescapable doubt concerning the reality of the prospect of B. No man by any precaution or ingenuity can guarantee to himself the exact realization of an imagined future satisfaction. Uncertainty must therefore, as Lord Keynes was the first to show us, be one of the main explanations of interest. But this proposition is only the first step towards the construction of a theory. Expectations are inexpressibly tricky and elusive material. For *stability* of interest-rates we have to postulate two 'camps' of divergent opinion, the Bulls and Bears of the *Treatise on Money*. But this again is not sufficient, for as I tried to show in my earlier book (on the business cycle) called *Expectation, Investment and Income*,* the long-term interest-rate must be looked on as an 'inherently restless variable'. I have not here developed that line of thought any further, but in Essay X I have tried to present in a fresh way the general notion that in a modern Western economy interest is mainly a manifestation, not of impatience nor of the higher technical productivity of roundabout methods of production, but of uncertainty. But the endeavour to re-examine from the beginning the whole question of the cause and nature of interest, which resulted in this essay, threw up one by-product to which I would draw the reader's attention, namely, the related concepts of possessor-satisfaction and the decision-interval.

The 'classical' theory, according to which interest is the price which equates the supply and demand of real resources for investment,

* Oxford, 1938, pp. 52, 53.

was able at one blow to explain both the causes and the consequences of interest-rate changes. But the uncertainty or liquidity-
preference theory of the origin of interest leaves us to deal separately
with its effects on the pace of investment. Here the main problem is
to reconcile the conclusions of theory with the testimony of business
men, who have appeared to deny to interest the role and importance,
in the calculations upon which they base their investment-decisions,
which theory suggests that it ought to have. Here again the explanation seems to be that the effect of a fall (for example) in the long-
term interest-rate in raising the 'present value' of durable equipment,
and the consequent stimulus given to the making of such equipment,
is overwhelmed and rendered negligible by the uncertainty regarding
the size or even the algebraic sign of those future profits upon which
the 'present value' depends. It still seems undeniable, however, that
interest-rate changes must sensibly affect the apparent profitability
of constructing those types of equipment, such as buildings and civil
engineering works, which may be deemed a secure source of profit
or valuable services for several decades ahead. Yet it is by no means
true in general that a given change in the interest-rate used for discounting all future net earnings of such assets will have its greatest
absolute effect on the present value of those instalments of such
earnings which are most distant in time. If all such instalments are
taken to be equal, the effect will in fact be greatest for those instalments whose futurity in years is the reciprocal of the annual interest.
This is very easily proved, but so far as I am aware it had not been
pointed out before the appearance of Essay XI in the *Economic Journal*
of March 1946.

If Lord Keynes had rewritten the *General Theory* after two or
three years, it seems possible that he would have made some use of
Myrdal's scheme of thought centred on the *ex ante–ex post* distinction.
Keynes had emancipated himself from the classical economists'
assumptions, but not from their static, non-expectational mode of
thinking; yet the dominant theme of his book is that 'A monetary
economy...is essentially one in which changing views about the
future are capable of influencing the quantity of employment and
not merely its direction'.* The whole emphasis of the book is on the
essential importance of expectations, yet the formal frame of concepts
is quite unsuited to that purpose. One part of the argument in
particular is crippled and confused by the lack of an explicit termin-

* *The General Theory of Employment, Interest and Money* (London, 1936), p. vii.

ology for distinguishing from each other quantities which are contingent, conjectural and plural because they refer to the future, and quantities belonging to the same economic context which, however, are known and unique because they belong to the past. This is the multiplier and the consumption function. Here consumption is said to depend on income and income on net investment and the propensity to consume, and we are offered the familiar concept of the simultaneous mutual determination of several variables. For a 'static' argument this is perfectly well, indeed it is, of course, the basis and essential principle of static analysis. But for an expectational analysis it is disastrous. What is that income in view of which consumption-spending is decided? Is it the realized income of a past period? Then, of course, we are abandoning the comparative statics framework in favour of period analysis. Or is it the expected income of the same period for which the consumption-spending is being decided? Then what happens if the realized income of that period, which will be partly governed by the consumption-spending, turns out to differ from the expected income which governed the consumption-spending? Some such difficulty, I think, must have been the source of the controversy which the multiplier idea aroused. In Essays XII and XIII I seek to disentangle the matter by using Myrdal's concepts.

Essay XIV is an attempt to distil the essence of that very difficult book in which the *ex ante–ex post* scheme of thought was first introduced. Myrdal's essay appeared first in Swedish in 1931 and then in German in 1933. In neither of these forms was it really accessible to English-speaking economists, and when at last it was translated into English the date was 1939, and a book which would have been a sensation before 1936 was hardly noticed. This book, *Monetary Equilibrium*,* is none the less a classic, and the justice of time will give it an honoured place alongside Wicksell's *Geldzins und Guterpreise* in the chief literature of economic dynamics.

Essay XV, which suggests a system of criteria for assessing the effects of Budgetary policies on price-levels, stands a little aside from the main concerns of Part III.

And lastly, Part IV. Some economists are content to work at particular problems without considering at all how their subject fits into the general body of knowledge and philosophical speculation; they would think it a waste of effort to ask themselves what we are doing when we create theories or offer explanations, and they would

* Hodge, 1939.

be impatient with anyone who suggested, for example, that an analysis of the meanings of the word 'time', and the role of various concepts which come under this heading, is any concern of the economist. But the philosophy of our business is far from being a side issue. When the claim is made by some, expressly or implicitly, that the way is now open for the economist to become a prophet and peer with assurance into distant years, or even to tell us within a few percentage points what the chief features of the situation will be in twelve months' time, it is clear that the most profound questions of the nature of human existence are not irrelevant to the economist's most practical duties and concerns.

G. L. S. SHACKLE

October 1954

AUTHOR'S NOTE FOR C.U.P.L.E. REPRINT

When plural rival hypotheses are entertained concerning some question, but it is recognised that the existing list of such hypotheses cannot be known to be exhaustive, and may even be by its nature indefinitely extensible, the use of probability to express the adjudged claim of any one such hypothesis to be taken seriously seems inappropriate. The properties of a non-distributional uncertainty variable to serve this purpose were suggested in a series of publications, including the *Economic Journal* 1939, *Oxford Economic Papers,* First Series No. 6, 1942, and *Expectation in Economics,* (Cambridge University Press, 1949 and 1952). The present volume contains some further expository approaches, theoretical extensions and special applications. The role of uncertainty in determining the essential nature of some central economic phenomena, including profit, the interest-rate and the effects of money, is also here explored. The whole theme was presented as a strand in a more general skein of ideas in my *Decision, Order and Time in Human Affairs* (Cambridge University Press, 1961) where a bibliography lists chapters and articles by other writers in which these suggestions have been extensively criticised and discussed.

G. L. S. SHACKLE

17 April 1968

ACKNOWLEDGEMENTS

I should scarcely have felt it excusable to add further, in Part I of this book, to the material already presented in the two editions of *Expectation in Economics*, had it not been for the continually repeated experience of meeting in person, or receiving letters from, economists and other scholars in many countries who have expressed in the kindest terms an interest in these ideas. I take this opportunity of expressing the warmest gratitude to those who have given this greatly valued encouragement, among them the following:

Monsieur Hubert Brochier of the University of Grenoble; Professor A. J. Brown of the University of Leeds; Mr Harald Dickson of the School of Forestry, Stockholm; Mr David C. Duncan of the National Institute of Industrial Psychology, London; Mr R. A. D. Egerton of the Queen's University, Belfast; Mr L. F. Emblem of the American University, Cairo; Mr S. H. Frowein, Assistant Editor, *The Bankers' Magazine*; Mr Bent Hansen of the University of Uppsala; Mr Hugo Hegeland of the University of Lund; Professor W. A. Jöhr of the Commercial University, St Gallen; Professor Erik Lindahl of the University of Uppsala; Professor Erik Lundberg of the University of Stockholm; Professor A. L. Macfie of the University of Glasgow; Mr A. T. Peacock of the London School of Economics; Professor Jürg Niehans of the University of Zurich; Professor Tord Palander of the University of Uppsala; Mr J. Pen of the Ministerie van Ekonomische Zaken, 'S-Gravenhage; Professor K. W. Rothschild of Oesterreichisches Institut für Wirtschaftsforsschung, Wien; Mr Paul Streeten of Balliol College, Oxford; Professor Ingvar Svennilson of the University of Stockholm; Professor V. Wagner of the University of Basel; Mr R. S. Weckstein of New York University.

At the 1953 meeting of the British Association for the Advancement of Science, part of the proceedings of Section F was a symposium on 'Uncertainty and Business Decisions', and I owe a very special debt for fresh insights and constructive criticism to those contributors to this colloquium who took *Expectation in Economics* as the text of their analyses. In this connection I wish especially to thank Professor W. B. Gallie, Professor of Philosophy in the Queen's University, Belfast; Professor D. J. O'Connor, Professor of Philosophy in the University of Liverpool; Professor G. P. Meredith, Professor of Psychology in the University of Leeds; and Professor B. R. Williams of the University College of North Staffordshire; as well as those other economists and mathematicians whom I have tried to thank elsewhere.

I wish to thank the editors of the journals where the essays in this book, except the last in the book, were originally published, for the permission which they have given for these essays to be reprinted. For permission to reprint that last essay I wish to thank the Committee of the University Press of Liverpool. The articles are listed below in order of the dates of their first appearance:

The multiplier in closed and open systems, *Oxford Economic Papers*, old series, no. 2 (1939).

Myrdal's analysis of monetary equilibrium, *Oxford Economic Papers*, old series, no. 7 (1945).

Interest-rates and the pace of investment, *Economic Journal*, vol. LVI (1946).

The deflative or inflative tendency of Government receipts and disbursements, *Oxford Economic Papers*, old series, no. 8 (1947).

The nature of interest-rates, *Oxford Economic Papers*, new series, vol. I (1949).

Probability and uncertainty, *Metroeconomica*, vol. I (1949).

Expectation in Economics: some critics answered, *Economica*, vol. XVI (1949).

A non-additive measure of uncertainty, *Review of Economic Studies*, vol. XVII (1) (1949–50).

Three versions of the ϕ-surface: some notes for a comparison, *Review of Economic Studies*, vol. XVIII (2) (1950–1).

Twenty years on: a survey of the theory of the multiplier, *Economic Journal*, vol. LXI (1951).

The nature and role of profit, *Metroeconomica*, vol. III (1951).

On the meaning and measure of uncertainty: I. *Metroeconomica*, vol. IV (1952).

On the meaning and measure of uncertainty: II, *Metroeconomica*, vol. V (1953).

A chart of economic theory, *Metroeconomica*, vol. V (1953).

The logic of surprise, *Economica*, vol. XX (1953).

The economist's view of profit, *The Company Accountant*, new series, no. 26 (1953).

Economics and sincerity, *Oxford Economic Papers*, new series, vol. V (1953).

What makes an economist? Liverpool University Press, 1953.

I wish, finally, to thank the staff of the Cambridge University Press for the endless care, skill and resource which they have lavished upon this book.

G. L. S. SHACKLE

October 1954

BIBLIOGRAPHY

The following is a list of books and articles in which the system of ideas proposed in my *Expectation in Economics*, and further treated in the essays of Part I of this book, have been discussed or applied:

A. BOOKS

TITLE	AUTHOR	PUBLISHER	DATE	CHAPTER, ETC.
A Survey of Contemporary Economics (volume II, edited by B. F. Haley)	Andreas G. Papandreou	Richard D. Irwin, Homewood, Illinois, U.S.A.	1952	Ch. 5
Die Konjunkturschwankungen	Walter Adolf Jöhr	J. C. B. Mohr, Tübingen	1952	Ch. 10
An Essay in the Theory of Profits and Income Distribution	B. S. Keirstead	Basil Blackwell, Oxford	1953	Ch. 3
Uncertainty and Business Decisions (edited by C. F. Carter, G. P. Meredith and G. L. S. Shackle)	W. B. Gallie, D. J. O'Connor, G. P. Meredith, C. F. Carter, B. R. Williams	Liverpool University Press	1954	Chs. 1, 2, 4, 5, 6, 8

B. ARTICLES

TITLE	AUTHOR	JOURNAL	VOLUME	NO.	DATE
Expectation in economics	C. F. Carter	*Economic Journal*	LX	237	Mar. 1950
Ovisshetens roll i ekonomisk planering	Harald Dickson	*Ekonomisk Tidskrift*	LII	[2]	June 1950
A study in expectations {Part I / Part II	J. Mars	*Yorkshire Bulletin of Economic and Social Research*	{2 / 3	[2] / [1]	July 1950 / Feb. 1951
A 3-dimensional model of the Shackle ϕ-surface	Harry G. Johnson	*Review of Economic Studies*	XVIII	46	1950–1
Alternative approaches to the theory of choice in risk-taking situations	Kenneth J. Arrow	*Econometrica*	19	[4]	Oct. 1951
Profitti, aspetative e impresa	B. S. Keirstead	*Economia Internazionale*	IV	[4]	Nov. 1951
Subjective probability and the economist	J. D. Sargan	*Yorkshire Bulletin of Economic and Social Research*	V	[1]	Feb. 1953
On the use of the theory of probability in economics	R. S. Weckstein	*Review of Economic Studies*	XX	53	1952–3
Expectations and economic stability	Melvin D. Brockie	*Weltwirtschaftliches Archiv*	70	[1]	1953
A revised theory of expectations	C. F. Carter	*Economic Journal*	LXIII	252	Dec. 1953
Shackle's ϕ-function and gambler indifference-map	B. R. Williams	*Metroeconomica*	VI	[3]	Dec. 1954
Investment, uncertainty and expectations	R. A. D. Egerton	*Review of Economic Studies*	XXII	[2]	Feb. 1955
Shackle's theory of expectation and the level of aspiration	David C. Duncan	[In the press]			
Expectation, surprise, and the theory of choice	W. E. Armstrong	[In the press]			

PART I

ON EXPECTATION AND UNCERTAINTY

PROBABILITY AND UNCERTAINTY*

In his novel *The Widows of the Magistrate*, Keith West tells how certain
Chinese officials once plotted rebellion against their Emperor. The
brief passage that I am going to reproduce describes the thoughts
of a certain sentry, who had to decide whether to obey his immediate
superior, the treacherous Captain of the Guard, or to stand alone
against the rebels in loyal defence of the Emperor's representative,
the Lady Hibiscus:

> In the room above, where the great drum stood, the sentry named
> Kwong Hui was testing the stacked bows of mulberry wood and setting
> the arrows in order.
>
> 'I am a man who seizes opportunity', he told the admiring women and
> the sleeping children.
>
> 'If I obey the Captain of the Guard, two things may happen. Either
> the rebellion succeeds, and I remain a soldier in the guard, or the rebellion
> fails, when I lose my head. Whereas if I obey the Lady Hibiscus, two
> things may happen. Either the rebellion succeeds, and I lose my head,
> or the rebellion fails, when I shall receive rewards quite beyond my
> imagination to conceive. Now of these four possibilities, the last only
> attracts me. So I shall strive to hold this tower unentered, as long as is
> possible, until the arrival of help from elsewhere. That is the course of
> wisdom, as well as the course of courage, and I am deficient in neither
> wisdom nor courage.'

This eminently wise and sensible decision, reached with such
incisive logic, might not have been so readily attained had the sentry
been acquainted with the theory of probability. For then he might
have argued thus: 'I find in the record of history a thousand cases
similar to my own, wherein the person concerned decided upon
treachery, and in only four hundred of these cases the rebellion failed
and he was beheaded. On balance, therefore, the advantage seems
to lie with treachery, provided one does it often enough.'

Having one's head cut off is, for the person concerned, rather final.
Had the sentry decided to support the rebellion, he might have had
time, just before the axe fell, to reflect that he would never, in fact,
be able to repeat his experiment a thousand times, and that thus the
guidance given him by actuarial considerations had proved illusory.

* *Metroeconomica*, vol. 1 (1949), pp. 161–73. Trieste.

When some kind of performance, such as the tossing of a coin or the throwing of a pair of dice, has been many times repeated in suitably uniform circumstances, we can establish for each possible result of such performance the approximate number of times it will occur in a given number of repetitions of the performance. If then some value is assigned to each possible result, so that with a tossed coin we count, for example, a head as worth 1 and a tail as worth 0, or with dice we value any throw by the number appearing on the upper faces of the dice, and if for each possible result we multiply its valuation by the number of times it will occur in some suitably large number of repetitions of the performance, we shall get a valuation of this series of performances considered as a whole. Provided our frequency-ratios are correct (it will be remembered that we have postulated 'suitably uniform' circumstances and a 'large' number of repetitions: I do not propose here to probe further into these terms), this valuation of the series of performances considered as a whole has nothing whatever to do with ignorance or uncertainty: it is knowledge. If each of the possible courses of action open to me in some situation consists in such a series of performances, and if the values assigned to various possible outcomes of any one type of performance properly reflect my tastes, then my choice can fall without hesitation on that series whose valuation is highest.

What conditions must be satisfied in order that this sort of knowledge may be applied when an individual decision-maker is faced with a choice (as every one of us is, every day and every hour) between a number of rival courses of action? The conditions can be epitomized by two statements:

(1) The frequency-ratios, unless derived *a priori*, must have been obtained from a set of performances sufficiently uniform and sufficiently numerous. This condition may be satisfied in varying degrees and will accordingly give answers of varying precision. We must notice that the experience or the set of performances from which the frequency-ratios are obtained need not have been suffered or made by the person who proposes to use the knowledge.

(2) The experiment, to the valuation of whose outcome the frequency-ratios are to be applied, must be what I shall call a *divisible* experiment.

It is this second condition which, in a great and fundamentally important class of cases, cannot be satisfied. The first condition may often, of course, be only very poorly met, and the valuation assigned to an experiment will not then fully deserve to be called knowledge. True uncertainty will have entered; not because frequency-ratios find a place in the calculation, but, on the contrary, because the strict conditions which justify their use are absent. Sometimes, as when a new invention is to be exploited, it is impossible in the nature of things to get strictly relevant frequency-ratios. Still we must remember that other people's experience, gathered at many times and places, may be as good as a man's own for determining frequency-ratios, and the difficulty of obtaining them is the lesser strand in my argument. That argument is really concerned with the question whether and when frequency-ratios have meaning and applicability for a contemplated future experiment, and I want, therefore, to attempt a classification of experiments from this point of view.

When an experiment is such that its result will be obtained by adding together the results of a series of separate performances, and when these performances are going to be sufficiently uniform in their circumstances, and sufficiently numerous, for frequency-ratios derived from a past series of similar performances to be applied, I shall call the experiment, which consists in the totality of the contemplated series of performances considered all together as one whole, a *divisible* experiment. Now it is plain that not every experiment is divisible in this sense. But when confronted with a non-divisible experiment, can we not handle the difficulty by seeking other experiments sufficiently like this one, sufficiently numerous, and able to be all performed at dates near enough in future time to provide us with the bricks for building up a divisible experiment? Can we not, in other words, treat any non-divisible experiment, not as something having an importance in its own right, as a particular, individual event, but as a mere anonymous contribution to a series or aggregation of performances, a series essentially similar to the tossing of a coin a thousand times? Can we not, in brief, treat it as what I shall call a *seriable* trial? It is plain that the Chinese sentry would have come to grief had he relied on such a solution, and his case gives us a clue. It does not matter whose past experience we use as a source of frequency-ratios, but the fears and hopes attached to future experiments only concern us if these fears and hopes are our own, only if we ourselves are going to be the gainers or losers by those experiments. There are two ways in which this condition can be met: either a great number of people must agree in advance to pool the results of the experiments which they as individuals will separately make; or else each individual must be able to feel sure that he himself as potential gainer or loser will in fact be able to repeat his own experiment many times. The former method is called insurance, and its scope as we know is very far from covering all the contingencies of life. Nor should we wish it to do so if it could, for to insure against failure would, in this hard and competitive world, mean also insuring against success. The second method is logically excluded from all that type of cases which I shall call *crucial* experiments.

By a crucial experiment I mean one where the person concerned cannot exclude from his mind the possibility that the very act of performing the experiment may destroy for ever the circumstances in which it was performed. We must remember that an essential part of these circumstances is the individual's own stock of experience and mental attitude. This does not, indeed, prevent a given act from being many times performed by him in relevantly uniform external, objective circumstances, but it does prevent the significance for him of the separate performances being uniform, for in strictness it is plain that every single thing we do changes our stock of experience. Part of the satisfaction we get by imagination of any contemplated act is the thrill of its success, if that should come. But this thrill cannot be the same on any later occasion as it was the first time.

Such thoughts may seem far from the pedestrian objectivity of business. So let us turn to a crucialness arising in a different way. Some experiments, like a chess move, must by their nature, whatever their outcome, inevitably change the whole course of relevant future events for the individual. If I stake my whole capital on a scheme for gold-prospecting, I may win a fortune that will transform my whole attitude and objective situation, or I may lose everything, so that by the time I have built up fresh savings I shall be an older and a different man with different ideas living in a different world. A general who adopts one scheme of tactics in a critical battle cannot expect to have his opportunity presented again should things go wrong. If I choose the wrong career when I am young, I cannot be young again. A political party which adopts a given 'platform' in an election campaign has made a choice that may well turn the course of history; there can be no repetition in relevantly identical conditions.

Let me return once more to my borrowed parable of the sentry. Here was a case where the decision-maker could not feel sure that he would be prevented from repeating his experiment many times. Had he supported the rebellion, it might have succeeded, and so he might have lived to change his allegiance again and again as the tide of affairs suggested. But does this mean that he could have applied actuarial principles on the first or any other occasion when this choice between loyalty and treachery was presented? Plainly not. Frequency-ratios give us foreknowledge of the outcome of an experiment which is going to consist of the aggregation of many separate but similar acts. But this phrase 'is going to' puts us in danger of begging the whole question. The application of frequency-ratios only makes sense if the individual can feel sure that there will be many repetitions, that there will be a divisible experiment in which the immediate act, with which he is now concerned, will be swallowed up. Thus what we may call a 'contingently crucial' experiment, that is, an act which, for all the decision-maker can tell, can have the consequence of making further similar acts impossible for him, is for all practical purposes as crucial as one where the impossibility of repetition is logically certain.

A crucial or even contingently crucial experiment must be treated by the decision-maker as in effect unique and never-to-be-repeated. But even when an experiment is not such that repetition is logically impossible, the individual may believe that some of the circumstances which affect the result will change away from the state of affairs prevailing at his viewpoint and never be restored. Speculation in building-land in the hope of a great migration to a supposed new goldfield is perhaps an example. Such opportunities may recur only at intervals of decades. Even with such long intervals, however, you may think we ought not to use the word 'unique'. If so, let us speak of *isolated* experiments. When a man must look down a long vista of future years to find any prospect of repeating the experiment he is about to make, such distant possible repetitions must be discounted, not only because he can feel no assurance that he will really be able to make them, but also because it is not in human nature to see a distantly future event so vividly, to give it a significance as great, as a like event in the immediate future. Whether the lack of assurance and the lack of vividness are two facets of the same thing I am not sure. But if experiments spaced widely out in future time are, as it were, a rapidly convergent series, we cannot by taking them all together make a divisible experiment.

What we have achieved so far is the distinction between an experiment of the kind I have called divisible, whose outcome is the result of adding the outcomes of many separate performances all in certain respects uniform, and an experiment of the kind we may call non-divisible non-seriable, which, so far as the individual is concerned who stands to gain or lose by it, can be neither itself broken down into a number of uniform additive parts nor treated as part of a divisible experiment. Now it is plain, I think, that for a non-divisible non-seriable experiment no frequency-ratio can have any meaning or relevance. Perhaps it is not difficult to see why the opposite view has sometimes been held. When any one of the separate performances of which a divisible experiment is composed is considered by itself as an experiment in its own right, as a particular event which for the time being is thought of in isolation from other performances, so that we are interested in the result of this performance for its own sake and not merely as an unidentified drop in an aggregative ocean, then this performance is, by assumption, non-seriable, and there is plainly an overwhelming presumption that it is, in that case, also non-divisible (for if it consisted itself of a series of more elementary performances, why cannot this latter series be prolonged?). Let us agree that even an instance of the tossing of a coin, by a man who has been tossing the same coin steadily for hours and intends to continue, can be looked on in this light as a non-divisible non-seriable experiment. But there will be in such a case a temptation to confuse the particular, mentally isolated performance with the divisible experiment in which it could be included, and to treat the 'known' outcome of the latter as though it were a guide to that of the isolated performance. The fact that out of 600 throws a die has shown an ace 100 times tells us that out of 6000 throws it will show an ace about 1000 times. But what does it tell us about the *next* throw, the 601st? Suppose the captains in a Test Match have agreed that instead of tossing a coin for choice of innings they will decide the matter by this next throw of the die, and that if it shows an ace Australia shall bat first, if any other number, then England shall bat first. Can we now give any meaningful answer whatever to the question 'Who will bat first?' except 'We do not know'? For a non-divisible non-seriable experiment the concept of frequency-ratios is wholly irrelevant. Yet because a seriable performance, one which is going to be treated as a mere item contributing to a divisible experiment, resembles a non-divisible non-seriable experiment in the fact that we can hold a number of different hypotheses as to what its own outcome will be, and because, when each of these contingencies is given a valuation, the process of forecasting the valuation of the divisible experiment consists precisely in taking each of these hypotheses in turn, multiplying its valuation by a frequency-ratio, and adding the various products together, we are tempted to think that this same additive procedure can be applied to the rival, mutually exclusive hypotheses concerning the non-seriable experiment. Such a transfer of method is plainly illegitimate, it does not make sense, and its result will be logically meaningless.

What basis is there left on which a person, faced with a set of rival courses of action each of which is a non-divisible non-seriable experiment, can make his choice? If we ask what in such a case it is rational to do there is no answer, if rationality means choosing the most preferred amongst a set of attainable ends. For he does not know what ends are attainable with the means at his disposal, indeed, in the face of this ignorance, his powers of action are not properly described as 'means' at all. But if we ask what it is sensible and natural for him to do, the example of the Chinese sentry again gives us the clue. The sentry saw two possible experiments, and for each of them there were two hypothetical outcomes; and for each experiment he saw no reason whatever to rely on one of its hypotheses rather than the other. For each experiment one of its two hypothetical results was agreeable and the other disagreeable, and it happened also that the two disagreeable hypotheses, one for each experiment, were identical. When he compared the two favourable hypotheses, however, one was incomparably more enjoyable to imagine than the other. Thus his choice was made.

Now I can imagine my readers saying: But this is a very special case. Two very special circumstances were present, which enabled the decision-maker to make his choice by a simple comparison of the pure *content* of the two agreeable hypotheses, leaving quite out of account, first, the question, which might arise most insistently in another case, of the relative *credibility* of the two hypotheses, and second, the whole matter of the disagreeable hypotheses. Am I saying, you may ask, that when we try to peer down our vista of future time we see nothing but the sharp clear-cut black lines of sure knowledge and the pure blank white spaces of sheer ignorance? Do our expectations resemble thus an engraving rather than a painting? Are there no greys, no half-tones? Those who may happen to have seen my *Expectation in Economics** will know that I am very far from neglecting that twilight zone between belief and disbelief without which the words 'hope and fear' would scarcely have any meaning. There is not time now to explain the nature of the measure of true uncertainty, the measure of acceptance of a hypothesis, that I there tried to adumbrate. Its chief characteristics are, first, that it is a measure of disbelief, of doubt, rather than of belief or positive confidence; and secondly, that it can be assigned to the various members of an exhaustive set of rival suggested answers to some question in degrees which are independent of each other. Thus in contrast to numerical probability, which is expressed in proper fractions which, taken over the entire set of possible contingencies, must sum to unity, the degrees of 'potential surprise' respectively assigned to the various members of a 'subjectively complete' set of

* Cambridge, 1949.

rival hypotheses need not sum to any particular total; the degree assigned to any one hypothesis can be altered without affecting the degree assigned to others; new additional hypotheses can be formed by splitting up what I have called in my book the 'residual hypothesis' (which is a mere formal recognition that, in the complex cases of real life, not all possibilities have necessarily been thought of) into additional explicit hypotheses, and the total number of rival hypotheses composing the exhaustive set can thus be increased, without the need to assign higher degrees of 'suspectness', i.e. of potential surprise, to the other, initially explicit hypotheses. These aspects of potential surprise, however, need not trouble us now. For the present purpose we are simply concerned with a variable which, when its value (in the algebraic sense) is high, makes the hypothesis to which it is assigned dimmer, less real, less interesting. I may perhaps be allowed to invoke an astronomical analogy. The brightness of the planet Venus, as seen from the earth, depends both upon its distance and upon its phase.* When the planet is at the full it is far away from us on the other side of the sun, and is therefore relatively dim. When it is at its nearest to us it lies between us and the sun, and so its visible face is wholly dark or illuminated only in a thin crescent. The planet appears to us brightest at an intermediate position, when a thick crescent is illuminated at a phase corresponding to that of the 5-day-old moon. Now these two variables which affect the brightness of the planet have their counterparts in the two variables which, I think we may say, affect the brightness, the interest, of a hypothesis. Those two variables are, first, the pure content of the hypothesis, and secondly, the degree of potential surprise assigned to it, the difficulty which the individual has in banishing from his mind, when contemplating in imagination a happy outcome, the thought that, after all, it may not come true. Upon these two variables there depends what we may call the degree of stimulus that a given hypothesis can impart.

If what I have been saying seems reasonable thus far, this is the position we have reached: a person faced with a set of rival courses of action amongst which he must choose will find that for each of them he has in mind a set of mutually exclusive hypotheses about what its outcome would be. For any one course of action, the hypotheses differ amongst themselves in their power to arouse his interest and release his mental energies: some, though exciting by their content, are too unplausible to be seriously interesting; others, though perfectly credible, are commonplace and dull. But from whatever

* These variables are of course not independent of each other.

combination of these two sources it springs, each has in some degree a power to stimulate the decision-maker's mind. If the content is agreeable, the stimulus, so far as it can influence the decision-maker, will pull him towards the course of action, if disagreeable it will push him away from it. Here we have apparently a situation of great complexity: whole terms of hypotheses are pulling and pushing the individual towards or away from each possible experiment, one might think his position would resemble that of a referee trying to manage ten games of football all being played simultaneously on the same pitch. How can he find for each experiment some single measure of its attractiveness?

Possible answers to this question fall, I think, into two classes. We can suppose that the decision-maker allows every one (or every member of some large subset) of the rival hypotheses, to which he concedes any plausibility, concerning the outcome of a course of action, to contribute something to his assessment of the merits of that course. Or we can suppose that a very few particular hypotheses will seem to him to subsume the significance of all the others, and will therefore select themselves as representatives of the entire set of rival hypotheses. Each of these two classes of answer can be exemplified by constructions using what I call potential surprise. We may call these two constructions respectively the integrative and the focus-values solutions.

In the conception that I have been outlining, each of the rival hypotheses that an individual has in mind concerning the outcome of some particular experiment can, if we like, be thought of as a very tiny plot of ground whose dimensions we shall not consider. Upon this tiny plot let us imagine a column to be erected, of a height which will represent the power of the hypothesis to stimulate the individual's mind. The little plots on which such columns are to be erected can be imagined, if you like, as forming a huge chequer-board with not just 64 squares but a very large number. As we move from left to right across this board we shall consider that we are moving towards hypotheses of successively more attractive content. As we move from the nearer to the farther edge of the board we shall consider that we are moving towards hypotheses carrying successively higher degrees of unplausibility, of potential surprise. Now it will be clear, I think, that every one of the entire set of hypotheses which the individual entertains in regard to some experiment will be able to find its appropriate, determinate place on such a board. Thus we shall see, stretching across the board, a collection of columns of varying height. How will these columns be arranged? Is it not plausible that the hypotheses of very high success will carry a rather high degree of 'suspectness', of potential surprise, while there will be many hypotheses of comparatively modest success which will all carry a zero potential surprise, that is, will be accepted by the individual as 'perfectly possible'? The columns belonging to these latter will together form a straight wall running along some part of the near edge of the board. The top of this wall will not be level but will be rising from left to right, because the farther to the right we go along it, the more interesting becomes the content of the hypotheses. At some point, however, we shall reach a hypothesis which, while not indeed 'too good to be true', is a little too good to be accepted on the same footing of perfect compatibility with everything that the individual knows of the relevant circumstances and of his own powers as those we have been reviewing. If it did come true, that would be a little surprising. It will therefore have to stand a little back from the near edge of the board. Its next neighbour will be a little harder still to regard as quite non-surprising if it were to come true, and the next one again harder still, and so on. Our wall of columns will therefore curl away towards the back of the board. What will be the shape of its upper edge in this curving and receding portion? At first each successive hypothesis that we come to, as we move towards the right, will still be so much more interesting in content that this advantage will outweigh the extra potential surprise assigned to the hypothesis, and its column will therefore be taller than that of the hypothesis we previously considered. But if we go far enough we shall eventually come to degrees of success which must appear to be dreams rather than reasonable hopes. They will seem too unreal to have much power over the individual's mind and decisions. When we have gone as far as that, therefore, we shall find successive columns getting shorter as we go still farther towards the right. Somewhere intermediately we must have passed a place where the wall was at its highest. Some hypothesis there will surely be which, on a balance between the difficulty of believing that it could come true and the intrinsic brilliance of the success it would represent if it did, will seem to out-top all others in its power of stimulus.

So far we have considered only the hypotheses of success, moderate or great. But there are also the hypotheses of misfortune or disaster. By a natural completion of our scheme, we shall arrange these unfavourable hypotheses so that they increase in badness as we go from right to left. Like the moderately good hypotheses, those moderately bad hypotheses whose occurrence would occasion no surprise will lie along the near edge of the chequer-board. Again there will be a point where the wall begins to curve away from the near edge of the board, and if we go far enough there will again be hypotheses too extravagant to command much of the decision-maker's attention; and again there will be a highest point of the wall, located some little way along its curving part. This wall corresponding to the bad hypotheses will thus in its general shape reflect as in a mirror the wall of the good hypotheses, and this mirror where the two walls meet will be located at a point representing an outcome neither good nor bad, neither enjoyable nor distressing to contemplate, an outcome which we may call *neutral*.

Until the experiment we have been discussing is actually performed it is, of course, not something external to the mind of the decision-maker but an idea that he has created in his mind, and in describing it we are describing an aspect of his own thoughts. None the less, for simplicity of language let us distinguish between this mental construct and his power of appraising it, so that we can speak of the experiment as attracting him through the influence of some or all of the agreeable hypotheses, those represented by that part of our wall lying to the right of the neutral outcome, and repelling him by some or all of its disagreeable hypotheses, represented by that part of our wall which lies to the left of the neutral outcome. Now if the height of each of the columns composing our wall represents the power of one or other of the hypotheses to stimulate and capture his attention, can we measure the experiment's total attractive power by measuring the area of the right-hand wing of the wall, and its total repellent power by the area of the left-hand wing? To attempt this would be one form of what I have called the integrative solution, but it would be a wholly fallacious and doubly mistaken one. When there are a number of candidates for one appointment, all very able and excellently qualified, we do not say 'What a strong team!' for, of course, they are not a team at all, they are rivals. To pick out any one of these candidates and assume that he will succeed is *ipso facto* to assume that the others will fail. Just so with the various hypotheses concerning the outcome of an experiment. They are mutually exclusive. To pick out one of them and say 'I shall assume this one is true' implies 'I shall assume that every one of the others is false'. If at any moment a man is deriving enjoyment and stimulus from imagining some future event which, for this purpose, he is for the time being implicitly assuming will come true, he cannot logically and without contradiction simultaneously derive enjoyment from imagining the coming true of another event incompatible with the first. But the act of decision, of choice between two rival experiments one or other of which, but not both, he can perform, surely requires him to take a view of each experiment which shall be internally coherent. Thus even if we assume that the respective degrees of stimulus derivable from the various hypotheses are measurable on some numerical scale, it would not make sense simply to take their sum. If on a given evening I have the choice of going to a concert, a dance, or an ice-hockey match, I cannot look forward to all these pleasures one piled on top of another, but to only one of them. But the truth that the packets, as it were, of stimulus are non-additive is even more obvious when we consider only that subset of the whole set of favourable hypotheses (or, alternatively, that subset of the whole set of unfavourable hypotheses) which carry zero potential surprise. For if it seems to me equally permissible (equally plausible or credible) to dream of winning £10—or of winning £1000—(but not both at once) I plainly shall not bother with thinking about the £10. It will be submerged in the greater hope. The same principle will apply to any set of hypotheses which all carry one and the same degree of potential surprise, whether this be zero or greater than zero, though usually the only such set in the individual's mind will be that of the hypotheses to which he assigns zero potential surprise.

How can this submergence of a good hypothesis in a better one, of a small hope in a greater one, which occurs when both carry equal degrees of potential surprise, when both, that is to say, seem to the individual equally easy or equally difficult to imagine coming true, be represented in our model consisting of the wall of columns? If the submergence were our only difficulty, the matter would be simple. It is as though the purpose of our wall was to catch the warmth of the sun, and only that part of it counted as useful which could receive the rays when they come in a direction parallel with what we have called the near edge of the chequer-board. Thus all that part of the wall which lies along this near edge will be quite useless, and can be ignored, except for its last and highest column, standing at the point where the wall begins to curve away towards the back of the board. If we imagine an observer standing and looking at, say, the 'favourable' wing of the wall, his line of sight lying parallel with what we have called the near edge of the chequer-board, the apparent area which will be visible to him will not be the actual area of the wall, because of its curvature, but by considering this apparent area we shall avoid counting additively the stimulus due to a lesser hope as well as that due to the greater hope in which it is submerged. But we shall still not have overcome the difficulty that even the remaining hypotheses, those whose height is not blocked from our observer's sight by a still taller column, are rivals and therefore their respective degrees of stimulus must not be added together. It is at this point of our argument that the choice between the integrative and the focus-values solutions must be made. The integrative solution supposes the decision-maker to allow every one of the hypotheses, except those which are submerged in more powerfully stimulating ones, to make some contribution to his decision. Amongst the favourable hypotheses carrying zero potential surprise, he will ignore all except the one having the most attractive content, the one located at that point of the 'favourable' wing of our wall where it begins to curve back from the near edge of the chequer-board. The influence of this hypothesis in attracting him towards the experiment in question will be the first term in an additive series. The next term will be contributed by the next hypothesis towards the right, one having even more attractive content, but carrying some degree of potential surprise greater than zero. However, the contribution made by this second hypothesis will by no means be the same as the influence it would have if it stood alone. The total influence exerted by the first and second hypotheses together will, we may suppose, be a little greater than that exerted by the first hypothesis alone. But it will not be equal to the sum of their separate influences. Thus the second term in the additive series will be the difference between the combined influence of the two hypotheses and the separate influence of the first hypothesis. When we proceed to a third hypothesis, its contribution will again be the difference between the combined influence of the first three hypotheses all considered together, and that of the first two considered together. So we can proceed through all the remaining hypotheses, writing down as an additive term in our series the difference which each successive hypothesis makes to the total influence of those we have already counted. The psychological, as well as the formal, nature of this process can perhaps be suggested by comparison with another kind of experience. The noise of a pneumatic drill outside our window can be extremely irritating. If a second drill starts, the noise of the two drills together may be a little worse than that of the first one alone, but it will be by no means twice as bad. Let us express the matter thus. We might be willing to give 10 shillings to have no noise at all, but if one of the drills was going to work in any case, we would not be willing to give 10 shillings merely to have the second one stopped. This, then, is the integrative solution. It supposes on the part of the decision-maker what is to my mind a rather unrealistic power and willingness to perform complicated and intensive introspections. Let me turn to my alternative, the focus-values solution.

Can a future event or situation contribute anything to a man's experience, to what is going on now in his mind as he ponders his decision? No. Only situations and events which are either present or else imagined can do so. To feel enjoyment or distress by anticipation is to feel it by imagination. Does a man set his heart on a bundle of various and conflicting hopes? Or will he set up some single coherent mental picture to represent what in his view he stands to gain if he decides on some specified course of action? If we believe that he will need some single self-consistent hypothesis as the focus of his hopes, and will also concentrate his fears on some one particular picture of misfortune, at what particular levels of success and of disaster will these two focus-points be found? I think there is a natural and obvious answer to this question. Surely he will choose what I have called the two most stimulating hypotheses, the ones represented by the highest points, respectively, of the favourable and of the unfavourable wing of our wall of columns. When the outcome of the course of action can be expressed and measured as a money gain or loss, we may call the two hypotheses the focus-gain and the focus-loss. Thus when, for example, the courses of action consist in various possible business ventures or investment opportunities the decision-maker will have for each such project a pair of measures, a gain and a loss. Choice amongst such pairs can be represented by an indifference-map.* Whether or not the specific solution I have outlined carries conviction, at least let us not allow anyone to claim to do away with the ineluctable, irreducible uncertainties that everywhere confront us in this life by means of frequency-ratio probability.

* *Expectation in Economics*, p. 30.

II

ON THE MEANING AND MEASURE
OF UNCERTAINTY: I*

Economic theory seeks to show how men's observed behaviour in the earning and spending of their incomes is a natural or inevitable consequence of some assumptions about human nature and about the essential circumstances of human life. Amongst these essential circumstances the main emphasis of value theory is placed on the scarcity of men's material resources, that is, the fact that their land, their own personal energies and skills, and their reserves of prepared goods are at any moment limited, while the quantities of these goods that they would like to have are virtually boundless. Faced with this scarcity, each man has constantly to be choosing and deciding between one thing and another, and value theory, leaping over a void without sparing it a glance, has assumed that these things between which men choose are the actual alternative satisfactions themselves. In value theory there is no slip 'twixt the cup and the lip, and the entire range of cups, containing every kind of beverage that ever can exist, is present to the mental eye of the chooser, who knows, moreover, the exact nature and degree of the effects that will be produced upon him by this or that measure of indulgence in each possible type of potation. Now even in that part of value theory called the theory of consumer's behaviour, this assumption of perfect knowledge is gravely unrealistic. All the goods that serve to educate or entertain us or enable us to communicate with one another, all the books, newspapers, films, theatrical performances, lectures, postal services and television sets, and all the apparatus of scientific research, could have no use or existence if the experiences they will give us could be known for certain beforehand in exact and complete detail. Why buy a book if you know in advance for certain precisely and completely what is in it? But if you do not know this, how can you gauge the precise effect that the reading of the book will have on you? To admit knowledge and information as one of the exchangeable goods is to expose a flank on which the theory of consumer's behaviour, as we find it in our literature, is defenceless; for knowledge would not be bought if it were already possessed; and when we buy

* *Metroeconomica*, vol. IV (1952), pp. 87–104.

knowledge, we do not know what we are going to get. But the theory of consumer's behaviour assumes that we always know what we are going to get.

Knowledge, then, is a very peculiar commodity, which can by no means fit into our accepted doctrines of the nature of value, and that is, perhaps, why those doctrines completely ignore knowledge, or rather, the possibility of its absence, and take perfect knowledge for granted. Even at the risk of wearying you, I feel it worth while to explain in still other words just what is here involved. The accepted theory of value assumes that the individual decision-maker, the chooser, our prime object of study whether in his capacity as consumer or producer, is solely and simply a chooser whose only function is to exercise his tastes and preferences in choosing among things whose qualities and powers are completely and perfectly known to him. And now we have found a thing, universally pursued and fiercely sought after, whose very nature is such that each specimen of it has special and individual characteristics and features which are logically incapable of being known in advance, namely, knowledge itself.

I have introduced this question of the character of knowledge considered as a commodity in order to make as vivid as possible the meaning, and establish the truth, of the following proposition: The things amongst which a man is free to choose are not satisfactions themselves, but actions designed to secure for him some sort of satisfaction; and except when he acts as a mere spender of income on familiar things for immediate consumption, there is no knowing whether any given course of action that he embarks on will secure him the sort of satisfaction he looks to it for, either in kind or in quantity. This is most strikingly true in regions of economic theory lying outside the theory of value, narrowly interpreted; and in particular it is true in the theory of investment.

The economic decision-maker, then, is a chooser among courses of action whose outcomes he does not know; or if this seems too sweeping, let us say that he is a chooser among courses of action concerning the outcome of each of which he entertains several non-excludable hypotheses. We need the notion of an *excludable* hypothesis, one, that is to say, which the decision-maker can reject absolutely as irrelevant and out of the question, because evidently even a man who feels perfectly certain that the outcome of a given course of action will be just such-and-such and nothing else, can nevertheless be said to entertain any number of *excluded* hypotheses about this course of action. Thus if we made no distinction between excludable and non-excludable* hypotheses, the mere plurality of hypotheses concerning any one course of action would not of itself give us a distinction between unique certainty concerning the outcome and uncertainty. And since I shall start the next stage of my argument by referring to the influence exerted on a man by a hypothesis that he regards as certainly true, I am bound to say clearly what I mean by a feeling of certainty. It could be said, perhaps, that the judgement which excludes a hypothesis, in my sense, is simply the extreme case of a range of judgements extending from unique certainty of the truth of a hypothesis, at one end, to certainty of its falsity, at the other, and it might then further be maintained that we have therefore no right to speak of excludable hypotheses before we have explained the nature or basis of this whole range of judgements. But I do not accept this argument; for it seems to me there can be differences of opinion concerning the nature of the judgements in the interior of the range (and indeed this very question is my central theme), but that the complete rejection of a hypothesis as not worthy of a moment's consideration means the same thing to all men in all circumstances.† I return, then, to my description of the economic decision-maker as one who has to decide upon one course of action out of a number which seem open to him, for each of which he has in mind a number of non-excluded hypotheses. How will he assess the comparative merit of each of these courses? What structure of judgements will underlie his choice of one course of action or experiment in preference to the others?

The hypotheses that he has in mind about the outcome of any one experiment are rivals, that is, they are mutually exclusive and the truth of one would imply the falsity of the rest. Each hypothesis can, therefore, be described for his purpose in terms of two characteristics: first, its *face-value*, that is, a measure of the gain or loss that it would bring to him if it came true, and secondly, the strength of its claim to be treated as if it *were* true. The two questions, closely bound together, that I want to discuss here are: first, what measure does the decision-maker use of the strength of the claim of a hypothesis to be true; and secondly, when to each hypothesis of a given gain or loss

---

* The excludability or non-excludability of any hypothesis is purely a matter for the individual's own judgement, not something on which someone else can pronounce 'objectively'.

† No reader, I am almost sure, will read this statement so carelessly as to confuse it with such absurd and totally unrelated assertions as that all men in given circumstances will reject the same hypotheses, or that all of those who reject any one hypothesis will do so on the same grounds or by the same process of explicit or intuitive reasoning.

that would accrue from a given course of action, he has assigned some particular value (in the algebraic sense) of the measure of its claim to be the true hypothesis, how does he combine the two characteristics of each hypothesis into an assessment of the power or importance, as it were, of that hypothesis, and how does he then construct, from these assessments of the hypotheses, a valuation of the course of action itself for comparison with valuations of his other possible courses of action? By 'valuation' I mean here his assessment of the attractiveness, or its contrary, of one course of action in comparison with others, as a motive for action; and some course or other he must evidently always adopt, even if it consists in 'doing nothing'. Let us sometimes use the word 'experiment' in place of 'course of action'.

The first of these questions can be expressed in a slightly different way as follows: Where he has a plurality of non-excluded hypotheses concerning any one experiment, the decision-maker surely cannot treat every one of these as making just that contribution to his valuation of the experiment as it would if it were his sole non-excluded hypothesis and were accordingly regarded by him as certain to prove true. The influence on him of a sole non-excluded hypothesis regarded as certainly true would depend, in a given environment, only on the face-value of this hypothesis, that is to say, on the size of the clear gain or loss in money, or other measure of the advantage, that would accrue in the actual event of this hypothesis proving true. He cannot regard each of several mutually exclusive hypotheses as certain to come true, and it seems reasonable to suppose that where there are several non-excluded hypotheses and each of them is accordingly held to be not certain, the influence of each will depend on a second independent variable (additional to the face-value) reflecting this fact of non-certainty. What will be the nature of this second independent variable?

To answer this we must ask: What is the function of this second independent variable, what essential service does it render to the individual, or to human society, what is its role in the scheme of things? Let me insist yet again on what seems to me a self-evident but much neglected truth: it is only in the present that we can experience things. We cannot experience the future itself but only our present imaginings of the future. And hence when I bring in the notion of enjoyment by anticipation, or distress by anticipation, to play so large and central a role in my argument, I am only asking you to agree that choice between alternative courses of action which seem open to a man must, by inexorable logic, be made on the basis of the feelings he gets from imagining the respective outcomes of these various possible courses. When a person imagines the future he provides himself both with immediate enjoyment or suffering and with an incentive to particular action. He imagines something which fills him with pleasure at the thought of it and desire to attain it, or with distress at the thought of it and desire to avoid it, and the very feeling of pleasure or distress at the contemplation of it moves him to action. Thus the two things, feelings experienced and motive to action, are one. Now if we assume, as seems to me reasonable, that the intensity of his experience of an imagined future will be partly a function of some definite, describable, and even quantifiable features of it, why should he not give himself licence to increase indefinitely the values he assigns to those independent variables and so increase his enjoyment *ad libitum*? Why set any bourne to the success that he imagines? Or what is to defend him from utter despair at the thought of nightmare possibilities? But, you will say, if he indulges in mere wishful thinking, or mere panic thinking, without restraint he will swiftly come to grief. And that is, of course, the answer. The conscience within, which compels him to try to relate his imagined future to the real scope and power of his present actions, is a device of the organism for self-preservation. The role of our 'second independent variable' is then, I suggest, to be a constraint upon the individual's imagination, preventing him from indulging in such wild hopes or fears as would invite early disaster in his career. In this role we can see it as one of two opposing sets of forces shaping the individual's imaginations of the future. On the one hand there is the fascination of the ideas of high success or of deep disaster, impelling him to heighten the colours and deepen the shadows of his picture of the potentialities of any one course of action. On the other there is the constraint exercised by our 'second independent variable', prolonging the economic careers of individuals and thus ensuring the economic survival of society.

If we accept this as the role or function of our 'second independent variable' what can we infer about its nature? In accepting this as the role, are we not in effect already saying that one test to be imposed on hypotheses concerning the outcome of any 'experiment' or course of action is simply that of conformity to the individual's own personal or vicarious experience in life and his conception of the general nature of things; that, in other words, he will begin by considering whether any given hypothesis is plausible, or credible, or possible?

Now the orthodox answer to the question: What will be the nature of the second independent variable? is this: We list the N hypotheses that the individual has in mind concerning the outcome of some one experiment and assign to each a proper fraction Q so that $\sum_{N} Q = 1$. Or if the hypotheses together form some range $a \leqslant x \leqslant b$ of a continuous variable x, we assign a probability-density function $f(x)$ such that $\int_{a}^{b} f(x) \, dx = 1$. Is this procedure of assigning numerical probabilities the same thing as the assigning of plausibilities? Let us consider what numerical probabilities are.

Suppose there is some class of performances, defined by means of some set of characteristics which each instance of this kind of performance has in common with all other instances, and let these performances be of such a kind that in each instance a recognizable stage is reached that we call the *result* of this instance of the performance. We explicitly specify that the result is to be a situation which can be wholly apprehended in a single act of observation and does not require to be built up from a number of separate and recorded acts of observation. Let us call each instance of this class of performances a *trial*. If, in a series of such trials, we are able to keep unchanged all those circumstances that we believe to be relevant, we shall expect the result of each trial in the series to be the same as that of every other. If we can keep only some of the relevant circumstances constant, or if we can do no more than confine each circumstance within certain bounds, and we conduct a number of trials in non-identical sets of circumstances, we shall expect the results of these trials to differ from one another, and we shall not expect to be able to predict the result of a proposed trial from those that have already been made. Knowledge of past results will not tell us the result of any *single* future trial. However, experience in many different contexts shows that even where only some of the circumstances can be held constant, or where we can only confine each circumstance to some range of variation, and where the state of each variable circumstance in any particular trial cannot be deliberately chosen at all, still there is knowledge to be had concerning the results of a *series* of trials when this series is treated as a whole. There proves in practice to be an eventual tendency, as the number of trials is increased beyond some perhaps rather indefinite minimum, for the relative frequency with which each distinct kind of result of the trials occurs to settle down to a near-constancy. Thus if we can define a set of types or classes into one or other of which the result of any trial must of logical necessity fall, and if we call each of these types or classes a *contingency*, then by making more and more trials while holding a given subset of the relevant conditions approximately constant we may be able to satisfy ourselves that out of any N trials, provided N be large enough, a given contingency will occur about P times. The whole set of such frequency-ratios P/N will by definition sum to unity. Two things can, I suggest, be said about such a set of frequency-ratios:

(1) When we treat the entire series of N trials as one whole and look on this series as constituting a single experiment, the frequency-ratios are knowledge, and this knowledge can legitimately be used to predict the result of a further similar series of trials conducted under the same limitations of the variability of the circumstances.

(2) But it is almost self-evident that the frequency-ratios cannot be used to predict the result of any one, particular, individual trial.

We have thus two headings under one or other of which we can classify all experiments or courses of action. First, there are those experiments which consist in a series of performances all in certain respects resembling one another, bounds being set to the range of variation of each circumstance in the total set of relevant circumstances under which all these performances are conducted. It is, let me specially insist, the series or set of trials all taken together as one whole which here constitutes the experiment; but since the result of this experiment is built up from a number of separate observations, let us call this type of experiment *divisible*. Secondly, there are those experiments whose result is seen in a single act of observation, the experiment being such as cannot be broken down into a number of more elementary performances all resembling one another in certain respects. Experiments of this type I will call non-divisible. Now evidently the context of a non-divisible experiment may be such that the latter can be treated by a decision-maker as one of the trials which together compose a divisible experiment; and further, a set of frequency-ratios applicable to this divisible experiment may be known to him, so that he can predict its result. Whether these things can be done or not will depend on the fulfilment of three conditions: first, there must be the prospect of a sufficient number of other trials about to be performed under circumstances each of which will lie within some pre-assigned range, the number of trials which is 'sufficient' depending on the narrowness of the ranges of possibility; secondly, there must be a record of a series of trials already performed under the same restrictions of circumstance, so that the proportions in which the result of the divisible experiment will be made up of this and that contingency can be known; and thirdly (and this is the condition on which I would lay special emphasis because of the tendency to overlook it) the result of the divisible experiment must be shared in by our particular individual decision-maker himself in proportion to the importance, in the divisible experiment, of the single trial which he will have contributed to it. It is only in so far as he himself will gain or lose according to the outcome of the divisible experiment as a whole, and not according to the outcome of the particular individual trial we are considering, that the latter can be effectively absorbed into the former and the frequency-ratios made use of by him. When a particular course of action can be treated by the decision-maker as one trial in a divisible experiment for which frequency-ratios are already known to him, I shall call it a *seriable trial*. It is evidently possible that one or more of the three necessary conditions for the decision-maker to treat his own non-divisible experiment as a seriable trial may not be satisfied, and so his own experiment may be what I will call *non-divisible non-seriable*. If it is, then there can be no straightforward use of frequency-ratios as knowledge which will enable him to predict with confidence the relevant outcome for himself of the experiment.

We are faced, then, with two questions: first, does real economic life consist preponderantly in having to choose amongst courses of action which are divisible or, if not divisible, then seriable, or does an important part of it consist in having to choose amongst courses of action each of which is non-divisible non-seriable? And secondly, if crises of decision amongst non-divisible non-seriable experiments do arise, can they be resolved by recourse in any sense to the procedure of assigning probabilities? It is clear, I think, that each daily occasion of purchasing familiar necessaries is a seriable experiment, and that when we feel ourselves to be living in an assured and stable environment the routine of private life is very largely amenable to probability calculations, formal and explicit or more often intuitive and subconscious. Even the matter of choosing where to go for the annual holiday could perhaps be drawn into this category, although it has two characteristics which tend to exclude it. First, it is almost too infrequent, and that in two senses: in an ordinary span of life the total number of annual holidays that anyone can look forward to is rather definitely limited; and then these occasions of deciding are for many of us what I call *isolated*; the question whether we shall enjoy or fail to enjoy a fortnight in Ireland in September next year has an importance in its own right, as concerning a distinct and individual portion of our life, and it is not quite easy to lump this question together with increasingly nebulous and remote occasions such as the holiday of the year after next, the year after that, and so on. In the isolation of some occasions of choosing, from other like occasions, through the fact that these occasions are distributed at long time-intervals stretching into remote future years, we have, I think, one important source of inappropriateness of the probability analysis. It is clear also that where the verdict upon the outcome of a given course of action is purely subjective and a matter of personal and private judgement, as in the question whether a holiday has been enjoyable or not, there can be no recourse to that famous expedient for rendering non-divisible experiments seriable, namely, insurance. Insurance consists in the prior agreement of many decision-makers to pool the results of the non-divisible experiments which they severally as individuals are about to make, and share the *total* outcome of the resulting *divisible* experiment which will be built up of the trials rendered seriable by this prior agreement. Now we know that there are many situations where insurance is impossible. Why should this be so, if the whole of economic life can really be brought within the scope of probability? There are, I think, it will be agreed, not merely some occasions of deciding which are rare and therefore each likely to claim in the decision-maker's eyes an individuality of its own, but also some which are for practical purposes unique in the life of the person concerned. Such are the occasions when a man chooses his life work, or his wife. But there is about some experiments something further, such as to render them logically incapable of absorption into a repetitive series. An experiment can be such that, whatever its outcome, the making of it will radically alter the situation of the individual decision-maker and his powers of action, so that it will subsequently be impossible for him to perform another experiment of a relevantly similar kind. Napoleon could not repeat the battle of Waterloo a hundred times in the hope that, in a certain proportion of cases, the Prussians would arrive too late. His decision to fight on the field of Waterloo was what I call a crucial experiment, using the word crucial in the sense of a parting of the ways. Had he won, repetition would for a long time have been unnecessary; when he lost, repetition was impossible.

Now there are, I believe, those who would admit the validity of the notion of experiments which are non-divisible non-seriable in the strict sense, but who would argue that none the less the man who can find some basis for assigning numerical probabilities, in some sense, to the rival hypotheses concerning the outcome of every experiment, no matter whether it be seriable or not, and who makes his valuations of rival courses of action in this way, will, as a result of consistently adopting this principle throughout life, come off better than he would otherwise. Those who maintain that, even when for the particular decision-maker each of the rival courses of action amongst which he must choose is non-divisible non-seriable, it is 'rational' for him to evaluate the relative attractiveness of the various courses by somehow assigning to their contingencies numerical probabilities indistinguishable in form from frequency-ratios, must, I think, have some such idea as the above in mind.

The position we have reached is this: Economic life consists to an important degree in having to choose amongst courses of action each of which is what I have called a non-divisible non-seriable experiment. On such occasions of choosing, frequency-distributions in the true sense, which if the experiments were divisible or seriable would provide knowledge of their outcomes, are instead non-existent, irrelevant and meaningless. Thus we might say without further ado that frequency-ratio probability has nothing to do with true uncertainty, and for the latter some new and different measure is required. But I do not wish to brush aside those arguments, that I referred to above, which suggest that frequency-ratios are brought in by a back door and used in some manner as if they were applicable. I now want to consider whether numerical probability is suitable in its formal properties to provide a measure of uncertainty and to express the state of mind of a decision-maker who is faced with non-divisible non-seriable experiments. I shall suggest that numerical probability, which in its formal and arithmetical properties is simply frequency-ratio probability, breaks down entirely as a means of interpreting and expressing some psychological aspects of the matter and encounters in this attempt some insuperable logical difficulties. These difficulties I will try to explain under five headings.

(1) Our study of the purpose or function of the 'second independent variable' led us to say that it ought to measure or indicate 'plausibility', 'credibility', 'possibility', and I further suggest that a hypothesis derives such an attribute from its own special features and from the decision-maker's conception of the general nature of things, and *not* from the consideration that it has few rather than many rivals in his mind. A 'perfectly plausible' or 'perfectly credible' hypothesis would be one in which the decision-maker could find nothing in the smallest degree incongruous with his experience of life and his notions of the laws of nature and of human nature, and nothing that conflicted with his information about the particular situation. To any and every hypothesis fulfilling this condition he would wish to assign such a value of the second independent variable as would stand for an absolute maximum of plausibility or possible-

ness, the highest degree conceivably attainable. But how could numerical probability serve this purpose? To assign to any hypothesis the probability 1 would imply that this hypothesis was held by the decision-maker to be certainly true and that all others were excluded. If he has in mind more than one non-excluded hypothesis then he must assign a probability of less than unity to even those which he regards as perfectly credible or perfectly possible. When there are many such hypotheses their 'perfect plausibility' will be very poorly suggested by the proper fraction representing their numerical probability.

(2) It may be felt that the difficulty just stated is not a great matter, and that so long as the decision-maker can point in any particular case to a specific proper fraction which he declares to be the probability corresponding to 'perfect plausibility' or 'perfect possibleness' we can be content. Suppose, however, that the decision-maker, having made what he takes to be a complete list of non-excludable hypotheses, judges all of these hypotheses to be 'perfectly plausible' and assigns to all of them equal probabilities; and that further reflection then suggests to him some additional hypotheses which also seem to him 'perfectly plausible'. 'Perfect plausibility' will now have to be represented by a lower numerical probability, a smaller fraction, than before. But can we be content to fill the role of our 'second independent variable' with a variable which does not provide a stable numerical value to represent 'perfect plausibility'? We are again driven to ask: Is there not a sense in which a hypothesis is 'likely' or 'unlikely', plausible, credible, acceptable, possible, regardless of whether there are few or many rival hypotheses? There is surely a sense in which the plausibility or acceptability of a hypothesis is independent of the plausibility, or the number, of its rivals. The use of numerical probabilities as the 'second independent variable' does not allow stability of the values of this variable against occurrences which, psychologically, ought to leave those values unaffected; does not give these values mutual independence; and does not make them independent of the number of rival hypotheses.

(3) The difficulty stated under (1) and (2) presents itself yet more vividly when two experiments are to be compared. For it can be contended, not merely that the decision-maker *may* assign to one or more hypothetical outcomes of any experiment a perfect or highest conceivable degree of plausibility, but that for every experiment he *must* select at least one such hypothesis. If, for any given experiment, he can think of no hypothetical outcome which does not seem to him to conflict with the nature of the universe as he conceives it, or with

the character of the particular existing situation as he conceives that, we can only say that he has not yet brought his thoughts into an internally self-consistent and harmonious picture; there is a logical contradiction within his own ideas. Now 'perfect plausibility' plainly ought to be represented for both experiments by the self-same value of the second independent variable. Yet with numerical probability this may not be possible. For by whatever process the probability-distribution for each experiment is arrived at, this distribution will assume a definite form involving definite ratios between the probabilities assigned respectively to various hypothetical outcomes. Consider, then, the two distributions (i) and (ii) in Fig. II 1. It is

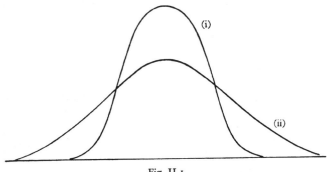

Fig. II 1

impossible to preserve the essential form of both these distributions while assigning the self-same probability to the two outcomes which are their respective modes.

(4) It is surely reasonable to require of the 'second independent variable' that it should not by its nature entail a verdict of 'faulty judgement' on the values of this variable assigned to certain hypothetical outcomes, should one of those hypotheses prove to be the truth. Yet if we use numerical probability as the second independent variable, any probability other than zero or unity must necessarily prove wrong in the event, while zero will prove wrong if one of the hypotheses to which it was assigned comes true, and unity will prove wrong unless the unique hypothesis to which it was assigned comes true. Suppose, for example, that a probability of 1/6 is assigned *ex ante* to some hypothesis concerning the outcome of a non-divisible non-seriable experiment. Then if this hypothesis proves false, the decision-maker was plainly wrong not to assign it a probability zero instead of 1/6, while if it proves true, he was plainly wrong not to assign it a probability of unity. For let us remind ourselves that we are now

speaking of a non-divisible non-seriable experiment, where frequency-ratios are meaningless and inapplicable, and where, therefore, there can be no question of justifying the judgement that the probability was, say, 1/6, by repeating the experiment many times and finding that in just 1/6 of these cases the hypothesis proves true.

(5) The objection which we brought under (4) against the adoption of numerical probability as our second independent variable is, I think, more purely a matter of logic, and makes less appeal to psychology, than the objections under (1), (2) and (3). Not that this fact, in my view, gives objection (4) a superior validity or greater importance. For psychological judgements are what we are essentially and centrally concerned with. It is, nevertheless, of some interest to make the distinction. But under (5), I return to a psychological basis for the objection, and it is this: When weighing a hypothesis, the decision-maker will surely often say to himself: 'I find no ground for inclining either towards or away from this hypothesis: I can perfectly well imagine that the hypothesis will prove true and I can perfectly well imagine that it will prove false.' In such a case the decision-maker is in effect saying: 'I find equally plausible both the hypothesis and its contradictory.' Now how can he translate this sentiment into terms of numerical probability? Not by assigning a probability 1/2 to the hypothesis and a probability 1/2 to its contradictory, for that contradictory may itself be capable of being split into a number of mutually exclusive hypotheses. Let the hypothesis be, for instance, that Mr S is an Englishman. If we know nothing of Mr S except that he is a native of Great Britain, we may feel inclined to give the probability 1/2 to the idea of his being an Englishman. This leaves a probability of 1/2 for the idea that he is a non-Englishman. On similar grounds we might assign a probability 1/2 to his being a Scotsman and the same to his being a non-Scotsman; and again we should have to say that the probabilities of his being a Welshman or a non-Welshman were each 1/2. But a native of Britain who is a non-Englishman can be either a Scotsman or a Welshman, and to all these three possibilities we have assigned a probability of 1/2, which of course is a contradiction in terms.

These are some of the dilemmas which, as it seems to me, we encounter when we carry over the language of frequency-ratio probability to the analysis of choice amongst non-divisible non-seriable experiments. Can we deduce from these failures the character that we shall require some new and different tool to have if it is to serve as our 'second independent variable'? Some writers, admitting that in some contexts the notion of objective frequency-ratios is incongruous, have suggested that nevertheless numerical probabilities can be used if we interpret them as subjective judgements. Does this mean that the probability assigned to a hypothesis about the outcome of some experiment measures the decision-maker's confidence that this hypothesis would prove true if that experiment were made? What else can it mean? But if so, subjective probability leaves us no better off. To have perfect confidence in the truth of one hypothesis is to have perfect confidence in the falsity of all its rivals. If several rivals each claim a share of 'confidence' it cannot be given in fullness and perfection to any one of them: it must be treated, just like frequency-ratio probability, as something limited in total amount so that, broadly speaking, the greater the number who share it the smaller will be the shares. Thus we are still confronted with the difficulties listed under our headings (1) to (5). These difficulties arise essentially because we have been using as our second independent variable something which is limited in amount and has to be shared out amongst the distinct non-excluded hypotheses; we have been using something which measures or indicates degrees of positive belief. Let us try instead the notion of degrees of *disbelief*, of doubt, rejection, or implausibility, interpreting this idea, however, in a sense especially designed to avoid our former difficulties. By disbelief I do not now mean the absence of perfect certainty, but the positive recognition of some disabling circumstance. If I am shown a closed hat-box and asked to guess what kind of hat is within, I shall attach no disbelief, in the sense in which I am now using the word, to the idea that the hat may be a topper, a ten-gallon hat from Texas, or a mortar-board, but I shall attach a high degree of disbelief to the hypothesis that the hat is of the three-foot diameter kind which ladies used to call a picture-hat: because such a hat would not go in the box; or at any rate, would not go in without being crumpled in a way that conflicts with my experience of how such hats are treated by their owners. Let me insist again on the distinction I wish to make between two entirely separate ideas: *certainty* that a particular hypothesis is true, and *absence of disbelief* in that hypothesis. By absence of disbelief in a given hypothesis I mean a state of mind such that, if the person concerned were suddenly to obtain knowledge of the matter and find that the hypothesis was in fact true, he would feel no mental discomfort or shock, he would not be in the least surprised. Now I think it will easily be agreed that while a person can only feel perfectly certain of the truth of one member of a set of mutually exclusive hypotheses at a time, he can, by contrast, feel a complete absence of disbelief in any number of mutually exclusive hypotheses simultaneously, in the sense in which I am using the word 'disbelief'. This will, perhaps become more immediately convincing if I may now switch over from the term 'disbelief' to a term designed to throw into relief the special meaning that I have in mind. To disbelieve in a given hypothesis means, in my definition, to perceive some distinct incongruity between that hypothesis and one's knowledge and general conception of the nature of things and one's detailed information concerning the immediate situation. If then the hypothesis should actually prove true, this event would be surprising, and so we can say that the event, viewed in imagination, is potentially surprising. Thus for the word 'disbelief' in the quite special sense in which I have been using it I propose now to substitute *potential surprise*.

Suppose, then, that a little distance from me in a tube train I see an English friend reading a book with easy enjoyment. I cannot see the title of the book. I shall not be in the least surprised if the book turns out to be in English or in French, and only a little surprised it it turns out to be in German. I shall be more surprised if the book proves to be in Italian or Spanish, still more surprised if it is in Dutch, and astonished if it is in Welsh. As to the possibility of its being a manuscript in my own handwriting, which I am conscious of having locked away in my desk a few minutes earlier, I feel able to exclude that hypothesis completely: should it prove true, the intensity of my surprise would be as great as I am capable of feeling. Now the two hypotheses, that the book is wholly in English and that it is wholly in French, are mutually exclusive. To feel certain at one and the same moment of the truth of both these hypotheses involves a logical contradiction, it does not make sense. But it is perfectly possible and indeed perfectly commonplace to have a complete absence of disbelief or, as I prefer to say, zero potential surprise about the hypothesis that the book is wholly in English and at the same time to attach zero potential surprise to the idea that it is wholly in French. And there is, in general, no limit to the number of mutually exclusive hypotheses to all of which simultaneously a person can, without logical contradiction, attach zero potential surprise. By this example I hope to have made clear what I mean when I say that *certainty of the truth* of a hypothesis, and *absence of disbelief* in that hypothesis, are totally different ideas. And this example will illustrate the more detailed definition and explanation I want to give you of the notion of potential surprise and of how I propose that we should use it as the 'second independent variable' that we have been seeking.

There is, I think, a definite range of possible intensities of potential surprise extending from zero at one end of the range to an absolute maximum intensity, corresponding to absolute disbelief, and rejection or exclusion of any idea to which it is attached, at the other end. Intensities outside this range are not defined, we do not give them any meaning, or if you prefer, they do not exist. Now I suggest that each of the two extreme levels of potential surprise, the zero level and the absolute maximum level, corresponds to a definite and real act of mind or state of mind. Each of these two psychic states or acts means in some sense, I think, the same thing for every man, and we have thus two bench-marks or, if you like, a surveyor's base-line, by means of which we can set up a scale of potential surprise. Mr W. E. Armstrong has suggested* that a scale for measuring utility can be constructed by each individual for himself by choosing two distinct experienced utilities and then considering for each of a number of intermediate levels of utilities (to discover such requires no more than the assumption that a man can arrange utilities in order of preference) whether it is nearer to one or to the other of his initially chosen pair. A utility for which he is unable to answer this question will divide his initial interval into two sub-intervals in some sense equal to each other. By successive repetitions of this procedure he can obtain a scale as fine as his own sensibility in the matter permits. A formally similar scheme will enable us to suppose in each man's mind a scale of potential surprise, and this scale will have an advantage over a similar utility scale in that the latter cannot, perhaps, claim any fixed anchorage or zero point, still less two definite levels which together provide a ready-made basic interval. The existence of these two datum points enables us, indeed, to claim that the scale of potential surprise is for some purposes interpersonal, but for my main application of it this further claim is unnecessary.

This idea of the two extremes which mark off the range of variation of potential surprise will allow us to give a final clarity to the distinction between certainty of the truth of a hypothesis and absence of disbelief in that hypothesis. To feel certain that one particular member of a set of mutually exclusive hypotheses is true is to feel certain that all its rivals are false, so that these rivals are completely excluded, or in the language I am proposing, every one of these rivals is to be assigned the absolute maximum degree of potential surprise. The particular hypothesis itself which is felt to be certainly true must of course be assigned *zero* potential surprise. Thus in the

* 'The determinateness of the utility function', *Economic Journal*, vol. LVIII (1939), pp. 453–67.

language of potential surprise we shall express the idea, that a particular person feels *perfectly certain* of the truth of a particular hypothesis, by means of two statements:

(1) that he assigns to this hypothesis zero potential surprise,

(2) that he assigns to every rival of this hypothesis the absolute maximum of potential surprise.

To make this pictorially vivid, let us put potential surprise on the vertical axis of a Cartesian diagram, and use various numbers on the horizontal axis to stand for the various members of the entire set of

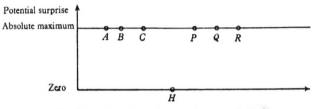

Fig. II 2A. Certainty of truth of hypothesis *H*.

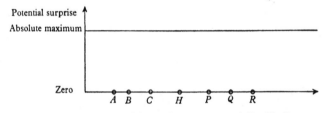

Fig. II 2B. Absence of disbelief in hypotheses *A, B...H...R*.

hypotheses in the mind of some individual about some question or experiment. This horizontal axis will stand for zero potential surprise, and above it a second horizontal line will mark the absolute maximum of potential surprise. In the region bounded by these two straight lines, understood as including the lines themselves, each of the points that we mark by a dot will stand for the assigning of some degree of potential surprise to one or other of the hypotheses of the set. Figs. II 2A and B illustrate in this way the distinction between certainty and absence of disbelief.

It remains for me to show that potential surprise can resolve my list of dilemmas. Objection (1) above calls for a measure which can express perfect plausibility or perfect credibility or perfect possibility without any implication or suggestion of perfect certainty. Zero-potential surprise assigned to any hypothesis does precisely this.

Objection (2) points out that when numerical probability is used to provide an index of the credence attached to a hypothesis by some individual, this index may need to be altered merely because the number of distinct and separately specified non-excluded hypotheses has been increased, although nothing may have happened to impugn more strongly than before the credibility of the hypothesis itself. By contrast with this, the degree of potential surprise attached to any hypothesis is independent of those assigned to all other hypotheses taken individually or together. Since potential surprise can thus resolve this difficulty, it can likewise resolve objection (3) which is essentially the same. The closed hat-box and the question what kind of hat is in it will illustrate this. If, having listed all the different types of moderate-sized hat I can think of, I assign to every one of them zero potential surprise, I am not in any way precluded from subsequently adding fresh items to my list and assigning to these also zero potential surprise. If, on the other hand, I had begun by naming five kinds of hat and assigning to each kind a probability of 1/5, and there had then occurred to me two additional types, I should have had to reduce the 1/5 to 1/7. But what would have been the justification for doing this? The hypothesis that the hat-box contains a topper is not rendered less plausible by the occurrence of the idea that it might, instead, contain a bowler. Objection (4) calls for a measure such that judgements expressed in terms of it can prove right in the event, and are not, like those expressed in terms of probability other than zero or unity, bound to prove wrong in the event. Potential surprise can improve on this requirement. An unlimited number of rival hypotheses concerning any one question or experiment can all simultaneously carry zero potential surprise, and when any one such proves true, the judgement is fully vindicated. Should a hypothesis prove true to which a degree of potential surprise greater than zero had been assigned, the degree of misjudgement is exactly measured and represented by this degree of potential surprise. Let me, at the risk of wearying you, once more remind you that we are concerned with non-divisible non-seriable experiments. Finally, objection (5) calls for a measure such that a hypothesis and its contradictory can both simultaneously be assigned an index implying that each of them is considered 'perfectly possible'. Now the contradictory of any hypothesis is the totality of all the rivals of that hypothesis, and since zero potential surprise can be assigned simultaneously to any number of hypotheses, all these rivals as well as the hypothesis itself can carry zero potential surprise and hence so can the contradictory. It will be realized that whereas numerical probability, at any rate in the frequency-ratio sense, is in some sense objective and public, potential surprise is subjective and private.

May I venture to quote briefly from a most fascinating and delightful broadcast talk by Professor M. G. Kendall on the subject of 'Nonsense'.* He is speaking of Lewis Carroll's epic *The Hunting of the Snark*:

> A number of characters whose names all begin with a B (for no reason at all) set out to hunt for an animal of dangerous habits called a Snark. One of the party, the Baker, is particularly susceptible to a subspecies of snark called a boojum, for if he sees one he must softly and suddenly vanish away. The whole interest of the chase depends on the question whether the snark they find will turn out to be a boojum—a completely nonsensical proposition....And if you think all this is ridiculous and beneath the notice of grave and serious-minded adults, you may care to know that the students of the theory of probability are still discussing the question whether one can take an even chance on the truth of any proposition whose meaning is not known.

I cannot pretend to answer this question. I can only suggest that by assigning zero potential surprise to the proposition whose meaning is not known, and zero potential surprise to the contradictory of this proposition, we can precisely express the appropriate and sensible state of mind of anyone who is asked his attitude to such a proposition. And so I think, if we cannot answer the question asked by the students of the theory of probability, we can instead cause this question to vanish away like the Baker himself.

* *The Listener*, 24 April 1952.

III

ON THE MEANING AND MEASURE
OF UNCERTAINTY: II*

In Essay II we suggested that the strength of the influence of any hypothesis, concerning the outcome of some contemplated course of action, on the decision whether or not to adopt that course in preference to other possible ones, must be thought of as depending on at least two independent variables. One of these is the *face-value* of the hypothesis, that is, some measure of what the decision-maker would gain from adopting the particular course of action, if the hypothesis were to turn out true. The other independent variable is some measure of the strength of the claim of the hypothesis to be true, as the decision-maker judges this claim in advance. In Essay II we proposed a specific meaning and character for this second independent variable, and called it *potential surprise*. This question of the nature of the 'second independent variable' was the first of two questions proposed in Essay II. The second of those questions asks:

When to each hypothesis of a given gain or loss that would accrue from a given course of action, the decision-maker has assigned some particular value (in the algebraic sense) of the measure of its claim to be the true hypothesis, how does he combine the two characteristics of each hypothesis into an assessment of the power or importance, as it were, of that hypothesis, and how does he then construct, from the assessments of the hypotheses, a valuation of the course of action itself for comparison with valuations of his other possible courses of action?

Those who adopt as their 'second independent variable' (the variable representing the decision-maker's degree of belief in or distrust of a hypothesis) some concept of numerical probability, are spared all further trouble in answering the above question. Whether the basis of their concept of probability is explicitly the notion of frequency-ratio, or whether it is a notion of subjective degree of belief axiomatized to behave in the same additive fashion as frequency-ratio probability, they have available (so they assume) the whole calculus by which actuaries arrive at well-founded predictions of the outcomes of divisible experiments. Having set up, for each course of action, an exhaustive system of contingencies, that is to say, a cabinet

* *Metroeconomica*, vol. v (1953), pp. 87–104.

of pigeon-holes such that any conceivable outcome falls into one or other of these pigeon-holes, they assign to each contingency a proper fraction as its probability, the fractions being such that the sum of them all is unity. They then multiply the face-value of each contingency by its probability and call the sum of the resulting products the *mathematical expectation* of gain or loss from the course of action in question. What justification of this procedure can be offered? If the course of action is a seriable trial, and if the decision-maker looks upon his probabilities as well-founded, then it is rational for him to say to himself: 'The outcome of the divisible experiment to which my present seriable trial contributes will be equal to the mathematical expectation of the result of any such trial, multiplied by the number of trials.' Thus when he is about to contribute to a divisible experiment by making one seriable trial, on the understanding that he will share equally with all other contributors of one seriable trial in the ultimate outcome of the divisible experiment, the mathematical expectation gives him a rational measure by which to compare the desirability of choosing a trial which belongs to this divisible experiment rather than a trial which belongs to some other divisible experiment. When, that is to say, the essential context is a divisible experiment, the probabilities in so far as they are well-founded give knowledge of the relevant consequences for the decision-maker of one choice or another. But what justification is there for comparing by means of 'mathematical expectation' the attractiveness of this and of that course of action, when these courses are non-divisible non-seriable experiments?

What justification is there for adding together mutually exclusive contingencies of an experiment which is for some reason essentially unique and non-seriable? The additive procedure by which we arrive at a mathematical expectation of the outcome of a divisible experiment depends for its rationality precisely on the belief that the various contingencies (in one or other of which each of the seriable trials making up the divisible experiment must result), so far from being mutually exclusive, will all be represented together in the total result of the divisible experiment, and will indeed each account for a foreknown proportion of the total number of trials making up that experiment. When the course of action is a non-divisible non-seriable experiment, such an additive procedure loses entirely the relevance it has for a divisible experiment, and has only one claim to fall back on: that of being a compromise. I shall suggest below that a policy for action in face of ignorance has two distinct rational objectives: one is to allow a man's hopes to rise to the height of his imagination, the other is to give him a feeling of 'limited liability' in case the worst should happen. He may, indeed, be best satisfied by some compromise between these two objectives; but the choice of the best compromise for this purpose has no connection with the mathematical expectation, which takes no account of either objective. The question at issue between those who believe that the compromise provided by the mathematical expectation is the reasonable solution (they have no right, in my view, to claim it as the rational solution) and those who disagree, is the question whether it is better to treat life as though it were an examination paper in arithmetic, where the problems have right answers if only we can work them out, or whether life is better looked on as the artist's canvas whereon, with such pigments as he possesses, he may freely attempt whatever picture he can imagine. But even this comparison is liable to mislead; for even when probabilities can be obtained from an appropriate series of trials in the past, the answers that can be worked out from these probabilities are not relevant unless there is to be repetition, effective for the individual decision-maker, in the future as well.

The foregoing argument concerns the relevance of the 'mathematical expectation' when the information exists for calculating it. But when does this information exist? In strictness, only in the illustrative examples of the text-books on numerical probability, or in games of chance; that is to say, in a context which is in two respects quite different from the real environment of human life. In that real environment there is, instead of the clear-cut simplicity of the games of chance, a fog of ignorance and confusion* arising not from remediable shortcomings of human organization, whose forces in a world of essential rivalry and struggle are partly directed to the very creation of this fog, but arising from the nature of things; and in that real environment it is for ever impossible for the decision-maker to say to himself 'I now possess all the relevant information'.

* The following passage is quoted by permission of Professor C. F. Carter from a letter written by him on 19 November 1949 to Mr J. de V. Graaff:

'I yesterday tried out on the [Emmanuel] College Economic Society the Balls in the Bag experiment proposed in your review of Shackle's book. The results confirm my impression that your rudimentary experiment will give different results to those to be expected in "real life". The point is that, even without prior knowledge of probability theory, a man is capable of working out something like the mathematical expectation of success when he is faced by only three equal chances. But as soon as I faced them with *four* balls a high proportion chose the wrong bag; and the more complexities I added to the experiment, the more plausible did it appear that regard should be had only to the focus-values. I think, therefore, that Shackle's treatment is valid for those situations which are likely in real life; or at any rate, is not proved invalid.'

It is because in the text-book examples of drawings from an urn, and in the games of chance, factors whose existence and nature are unknown are excluded by the rules of the game, that these examples and games are irrelevant to reality.

The view that I seek to combat is that we can analyse and understand the conduct that men adopt in face of uncertainty, that is, in the kind of situation which confronts them when their choice of action must be made amongst non-divisible non-seriable experiments, by supposing them to use an actuarial outlook and procedure. My case against the usefulness of this supposition fall under three heads. First, that the actuarial procedure, the calculation and comparison of a mathematical expectation for each possible course of action, is logically irrelevant. Secondly, that the belief that men use this procedure implies that they are seeking to compare objective facts, results, advantages and disadvantages, by means of an available objective procedure; whereas I contend that men cannot compare future events themselves but only their own present, subjective, imaginations of these events, and that it is the feelings that these imaginations give them that will decide their choice; and thirdly, that what experience and knowledge of how the world works does for men is not to enable them to select one particular hypothetical outcome of each proposed course of action as more 'probable', or deserving of a larger share of positive confidence than any other, nor to enable them to allocate shares of such positive confidence amongst all the rival hypotheses; but to enable them, as it were, to pass the hypotheses which present themselves through a series of sieves of increasing fineness, leaving at last a perhaps large number of very various hypotheses which all now stand on an equal footing of 'perfect plausibility', which have all been accorded the status of 'absence of disbelief'.

When all those hypotheses which fail to pass the test of 'perfect plausibility' have been set aside, those that remain will not usually make a compact set of closely similar outcomes, but a set or range whose extremes would represent for the decision-maker high success and serious embarrassment. To say this is simply to say again in different words that men's knowledge and insight do not usually enable them to specify narrowly what is positively probable, but only to discountenance what is implausible and far-fetched. When the decision-maker's aim is an economic one, as when he seeks the most profitable amongst a number of investment projects, the set of all conceivable hypotheses about the outcome of any one project can often be treated as a continuous variable, and each value of this variable x will then be assigned by him some degree y of potential surprise. My contention in this and the preceding paragraph can be expressed by saying that the typical form of the function $y = y(x)$ will resemble that of Fig. III 1, having a considerable segment where y is zero, merging at either end into monotonic increasing or decreasing segments leading to those values of x above the upper and below the lower of which y takes everywhere the absolute maximum value $y = \bar{y}$.

For the sake of having a concrete subject-matter, let us from now on take the continuous variable x to stand for hypotheses concerning

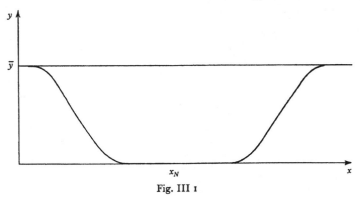

Fig. III 1

the size of the investment-profit from constructing or buying some system of productive equipment: let us say a farm, a natural-gas pipe-line, or a ship. If t measures futurity from the instant when this equipment is bought by the decision-maker, $s(t)$ the money-outlay per time-unit on operating the equipment and keeping it in repair, and $z(t)$ the sale-proceeds per time-unit of its produce of goods or services, and if $\rho = \log_e (1 + r)$, where r is the market rate of interest on long-term loans of money, and if u is the purchase-price or construction-cost of the equipment, then let

$$v = \int_0^\infty \{z(t) - s(t)\} e^{-\rho t} dt \quad \text{and} \quad x = v - u.$$

x is plainly conjectural and it will not be unrealistic to assume that its highest algebraic value for which $y(x) = 0$ will represent a large profit perhaps several times u, while its lowest algebraic value for which $y(x) = 0$ will be negative and will represent the loss of most of the purchase-price u. The decision-maker, we suppose, has in hand a large sum of money which he can use for the purchase of any one of a number of various systems of equipment, or can retain as money. His choice amongst these various courses of action or experiments will be based on a comparison of the forms of the potential surprise curves, $y = y_1(x)$, $y = y_2(x)$, ..., which he has mentally constructed, one for each of the n different ways of investing his money. Our problem concerns the manner in which this comparison will be made.

Possible methods fall, I think, under two main headings, between which perhaps various compromises or combinations are possible. These methods we can call the *integrative* and the *focus-values* types of solution. By an integrative solution I mean one which allows every point (x, y) of the curve $y = y(x)$ for which $y < \bar{y}$, with the possible exception of one or two particular points, such as, perhaps, that where $x = 0$, to make some contribution to the decision-maker's

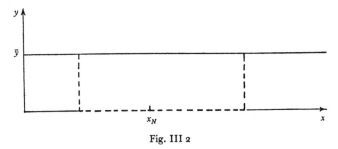

Fig. III 2

judgement of the merits of the project in comparison with those of another project. By a focus-values solution I mean one where the judgement of a project is based upon two points only of its y-curve. The propriety of supposing enterprisers to compare projects by the focus-values method is suggested by the following line of thought:

Let us consider a y-curve where $y = 0$ for every value of x in some continuous 'inner range' extending on either side of $x = 0$, and elsewhere takes its 'absolute maximum' value $y = \bar{y}$, so that the curve resembles Fig. III 2. All hypotheses which the decision-maker has in mind concerning the outcome of the project thus fall into two classes, those (belonging to the 'inner range') which he regards as perfectly plausible, and those which he altogether excludes as impossible. He will surely allow to these latter no influence on his decision, and will concern himself at most with the hypotheses belonging to the 'inner range'. But my contention is that he will indeed be concerned only with the *extremes* of the inner range, that is to say, with the two numerically largest values of x, one positive and one negative, for which $y = 0$. These two values of x represent respectively the largest profit and the largest loss that he looks upon as possible. The former is his highest hope from the project in question, the latter his worst fear from it. Let us now remind ourselves that all the hypotheses in the inner range are mutually exclusive. If the decision-maker considers that a particular size of profit, x_F, is perfectly possible, what difference will be made to his feelings about the project by the fact that some smaller positive profit is also perfectly possible? The difference of character, relevant to this question, between a divisible experiment and a non-divisible non-seriable experiment is quite fundamental. The merit of a 'divisible' project can be judged from the outcome which it is known to be going to yield; 'known', that is to say, in so far as the actuarial calculation of its result is based on well-founded frequency-ratios; the merit of a 'non-divisible' project depends not on what it will do, for this is unknown, but on what the decision-maker judges it can do at best or at worst. But, the reader may object, is not the presence of lesser gains, amongst the decision-maker's non-excluded hypotheses, a comfort to him against the thought that the best possibility may not come true? Do not the positive values of x interior to the inner range, the hypotheses of profit still positive but smaller than the largest to which zero potential surprise is attached, constitute a second and a third, etc., line of defence? No. For all these hypotheses are taken in rear, as it were, by the hypotheses of loss which are equally regarded as 'perfectly possible'.

Those accustomed to think in terms of the actuarial calculation of the result of a divisible experiment will find this point exceedingly hard to appreciate. Suppose, for the sake of argument, that the decision-maker does fix his attention momentarily on one of the interior hypotheses, the idea of a small gain. Such a gain, by hypothesis, is perfectly easy to imagine as the outcome of the project. But his attention will not rest on that hypothesis. His mind will be immediately challenged by the thought that much larger gains are equally easy to imagine: why then stop at a relatively small one? And in the other direction, is there any point in contemplating a modest possible loss, if a larger loss is equally possible; equally capable, so far as plausibility is concerned, of arousing his anxiety, and much more capable of arousing it, so far as face-value is concerned?

The fundamental hypothesis of Neumann and Morgenstern's Theory of Games is that a decision-maker will choose that action (strategy) whose worst possible outcome is the least bad amongst the respective worst possible outcomes of all the actions open to him. The context of this assumption is a game where each player knows for certain exactly what would be the upshot of any combination of strategies, one chosen by himself and one by his opponent. In a context where the players have not this comprehensive, exact and certain knowledge (which moreover they know to be such), would the Neumann and Morgenstern hypothesis be more plausible than that the decision-maker will choose that action whose best possible outcome is the best amongst the respective best possible outcomes of all the actions open to him? Whether we answer yes or no to this question, there is surely a third hypothesis which is more plausible, and of more general analytic power, than either of the two former, namely, that he will take into account both the 'best possible' and the 'worst possible' outcome of each course of action and make these *pairs* of outcomes the basis of his decision. If this be accepted, it remains to discuss under less restrictive assumptions than those of the 'rectangular' potential surprise curve of Fig. III 2, what we can best mean by the 'best possible' and 'worst possible' outcomes of a project or course of action for which the decision-maker has set up a potential-surprise curve.

Let us therefore return to y-curves of the type of Fig. III 1, where above the upper extreme of the inner range, and below its lower extreme, potential surprise increases slowly at first with increase in the numerical value of x. A hypothetical outcome of given face-value will, I think, seem to the decision-maker less interesting if it carries some potential surprise than if it carries none. If it is a desirable outcome the association with it of some potential surprise will dim in some degree the pleasure of imagination which this idea can afford; and if it is a bad or disastrous outcome, again its impact on the decision-maker's mind will be softened if it carries some potential surprise. Now this effect of potential surprise will be working in opposition to the direct effect of the numerical increase in face-value, for the latter will tend to make the hypothesis more interesting, more capable of attracting and holding the decision-maker's attention. Thus as we suppose him to pass in review hypotheses of successively larger numerical face-value, above the upper or below the lower extreme of the inner range, there will at first be a continuing increase in the degree of 'stimulus' that these hypotheses provide, in spite of the growing effect of the increasing potential surprise with which hypotheses of successively larger numerical face-value are associated. But since when potential surprise has reached the 'absolute maximum' level the degree of stimulus or 'interesting-ness' of the relevant hypotheses will have fallen to zero, it follows that as, say, the 'profit' branch of the y-curve is traced continually outwards a value of x will eventually be reached whose associated degree of stimulus is not going to be exceeded, and beyond this point the degrees of stimulus must somewhere begin to decline; and similarly on the 'loss' branch of the y-curve a hypothesis, or a range of hypotheses, will be found for which the degree of stimulus is greater than anywhere else on that branch of the curve. If, indeed, we assume that the degree of stimulus is a monotonic increasing function of numerical face-value, and a monotonic decreasing function of potential surprise, we can expect to obtain two determinate hypotheses or values of x (of profit and loss respectively) whose power of capturing or stimulating the decision-maker's interest or attention is a maximum, and these, I suggest, are what we can most usefully mean by his 'best' and 'worst' hypothetical outcomes.

In this construction we have introduced a variable denoting the 'interestingness' or power of stimulus possessed by the combination of a particular face-value x of hypothetical gain or loss and the degree y of potential surprise which, according to the y-curve belonging to some particular project, is associated with it. Let ϕ stand for this degree of stimulus. Then we wish to consider the characteristics of the function $\phi = \phi\{x, y(x)\}$, or rather, of the surface $\phi = \phi(x, y)$, in which, for the given individual, all such twisted curves, or 'space-curves', as $\phi = \phi\{x, y(x)\}$ will lie.

Let us define $\phi(x, y)$ more precisely as the *excess* of the power of stimulus possessed by any given 'point' (x, y) over the least such power that any point can be found to possess. We have assumed that any hypothesis which is coupled with the absolute maximum of potential surprise, $y = \bar{y}$, will be quite without interest for the decision-maker, and thus ϕ will be zero everywhere on the line $y = \bar{y}$. But it also seems plausible that even where $y = 0$ there will be some values of x which seem to the decision-maker to represent so little in the way of added wealth or reputation, or so little in the way of lost ground or danger increased, that these hypothetical outcomes will have no power of stimulus. If, indeed, we are to be able to attach any meaning to the expressions 'a good outcome', 'a better outcome', 'a bad outcome', 'a worse outcome', there must for each decision-maker be some value of x above which outcomes are 'good' and another below* which they are 'bad'; and it is perhaps a defensible simplification to assume that his discrimination is fine enough for us to treat these two values as one and the same and to call them the 'neutral' value $x = x_N$. And we shall not, I think, lose anything important in generality by further assuming, when x stands

* That is, 'at a lower algebraic value than which....'.

for investment-profit in the sense defined above, that $x_N = 0$, the neutral outcome is a zero profit.

Let us now assume, in accordance with the arguments of earlier paragraphs, that

$$\frac{\partial \phi}{\partial x} > 0 \quad \text{for all } x > 0 \text{ and } y < \bar{y},$$

and that

$$\frac{\partial \phi}{\partial x} < 0 \quad \text{for all } x < 0 \text{ and } y < \bar{y},$$

and that

$$\frac{\partial \phi}{\partial y} < 0 \quad \text{everywhere.}$$

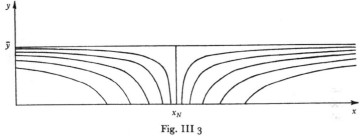

Fig. III 3

Then if the surface $\phi = \phi(x, y)$ is pictured by a set of contours $\phi \equiv \text{constant} > 0$, and a member of this set is written explicitly $y = F(x)$, we have $\phi\{x, F(x)\} \equiv \text{constant} > 0$ and along each such contour

$$\frac{d\phi}{dx} \equiv \frac{\partial \phi}{\partial x} + \frac{\partial \phi}{\partial F}\frac{dF}{dx} \equiv 0, \quad \text{so that} \quad \frac{dF}{dx} = -\frac{\partial \phi}{\partial x}\bigg/\frac{\partial \phi}{\partial F}.$$

Since here F is another name for the variable y and we have assumed that $\partial \phi/\partial y$ is everywhere negative, while for $x > 0$ we have assumed that $\partial \phi/\partial x$ is positive, it follows that where x is positive, dF/dx is also positive and the contour $y = F(x)$ slopes from lesser to greater values of y as x increases. But since we assume $\phi(x, \bar{y}) \equiv 0$ no contour $\phi > 0$ can ever attain the line $y = \bar{y}$, and it follows that each contour must approach this line asymptotically. By a parallel argument the contour lines where x is negative will have dF/dx negative and will also approach the line $y = \bar{y}$ asymptotically. Thus the representation of the surface $\phi = \phi(x, y)$ by a contour-map will resemble Fig. III 3.

We can now give a precise meaning to the notion of a pair of hypothetical outcomes, one standing for the 'worst threat' and the other for the 'best promise' of a given enterprise or experiment, into which pair of outcomes the quality of the enterprise is, for the decision-maker, wholly concentrated and which provides the basis for his comparison of the attractiveness of this enterprise with that of others. (The quality or attractiveness of the enterprise is of course subjective and personal to the particular enterpriser in whose mind the project is imagined; we might say, perhaps, that it is a 'tension' which would be of different strength if either the mind or the mental construct were different.) Upon the contour-map described above, whose form in detail is special to the individual decision-maker, we imagine the particular potential surprise curve (y-curve) which he assigns to some particular project to be superposed as in Fig. III 4. As we trace the y-curve outwards from x_N towards the right or left along the x-axis, we ascend a ladder of contours representing successively

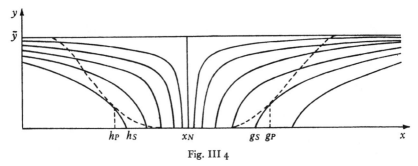

Fig. III 4

higher values of ϕ. At some distance from x_N the y-curve bends away from the x-axis, but gently at first, so that over some further range of x beyond the upper or the lower extreme of the inner range it will continue to cross successively higher contours as it reaches values of x successively more remote from x_N. But since eventually in each direction the y-curve attains the line $y = \bar{y}$, where $\phi = 0$, it must somewhere begin to cross successively lower contours as we trace it continually outwards from the neutral value of x; and it follows that amongst all the contours that the y-curve crosses or touches at positive values of x there must be a highest contour; and likewise amongst all those that it encounters at negative values of x there must be a highest contour.

If the y-curve has only one point in common with each of these two highest contours, it will meet each of them in a point of tangency. These points, which are of course constrained maxima of ϕ, represent by definition the *highest bids* which the particular project in question can make for the decision-maker's attention and interest. One of these bids is the most powerful suggestion of success and the other the most powerful suggestion of disaster that the conception of the project conveys to him; the 'power' of each suggestion being the net effect of face-value and of associated doubt or potential surprise. Let us recall that because the project is a non-divisible non-seriable experiment, his various hypotheses as to its outcome are mutually exclusive and that therefore there is here no logical basis for the additive procedure by which a 'mathematical expectation' is assigned to a divisible experiment. The project stimulates the decision-maker by the highest hope he can entertain about it, subject to the constraint of plausibility, and, on the other hand, by the worst fear he must feel about it, again subject to the constraint of plausibility. If two university teams of athletes are competing in a race, the question which university will win the race depends not on whose team is the fastest on the average of all its members, but on whose team contains the fastest individual runner.

In order to suggest that the two points on the y-curve where ϕ has its maxima will concentrate upon themselves the decision-maker's whole concern and attention, I call them *focus-points*. But such pairs of points will not themselves serve for the comparison of different projects, for not only will the two members of each pair usually have different values of y, but the values of y will also differ in general between the two respective 'favourable' focus-points of any two projects, and also between their respective 'unfavourable' focus-points. Thus we must conceive of the decision-maker as performing a mental process equivalent to 'standardizing' the focus-outcomes of all projects under review, by finding for each focus-point (x, y) an *equivalent* point (x, o). What must we mean here by 'equivalent'? Evidently the relevant sense is that of giving rise to equal values of ϕ, and so we seek for each point (x_P, y_P) or 'primary' focus-point a *standardized* focus-point (x_S, o) such that $\phi(x_S, o) = \phi(x_P, y_P)$. In terms of the contour-map of the surface $\phi = \phi(x, y)$ this process of standardizing consists simply in tracing that contour $\phi = \text{constant}$, which has a point of tangency with the y-curve, from this point of tangency back to the x-axis, the line $y = o$. To distinguish between an original focus-point and its standardized equivalent we shall call the former a *primary* focus-point and the latter a *standardized* focus-point or focus outcome. The two such points belonging to any one project we can distinguish from each other by calling one the *standardized focus-gain* and the other the *standardized focus-loss*.

It remains to consider by what construction we can represent the mental process of comparing with one another two projects for each of which a pair of 'focus-outcomes' has been determined. The parallel which suggests itself is that of the consumer's process of choosing between two combinations of quantities of two goods, and the indifference-map apparatus which has been evolved to illuminate his behaviour will also serve, with suitable modifications, to complete our analysis of the conduct of the enterpriser.* It will be realized that since every standardized focus-outcome is a point whose y-coordinate is zero, each standardized focus-outcome can be treated as simply a scalar number, rather than a point, and its meaning is indeed simply a number of the money units in which profit and loss are reckoned. Thus any pair of standardized focus-outcomes can be transferred to a new diagram, entirely distinct from that of the ϕ-surface where they were determined, and used as Cartesian coordinates of a point on what we may call the *gambler indifference-map*. Here distances on the horizontal axis will represent standardized focus-losses and those on the vertical axis standardized focus-gains. The points in the plane of this diagram will fall into sets such that the enterpriser is *indifferent* between the points of any one such set, and it is natural to suppose that each such set will form a smooth continuous curve. These curves, the enterpriser's gambler indifference-curves, will evidently slope upwards from left to right (in contrast to the consumer's indifference-curves) because in order that two points may be equally attractive to him, that one which represents a greater focus-gain must surely also represent a greater focus-loss.

We must now distinguish between a partial and a general formulation of the enterpriser's problem. We can think of him either as deciding which of several equipment-systems he shall construct or buy; for example, whether he shall build a natural-gas pipe-line or a ship, and whether a ship of this type and size or that; or we can think of him as deciding which of several comprehensive plans he shall adopt for disposing of his entire 'fortune', the sum of money which, either because he owns it or because it has been placed in his hands by others to be used at his discretion,† he has at command.

---

* Since we are now taking the investing enterpriser as our representative of the decision-maker, I shall henceforth use the term 'enterpriser' instead of 'decision-maker'.

† It is sometimes held that the analysis of business men's motives and decisions must proceed on a radically different basis when the business man is an executive controlling assets mainly owned by other people, from what is appropriate when he is the owner as well as the policy-maker of the firm. This view neglects the consideration that if the executive's main concern is for the security, power and prestige of his personal position, then all these things are promoted and measured by the success of the business that he guides, as reflected by its profit. This question finds a place in a brilliant analysis of the relations between different types of expectations, policy decisions, market conditions, and degrees of uncertainty, by Professor B. S.

We need not concern ourselves here with the distinction between the enterpriser's ownership of a given sum of money and his command of it through his being the active member of a partnership of venturing owners of capital, with whose interests and advantage he identifies his own success and reputation; though we shall later need to distinguish between such funds and those he might borrow at fixed interest. By the enterpriser's *fortune* I shall mean hereafter the whole market value of the assets which he has at his sole discretionary command; it will exclude any money which he borrows at fixed interest. Now it is clear that his decision to buy or construct some particular, technically specified, equipment-system may not require the whole of his fortune, and so at any time the two problems, first, what set of assets (including, perhaps, several distinct equipment-systems) shall represent his whole fortune, and secondly, whether he shall at that time exchange or spend some part of his assets, a certain sum of money, for a particular newly constructed equipment-system, are conceptually distinct.

The relevance of this distinction for us is the following: If the remainder of his fortune, which would be left after he had constructed equipment-system A, is of different size, or would for some reason be differently disposed of (represented by a type of asset differing in the ratio of its focus-gain to its focus-loss) from what would be the case if instead he constructed equipment-system B, then when he considers the focus-gain and focus-loss of his fortune as a whole, as these focus-outcomes would be in case he chooses A and in case he chooses B, part of the difference between the two situations will be imputable to the different disposal of the remainder of his fortune, rather than to the direct difference between equipment-system A and equipment-system B. Now it is the standardized focus-outcomes of his fortune as a whole which are really of concern to him. Thus when we use the idea of the gambler indifference-map as a model of the enterpriser's mental process in deciding between two investment-opportunities, let us say the construction of A or B, it will be appropriate to interpret the gambler indifference-map as relating to his fortune as a whole, and the points plotted on it, corresponding respectively to the two equipment-systems A and B, will have coordinates which are the standardized focus-outcomes belonging to his whole fortune when it incorporates system A and when it incorporates system B. To say this evidently implies that each of the two equipment-systems A and

Keirstead in *An Essay in the Theory of Profits and Income Distribution*. (See on the above question §ii of Chapter IV, and p. 57, l. 18 to p. 59, l. 14.) This book is a major contribution to the literature of the theory of profit.

B, considered as a means of employing part of the enterpriser's fortune, will have associated with it some specified means (not in general the same for both A and B) of employing whatever remainder of that fortune will not be required for the construction of A or B. In the last section of this essay, in order to attack a particular problem, we shall make the special assumption that the remainder of the fortune is used in such a way as to have zero focus-gain and focus-loss of its own. Meanwhile we can say something further about the shapes of the gambler indifference-curves.

It seems reasonable to suppose that the gambler indifference-curves will become steeper towards the right. That is to say, the greater the standardized focus-loss, the greater will be the increment in the corresponding standardized focus-gain necessary to compensate precisely a given (small) increment of the standardized focus-loss. Two types of gambler indifference-map, corresponding to two types of entrepreneurial temperament, can perhaps be usefully distinguished. Since the enterpriser cannot lose more than his entire fortune, a perpendicular is dropped on to the loss axis at the point corresponding to that fortune, and to the right of this perpendicular the indifference-curves have no meaning and are not drawn. The shape of the indifference-curves in the neighbourhood of this barrier is important. For some people, the thought of losing everything would not be made up for by the thought of any hoped-for gain, however large. For them the gambler indifference-curves must approach the barrier asymptotically, bending upwards more and more steeply as they approach it. But there are some, I think, who will embrace a venture where they must regard the loss of all they possess as perfectly possible, provided that this venture makes a very large gain indeed seem also possible. In such cases the gambler indifference-curves will actually meet the barrier at some finite gain. The two types of map are illustrated in Figs. III 5 and III 6. In both types we draw the curves with their slope becoming steeper as we consider larger and larger values of the standardized focus-loss; we assume, that is, that focus-loss has 'increasing marginal disutility', which is the same as to say that the remainder of the enterpriser's fortune, which would be left to him if he were in fact to suffer a loss equal to his standardized focus-loss, has decreasing marginal utility.

The meaning of a gambler indifference-map of either type is, of course, that of two courses of action the enterpriser will prefer the one represented by a point on an indifference-curve lying above and to the left of the indifference-curve containing the point representing the other course of action.

By way of illustration of the use of the constructions we have developed above, it may be interesting to apply them to the problem of the rational determination by a particular enterpriser, given his temperament and expectations, of the scale to which an equipment-system of given technical design should be built.* For this purpose we shall assimilate to each other the 'general' and the 'partial' formulations of the enterpriser's investment problem by assuming that he will keep in his bank any part of his fortune not needed to pay for the equipment-system. Since we are speaking throughout of losses and gains of money, any wealth kept in the form of money (bank deposits or currency) cannot yield any gain nor suffer any loss, and the focus-gains and focus-losses for his fortune as a whole, when

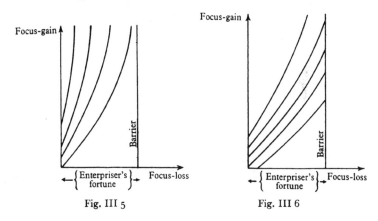

Fig. III 5   Fig. III 6

part of it is imagined to be used to construct an equipment-system of this type or that, will be simply those assigned by the enterpriser to the equipment-system itself. We exclude at first any borrowing by the enterpriser of money at fixed interest.

The difference between one equipment-system and another can range from total dissimilarity of purpose and method to a simple difference of scale. Whatever may be the kinds and degrees of difference between a number of investment-opportunities which an enterpriser is comparing, each of them, after due examination, will find a place on his gambler indifference-map. When the choice is simply between equipment-systems of different scale but similar purpose and design, the points will presumably lie on a segment of

* What follows from this point to the end of this essay formed part of a paper written in March 1950 and read by the author at the University of Nottingham in October 1951, which has remained unpublished.

a smooth curve, which we may call the *scale-opportunity curve*, and which in perfect competition will tend to approximate to a straight line passing through the origin. For it seems plausible that an increase of the productive capacity of the proposed equipment-system in a ratio R will, in perfect competition, increase both the standardized focus-gain and the standardized focus-loss in roughly that same proportion R. In other market conditions the choice between a small and a large scale may imply, for example, a choice between a small local market which could perhaps be firmly mono-polized and a more precarious attempt to invade other areas. In this example the curve might be concave downwards, since mono-poly profits might seem more assured, and loss due to successful counter-attack by others less likely, in a small local market than in a larger one. On the other hand a small and therefore perhaps specialized geographical region is more vulnerable to shocks from without, such as a weakening of demand for its staple products, aggravated by the corresponding 'regional multiplier' effect, than a very large and diversified region. Large scale would from that point of view bring a feeling of greater safety, that is, the focus-loss would not increase proportionately to the scale. When we relax the assumption of perfect similarity of design between equipment-systems of different scale, and admit the possibility of changes of detailed technique and physical lay-out to exploit economies of scale, still another set of influences on the shape of the scale opportunity curve is introduced. If economies of scale involve highly specialized methods, exceedingly efficient, perhaps, at some particular optimum output but rather narrowly and inflexibly confined to it* (as is, I think, the case with, for example, some flow production methods in the automobile industry), then the exploitation of such economies might conceivably bend the scale-opportunity curve downwards, because the economies which would be achieved if all went well would not increase profits by as much as the closing of the plant, in case of a falling-off in demand, would increase losses. The shape of the scale-opportunity curve under various assumed types of market imperfection and under various assumptions concerning economies of scale might I think prove an interesting study. Meanwhile, by assuming that market conditions do not depart very widely from perfect competition (and remembering our assumption that the

* The question how enterprisers respond in shaping their investment-plans to such a situation was introduced into economic theory by Professor A. G. Hart; see *Anticipations, Uncertainty, and Dynamic Planning* (Chicago, 1940) (second edition published by Augustus M. Kelley, 1951).

enterpriser does not borrow any money at fixed interest) we can take the curve to be approximately a straight line.

It is plain that, like the gambler indifference-curves, the scale-opportunity curve cannot extend to the right of the 'barrier' representing the loss of the enterpriser's whole fortune, and thus the scale-opportunity curve will consist of a straight segment bounded by this barrier on the right and by the origin on the left. The preferred scale for his new equipment-system will be the scale corresponding to the point (if unique) which the scale-opportunity curve has in common with the highest amongst all the gambler indifference-curves which it encounters. When the gambler indifference-curves are concave upwards and approach the barrier asymptotically, and the scale-opportunity curve is straight, the preferred point will evidently be a point of tangency between the scale-opportunity curve and an indifference-curve, as illustrated in Fig. III 7. Even when the indifference-curves attain the barrier at finite ordinates, the same may still be true, or the preferred point may lie on the barrier. But when we relax the assumption that the enterpriser does not borrow at fixed interest, a further possibility arises.

If the enterpriser can augment his resources beyond the amount of his fortune by borrowing at fixed interest, it will still be impossible for him to lose more than his fortune (any loss beyond that will fall on his fixed-interest creditors); but the scale of his new equipment-system will no longer be confined to what can be paid for by his fortune; and since there is nothing in our assumptions to prevent us from supposing that each increase of scale brings an increase, in some fixed proportion, in his standardized focus-gain, the result of supposing him to be able to borrow at fixed interest is that the scale-opportunity curve where it approaches the barrier will bend upwards and coincide with the barrier for some distance. If the enterpriser's temperament is such that his gambler indifference-curves approach the barrier asymptotically, he will not, in fact, have any incentive to borrow at fixed interest because the highest attainable gambler indifference-curve will still be the one with which the scale-opportunity curve has a point of tangency. But if the gambler indifference-curves actually reach the barrier, then the enterpriser may be able to borrow at fixed interest enough extra funds to carry his scale-opportunity curve up the barrier to reach a better indifference-curve than the one with which it has a point of tangency. This possibility is illustrated in Fig. III 8.

The problem we have attempted in the foregoing paragraphs is essentially the one for whose solution Mr Kalecki proposed his

Principle of Increasing Risk,* the question, that is to say, what factors will proximately govern the size of the equipment-system that an enterpriser will elect to build at any one time for a given business purpose. If this problem were confined to cases where the enterpriser only considers investing what we have called his fortune, and excludes from consideration the possibility of borrowing at fixed interest, we should claim to have answered that problem by pointing to the upward concavity of the gambler indifference-curves and the relative straightness of the scale-opportunity curve. This part of our

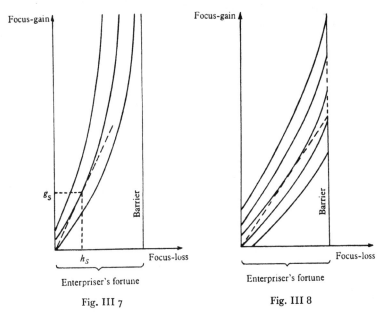

Fig. III 7   Fig. III 8

solution is simply a reinterpretation of Mr Kalecki's Principle of Increasing Risk in terms of a different apparatus. But can it be true, as would follow from the second part of our solution, that an enterpriser will only consider it worth while to borrow at fixed interest if he is of that temperament for which the possibility of losing his entire fortune can be contemplated, provided this affords the possibility of contemplating also a sufficiently great gain? We must remember, in this regard, the rather restrictive assumptions on which our analysis rests; these assumptions belong really to the case of an enterpriser with a 'fortune' not yet very large embarking on his first

* *Essays in the Theory of Economic Fluctuations* (London, 1939), p. 95.

entrepreneurial venture, or on one which comes early in his personal entrepreneurial career (for it would be difficult else to accept the assumption that the rest of his fortune is to be kept in the bank); and for such a case as this the second part of our solution may in itself be thought by no means unrealistic.*

* A highly suggestive discussion of the evolution of the enterpriser's attitude to uncertainty as it is moulded and conditioned by his entrepreneurial experience of success or failure and by the resulting development of his economic situation will be found in 'Some Notes on Risk' by H. R. Parker in *Metroeconomica*, vol. v (1953), pp. 138–44. Mr Parker has advanced into a field at present almost untouched in economic literature.

IV

THE LOGIC OF SURPRISE*

'A surprise is expected.' These words on a newspaper placard carry at first sight the suggestion of a contradiction in terms. *Surprise* is what we feel when an expectation has gone wrong, has proved in the event to have been ill-founded and false. How then can one *expect* to be surprised? One possible explanation is trivial: the expectation was in the mind of person *A* and concerned a feeling to be experienced by person *B*. But let us ask whether in any sense a man can expect that he himself will on some specific occasion experience surprise. On broad grounds of common experience and common sense we may well be inclined to start by saying that we all know that there is such a thing as a feeling of surprise, we have all experienced it at one time and another, and it would be absurd to say to oneself at any stage of life: 'I shall never again be surprised.' So at least in a vague and general sense we do assume, and accept the fact, that life has surprises in store for us, though whether this is more than the inescapable result of cold reflection, whether it really represents a lively and insistent conviction, is perhaps more doubtful. But plainly there is here a paradox: on the one hand there is the fact that each one of us feels sure that he will in the future experience surprise, on the other hand there is the fact that surprise is what we feel when that has occurred which we did *not* expect. It may be asked: Is the indefiniteness of the future occasion, its being quite unspecified as to date or circumstances, an essential condition for the possibility of entertaining a belief that we shall feel surprise? No: it is, I think, possible to expect to be surprised by what will happen on an occasion which is in some sense particularized. The paradox is a close-knit and definite one. To resolve it we need first some definitions.

There are two things that I think we can reasonably mean when we say that a person expects such and such a state of affairs or such and such an event. The state of affairs being specified, and its location in future history being stated by naming a calendar date or by describing an organic sequence of situations of which the particular state of affairs is the end-product, or by naming some, so to speak, pigeon-hole in future history such as 'the next General Election' or 'the next debate in the Commons on economic affairs', we can mean, when

* *Economica*, vol. XX (1953), pp. 112–17.

we say that a given person 'expects' this state of affairs to arise at the named 'cue', either that he attaches zero potential surprise to this as well as to many other mutually exclusive hypotheses, or else that he attaches some degree greater than zero of potential surprise to all hypotheses other than this one. Even with the first, and weaker, of these two meanings our paradox appears.

In conversation we use such words as 'surprising' and 'unexpected' with little heed to fine shades of meaning or to precision and consistency. But for my present theme I must recall a distinction which I suggested some years ago* and which is not, I should maintain, a fine or subtle difference of meaning but a plain and essential one. By a *counter-expected event* I mean an event which has figured as a member of the set of hypotheses provisionally entertained by some individual about the outcome of some course of action or some 'experiment', or about the answer to some question, and which has been carefully examined by him in that context and as a consequence has been assigned a high degree of potential surprise. A counter-expected hypothesis, that is to say, is in rough language a hypothesis that has been looked at and rejected. In contrast with this I define an *unexpected event* as one which has never been formulated in the individual's imagination, which has never entered his mind or been in any way envisaged. But here we must be careful. Evidently the question whether an event has been thought of or not may depend on the degree of exactness and detail in which it is specified. If I lose my latch-key, the possibility that I shall find it 'at home' will no doubt be in my mind; but the idea that it could have found its way into my three-year-old daughter's money-box may have escaped me in that explicit form. Yet this also answers to the description of finding the key 'at home'.

These two categories, counter-expected and unexpected situations or events, are exhaustive in the sense that under one or other of these heads can be included every kind of event or state of affairs which does not conform fully and precisely to an imagined situation or event pre-existing in the individual's mind and carrying zero potential surprise. Now to say that someone expects to be surprised by a counter-expected event involves a logical contradiction. Some precisely specified future event is imagined, and some degree, zero or greater than zero, of potential surprise is attached to the hypothesis of its occurrence. To expect this event means, at any rate, to assign to it zero potential surprise; but in that case this zero degree of

* 'The expectational dynamics of the individual', *Economica*, vol. x (1943), p. 117. See also *Expectation in Economics*, pp. 73, 74, 76.

surprise is what is expected to be experienced if this event occurs. Thus it follows that our paradox can only be resolved by supposing that one can expect to be surprised by an unexpected event. In what circumstances will this be possible? This latter question is really two questions:

(1) What circumstances expose a man to the occurrence of an unexpected event?

(2) In what circumstances will he be aware of this exposure?

Here we are not thinking, of course, of events in general, but of the outcome of specified antecedents, the result of an 'experiment' defined in some respects as to its character and particular occasion. All of us, needless to say, are at all times exposed to unexpected occurrences in general. Question (1) asks in what circumstances, when a man has been looking at some particular pigeon-hole of future history, what actually happens can have altogether escaped his survey of possibilities, so that the degree of potential surprise he assigned to it was neither zero nor greater than zero, but was non-existent, a sheer blank. If the question to which the event will provide the answer is a very simple one, so that the answer will be, for example, simply Yes or No, or a single number, then it is plainly almost impossible that the individual should fail to survey, at least in principle and by implication, all outcomes which are logically conceivable, so that no loophole will be left for anything to occur which he has not thought of and to which he has not assigned some degree of potential surprise. When the question is a Yes or No question or a 'one-dimensional' question, there can scarcely be any possibility of an occurrence which is unexpected in my special sense. It is when the answer must consist in a catologue of a great many particulars and details that the very existence of some of the individual characteristics, or the possibility of certain combinations of them, may be overlooked by the individual when he considers the matter in advance. Complexity of the event is therefore, I think, a circumstance which must be present if the individual is to be in fact exposed to the occurrence of an unexpected event. Thus, for example, the size of a dividend could not be un-expected in my sense, though it could of course be counter-expected. But a Budget, or some of its proposals, could be unexpected, because the variety of possible combinations of measures is so great. We come, then, to question (2).

By an exhaustive set of rival hypotheses about some question I mean a set of headings under one or other of which the individual feels certain that he will be able to place the true answer to the question when it shall become known. Some at least of these headings will ordinarily be stated with some precision and fullness of detail, but the individual may not feel certain that the true answer will be found amongst these accurately stated hypotheses. If so, in order to make the set of hypotheses exhaustive he will have to include a *residual hypothesis*, which will be simply a recognition of the non-exhaustiveness of his list of precisely stated hypotheses. Since, if the question is meaningful, it must necessarily have some true answer, the individual will acknowledge that one at least of his exhaustive set of rival hypotheses must be assigned zero potential surprise. But there is nothing in general which compels him to attach zero potential surprise to any of his fully stated hypotheses; every one of these may carry potential surprise greater than zero, and the zero degree be attached only to the residual hypothesis. If so, there is no logical contradiction in his believing it possible that when the true answer shall become known, its character in detail will surprise him. More precisely we can say that no logical contradiction is involved in the individual's assigning zero potential surprise simultaneously to each of the ideas (1) that the true answer when it shall become known will fall under his residual heading, and (2) that its character in detail will cause him surprise.

By way of illustration, suppose that a nineteenth-century physicist had been shown an electronic digital computer performing in a matter of minutes calculations that no human computer could execute in a lifetime. Unable to conceive how the miracle was wrought, yet convinced that the apparently impossible was in fact being done, he might well have attached potential surprise greater than zero to any conjectured, but plainly unsatisfactory, explanations that had occurred to him, and so have been compelled to reserve zero potential surprise for a residual hypothesis. And he might well have admitted to himself that the true explanation when it should be revealed was almost bound to surprise him.

It is evident that the existence, amongst his exhaustive set of rival hypotheses, of a residual hypothesis is a necessary condition of his being able to attach zero potential surprise to the idea that the eventual true answer will surprise him. For if all the hypotheses which together compose the exhaustive set were each fully specified in detail, he would, by the meaning of the words, not expect to be surprised by any one of those which he expected to occur. But is the existence, in his exhaustive set, of a residual hypothesis a *sufficient* condition for him to 'expect to be surprised'? I think the very fact that he has been baffled in his attempt to formulate in detail an exhaustive set of rival hypotheses indicates that he will necessarily be surprised by the truth which resolves his bafflement; anything not capable of surprising him would have occurred to him. If we say that the existence of a residual hypothesis is a sufficient (as well as a necessary) condition for the individual to be able without logical contradiction to 'expect to be surprised' by the true answer, we are giving to the word 'expect' the stronger of the two meanings mentioned above. For we are saying that the individual will attach potential surprise greater than zero to the idea that the true answer, when it shall become known, will *not* surprise him; we are making the word 'expect' mean that the individual has some positive degree of confidence in the idea that he will be surprised.

The argument to this point may be summarized thus: an actual experience will cause surprise when an imperfect image of it has been formed in advance; and the imperfectness can consist either in some wrong characteristics or details being specified in place of right ones, or in blanks having been left in the picture, that is, it can consist in characteristics or details which in fact belong to the experience having been omitted altogether; or again we can say, in the experience having 'dimensions' beyond the list of those which the individual could specify in advance. If the existence of these blanks, and the individual's inability to fill them in, has been recognized by him in advance, and if he also recognizes that their existence exposes him at least to the possibility of being surprised when the actual event fills them in, he can be said to 'expect to be surprised'. For he will then attach zero potential surprise to the hypothesis that the filling of the blanks will, by its manner or matter, not by its occurrence, surprise him; and to attach zero potential surprise to a hypothetical future event is one thing that we can mean by 'to expect it'.

Our argument regarding the possibility of 'expecting to be surprised' has had as one of its central ideas the concept of residual hypothesis. The part that this idea can play in the analysis of real situations may be illustrated in conclusion of this note. We have seen that the individual will only be driven back on a residual hypothesis when the question: What will be the outcome of this course of action? presents itself to him in a rather complex form, calling for an intricate schedule of information rather than a single number or a simple Yes or No. But it may be that this complicated kind of answer is going to be treated as a means to a simpler kind, which will sum up in some values of a single variable the happy or unhappy possibilities implied by the complex answer. The values of this variable corresponding to different hypothetical answers of the complex kind, each associated by the individual with some degree of potential surprise, will constitute a set from which he can select two focus-outcomes which, when standardized, he can use as coordinates to plot a point, representing the course of action in question, on his gambler indifference-map. Now it seems evident that the only way in which a residual hypothesis concerning the complex type of question can be 'summarized' by means of a single variable is by two very widely separated values* of that variable, one of them representing a highly desirable and the other a highly undesirable outcome. If two such values select themselves as the focus-values of a course of action concerning whose detailed outcome a residual hypothesis is entertained, the point representing this course will lie far from the origin of the gambler indifference-map, and, if losses are measured on its horizontal axis, far towards the right where focus-losses approach the maximum possible size represented by the individual's whole fortune. Now there is reason to suppose that the slopes of the gambler indifference-curves on such a map become steeper towards the right. Thus a point whose location is determined by a residual hypothesis is very likely to lie below the origin indifference-curve, that is, the gambler indifference-curve on which all points are esteemed by the individual as neither more nor less desirable than an assurance of neither gain nor loss, a situation which, in the context of gains or losses measured in money, he can attain by simply keeping his whole fortune in the form of a bank-balance. However, if only some of his possible courses of action have a residual hypothesis, does the conclusion we have just reached have any practical bearing?

The state of mind in which the individual can only render exhaustive his set of hypotheses concerning some one or more questions or courses of action, by including in each such set a residual hypothesis, can arise in two ways. The feeling of unplumbed ignorance or lost bearings can be concerned with the situation of which some particular actions of the individual would be the 'proximate cause'. Or it can be concerned with the framework of events which will happen 'in any case', the things which are altogether outside his control, such as the weather or the political situation. In the latter case it may well happen that not one of the more adventurous of the courses of action open to him escapes the need of a residual hypothesis to render exhaustive his set of rival hypotheses concerning its outcome. If he attaches low or zero potential surprise to these residual hypotheses, all the points representing active and 'positive' policies may lie below the origin indifference-curve, and only those

---

* Their separation can of course only be meaningfully described as 'wide' in relation to a particular context.

representing passive policies, typically that of keeping his fortune in cash, may lie on or above it. Thus we should expect that when the news seems to provide internally inconsistent or conflicting evidence about the policies or intentions of powerful persons, or concerning the degree of knowledge they possess, or is for any reason especially difficult to interpret, the consequence would be to inhibit some kinds of business activity; not because the news was regarded as *bad* from the point of view of those engaged in this activity (often they are divided into two camps with opposing momentary interests, like the Stock Exchange bulls and bears), but because it is *unintelligible*. And this we actually observe to happen.

V

'EXPECTATION IN ECONOMICS':
SOME CRITICS ANSWERED*

By a *unique* trial (experiment, question about the future) I mean one which is unique in its effect on the life of the individual who makes it; that is, a trial whose character and circumstances are not sufficiently like those of other trials which he expects to make for him to treat all these trials as parts of a larger whole, with whose outcome as a whole, and not with those of the separate trials composing it, he is really concerned. It may also be true of a trial, whether or not it is unique in the above sense, that the individual's own experience or the available record of history do not provide instances similar and numerous enough for frequency-ratios to be obtained; this is a separate, and for the logic of my case a minor, matter. The most fundamental and essential source of uniqueness in a trial is *crucialness* (see below).

By an *isolated* trial I mean one which is rendered virtually unique by time-separation from expected trials resembling it, so that the latter cannot loom large enough in the individual's time-perspective, compared with the immediately future trial, to be combined with the latter into a larger whole whose outcome as a whole, and not that of the separate trials composing it, is what matters to him.

By a *crucial* trial I mean one whose outcome, like a chess-move, will affect the whole future course of relevant events for the individual. A crucial trial is necessarily unique. By making it the individual gives himself a new set of circumstances and opportunities, so that it is logically impossible for him ever to repeat the experiment which brought this new situation about. *Crucialness* is the real and important source of uniqueness in any occasion of choosing: and far from being unusual, it is all-pervasive; perhaps it is not too much to say that every choice I make is crucial, and steers my life into a path different from what it would otherwise have followed.

It is because I believe most occasions of choosing are, and are felt to be, crucial that I attach so much more importance to the unique or isolated experiment than to the kind typified by drawing balls from an urn or tossing a coin (except when the latter is for choice of stations in the Boat Race or of innings in a Test Match).

* *Economica*, vol. XVI (1949), pp. 343–6. Originally entitled 'Three notes on *Expectation in Economics*'.

Now when an experiment, a question about the future, is unique, isolated, or crucial, it does not make sense to add together its rival hypothetical outcomes or answers. They are mutually exclusive. One alone will come true, the others will be for ever false. This is in absolute contrast to what we can say of each of a series of trials all in some sense alike and each important only as it contributes to the total result of the series. To decide between rival courses of action when each is a crucial or unique experiment, a man must surely choose for each some single clear-cut hypothesis to give him that enjoyment by imagination which is all the good that something in the future can give him. He cannot add the rival hypotheses, he must choose between them. How are we to introduce, as we must, his doubt and uncertainty into his process of choosing? The traditional view, I suggest, substitutes the idea of confusion for that of uncertainty; all the rival hypotheses, shouting together with their many voices, give him a confused impression that he should move one way rather than the other. Since all of them necessarily are liars but one, this procedure is an irrational compromise. My own suggestion is that of focus-values described in *Expectation in Economics*, Chapter II, and Appendix C and the final Appendix, and the first point I have to deal with is my view, contested by my critics, that the individual, once he has selected the 'most powerful element' amongst the hypotheses of gain and similarly amongst those of loss, will confine his attention to these two 'elements' exclusively.

He cannot add the rival hypotheses; how then is he to use them except by selecting distinguished individuals from amongst them? Are we to suppose that he vacillates between them? This is merely another version of the confusion of voices. Or that, distrusting the focus-gain, he keeps in reserve at the back of his mind other hypotheses, less attractive in pure content but carrying lower potential surprise, to comfort him against the idea that the focus-gain may not be realized? To think this is to misunderstand the nature of potential surprise as I conceive it, and of enjoyment by imagination.

All hypotheses to which a man assigns zero potential surprise have perfect and undulled access to his mind, and he is not rendered less sensitive to any one of them by an increase in their number. He cannot rationally, I think, 'crowd out' a disagreeable hypothesis by having also in mind other less disagreeable or positively agreeable ones. These would indeed take away from the disagreeable hypothesis some of its numerical probability, and therefore the latter concept thus misapplied distorts the truth. Against a hypothesis of disaster, rival hypotheses can provide no defence, no barrier or analgesic; only (if they are hypotheses of success) a counterpoise. Such an analgesic, if the circumstances provide one, must consist in high potential surprise, a denial of plausibility, attached to the unpleasant hypothesis itself. Amongst gain-hypotheses, therefore, none smaller than the focus-gain can contribute anything to the venture's attractiveness. What of gain-hypotheses larger than the focus-gain, that is, those elements which are weaker than the most powerful element through carrying too high a degree of potential surprise? The very fact that they are weaker means that, having assigned to each rival hypothesis the degree of potential surprise that intuition suggests, the individual finds that the venture looks most powerfully attractive when he thinks of it as the possible (though slightly doubtful) provider of gain x_1, than as the more doubtful provider of gain $x_2 > x_1$. (He must think of it as one or the other.) The larger but weaker gain-hypotheses could influence the individual, I think, only through vacillation. Plainly, when he makes his decision, vacillation is at an end.

In sum, I must ask my critics: Can one really entertain two mutually exclusive hypotheses at one and the same time in such a way that they reinforce each other in giving enjoyment?*

What is the source of my critics' feeling that other elements besides the two 'most powerful' are taken account of in the individual's final decision? I think it is that they are still unconsciously thinking in terms of numerical probability and of repeated trials forming parts of a larger whole which alone is significant. They may even feel that I exaggerate the importance and pervasiveness in life of unique occasions of choosing as compared with those which can be all thrown together into an actuarial cauldron until the uncertainty belonging to each comes out in the wash. But do not all those moments which have some quality or savour that makes up the worth-while part of life seem to us unique? A child who is prevented by some last-minute hitch from going to a party can by no means be consoled by being told that there will be plenty of other parties in future months and years. We live in the present moment. If I fail to make a success of *this* moment, my whole faith in my capacity for dealing with life is to some degree undermined.

How does my system discriminate between the respective degrees

* The uncertainty inherent for the individual in a situation where he feels that either hypothesis *can* be entertained need not be given expression by the rationally impossible feat of enjoying by anticipation *both* the mutually exclusive outcomes at the same time. The uncertainty can be expressed by potential surprise assigned individually and independently to *each* hypothesis regardless of others.

of attractiveness to a man of two alternative courses of action, of which one will yield him £1 for certain, and the other will yield him £1 or nothing according as a tossed coin shows heads or tails? This illustrates a class of cases which I ought to have considered amongst the Special Cases of Appendix B,* viz. those where the only outcomes carrying zero potential surprise are gains (or at least do not include any losses). Mr Graaff has suggested to me that the ϕ-function should be made to depend on the individual's degree of belief as I have defined it in the final Appendix,† by the introduction, as a third independent variable, of the degree of potential surprise

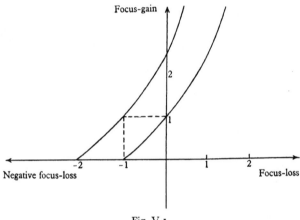

Fig. V 1

attached to the contradictory of a hypothesis. But this remedy will not serve for the *general* case of y-curves whose inner range includes no losses; it is useful only for those cases (rare, I have assumed, in economic subject-matter) where one particular hypothesis is looked on as 'more likely' than *any* other. For if there is any other hypothesis also carrying zero potential surprise, i.e. if the inner range is not merely one single value of x, then the potential surprise attached to our contradictory will be *zero*, and cannot, therefore, help the ϕ-function to discriminate between y-curves having different 'loss-excluding' inner ranges. (This point illustrates a quite basic and essential aspect of the very *raison d'être* of my whole construction, viz. the uselessness in general of any concept of positive belief or confidence in a hypothesis: you cannot at one and the same time believe positively in (have more than zero confidence in) both (all) of two

* *Expectation in Economics*, p. 36.   † Ibid. p. 128.

or more rival (mutually exclusive) hypotheses. Hence we must use a measure of disbelief.) Degree of belief is no remedy; but no remedy is needed. My ϕ-function as it stands can discriminate perfectly between the two alternatives in the case proposed by Mr Baumol and Mr Graaff. For just as we insist that a quadratic equation always has *two* roots, and in such a case as $(x-a)(x-a) = 0$ we say it has two equal roots, so we must suppose the individual to ask himself always what is the 'least good' hypothetical outcome that he need consider as well as what is the best one. When he is offered £1 with certainty the 'least good' hypothesis is a negative loss of £1, and the best hypothesis is a positive gain of £1. The fact that these two outcomes are identical does not prevent us from plotting on the individual's gambler indifference-map the point which corresponds to them. This point $(-1, 1)$ will lie in the upper left-hand quadrant of the map (see Fig. V 1) on a gambler indifference-curve above and to the left of (i.e. preferable to) the one containing the point $(0, 1)$ which corresponds to the other alternative, viz. a focus-gain of £1 and a focus-loss of £ zero. In a more general situation where we have two bell-shaped y-curves whose inner ranges both lie wholly on the gain side of the neutral outcome, one curve enclosing the other, the question how the individual will select a 'least-favourable' hypothesis for each in order to plot for each a point on his gambler indifference-map is an important and interesting one which I must hope to deal with elsewhere.

VI

A NON-ADDITIVE MEASURE OF UNCERTAINTY*

In very kindly writing to me about the system proposed in *Expectation in Economics*, Professor C. F. Carter and Dr Lawrence R. Klein have both pointed to *non-additivity* as one of its most essential characteristics. The nature and necessity of a non-additive system are the theme of Appendix C to Chapter II of my book, and I wish to give all possible emphasis to this central strand of my theory.

My system is non-additive in two entirely different ways. First, when some kind of performance, such as the tossing of a coin or the throwing of a pair of dice, is repeated indefinitely in suitably uniform conditions, we can establish for each possible result of such performance the number of times it will occur in a given number of repetitions of the performance. These frequency-ratios, one for each possible result, must plainly sum to unity. This necessity alone (quite apart from the logical impossibility of using frequency-ratio to discuss the outcome of a unique or isolated experiment) would make numerical probability quite unsuitable for describing mental states of uncertainty. For this purpose we need a measure of acceptance, of a hypothesis proposed in answer to some question, which shall be independent of the degrees of acceptance simultaneously accorded to rival hypotheses. The need for such independence appears perhaps most strikingly when we select one such hypothesis and gather together all its rivals to constitute its contradictory.

There is no psychological reason why equal degrees of acceptance should not be accorded to a hypothesis and its contradictory, but when the contradictory itself consists of two or more mutually incompatible hypotheses, we plainly cannot give the probability half to each hypothesis and its contradictory, for we have several such pairs. More generally, we need a measure of acceptance by which the individual can give to new rival hypotheses, which did not at first occur to him, some degree, and even the highest degree, of acceptance without reducing the degrees of acceptance accorded to any of those already in his mind. And this leads on to the suggestion that what we need is a measure, not of positive belief or confidence in given hypotheses (for it is plain that the more numerous are the hypotheses claiming a share of such positive 'confidence' the more thinly it must

* *Review of Economic Studies*, vol. XVII (1) (1949–50), pp. 70–4.

be spread over them; we cannot have high degrees of confidence in two or more mutually exclusive hypotheses simultaneously) but a measure of disbelief; for this can be put at zero for as many rival hypotheses as we like. Thus while the additive character of numerical probability is fatal to its use for describing mental states of uncertainty (that is, states of acknowledgement of ignorance), we have with potential surprise an absolute release from any such requirement. The degrees of potential surprise assigned to the members of an exhaustive* set of rival hypotheses are independent of each other and need not sum to any particular total. They can, for example, all be zero, and thus express the individual's feeling, which cannot be expressed by frequency-ratio probability, that every one of the rival hypotheses has 'nothing known against it'. For it is also true that numerical probability cannot distinguish between perfect possibility and perfect certainty. If a hypothesis appears to a person to be wholly consistent with all that he knows about the relevant situation, we may say that this hypothesis is for him perfectly possible. It is my contention that, in general, there is no logical impossibility for him thus to entertain any number of rival suggested answers to some question. But the numerical probability $1/n$ assigned to each of n hypotheses each regarded as perfectly possible does not well convey that state of mind; and, indeed, if a hypothesis is looked on as 'perfectly possible' and continues to be so esteemed when new hypotheses are thought of which also seem perfectly possible, why should the measure of acceptance that we give to it be diminished by their arrival?

This characteristic of potential surprise, that the degrees in which it is assigned to the various members of an exhaustive set of rival hypotheses do not have to sum to any particular total, is, then, the first of the ways in which my system is non-additive.

If potential surprise is chosen as the appropriate measure of the degrees of acceptance that an individual gives to his rival hypotheses about the outcome of some course of action, and we suppose him to assign a degree of potential surprise to each rival hypothesis about each of the various courses of action that seem open to him, how does he then decide which course he prefers? In those cases where it makes sense to use frequency-ratio probability as the measure of acceptance (I shall argue that these are not cases of true uncertainty at all), the appropriate procedure is additive. This is the second kind of additiveness that my system abandons. We have to consider why the notion of frequency-ratio has no relevance or meaning for the analysis of true uncertainty.

* See *Expectation in Economics*, final Appendix.

Our starting-point is the distinction between what I shall call a *divisible* and a *non-divisible* experiment. The outcome of a divisible experiment is the result of adding the outcomes of indefinitely many separate trials all in certain respects uniform; for example, we may throw a pair of dice indefinitely many times and add the numbers obtained in the separate throws. Regarding any one trial we may only be able to say that its result will be one or other of a certain set of contingencies; but if *a priori* or by experience we can establish for each contingency the number of its occurrences in a given number of trials (its frequency-ratio), we then know* the outcome of the divisible experiment as a whole. By a non-divisible experiment I mean one which, through its being crucial for the whole relevant future course of events or in some other way inherently unique,† or through its being isolated so far as the life of the individual decision-maker is concerned, can be neither itself broken down into a number of uniform additive parts nor treated as part of a divisible experiment. For a non-divisible, unique experiment it is plain that no frequency-ratio can have any meaning or relevance. Now when any one of the separate trials of which a divisible experiment is composed is considered by itself in its own right, as an isolated, particular event, so that we are concerned with the result of this particular trial and not with an anonymous contribution to the total result of a divisible experiment, then this trial is itself a non-divisible experiment, and its result cannot be predicted by any additive, frequency-ratio procedure. But there is a temptation to confuse the particular, isolated trial with the divisible experiment in which it could be included, and to treat the known outcome of the latter as though it were a guide to that of the isolated trial. When we are about to make a non-divisible experiment we have in mind a number of rival, that is, mutually exclusive, hypotheses concerning its outcome. Not only are there no objectively obtainable frequency-ratios by which to multiply these, but the very notion of frequency-ratio is wholly out of place; it does not make sense to assign even subjectively determined 'frequency-ratios' to the various hypotheses, multiply, and add the products. The result will be logically meaningless. Yet because frequency-ratios, meaningful for a *divisible* experiment, are at hand to be stolen for illegitimate application to one of the particular trials composing that divisible experiment, we are tempted to suppose

---

* I am not here concerned with subtleties of the theory of knowledge; I only wish to contrast 'knowlege' with 'ignorance' in a simple-minded and vernacular sense of these words.

† See Essay V above.

that every experiment, even when unique and non-divisible, can be assigned an 'outcome' obtained by an additive, frequency-ratio procedure.

The outcome of a divisible experiment, if frequency-ratios can be established, can be known in advance. It is a non-divisible experiment that confronts us with true uncertainty, that is, ignorance, about its outcome. But since in practical life it is continually necessary to choose between experiments, i.e. to decide whether to follow this course of action or that in given circumstances, some substitute must be found for knowledge. Whether any such substitute can have a rational basis is not our concern here. A variety of hypotheses will usually be entertained by the decision-maker about the outcome of a non-divisible experiment, and to each he will, I think we may assume, assign some coefficient expressing the degree to which it seems to him, on whatever grounds, 'possible', 'plausible', 'non-absurd', 'acceptable', or whatever we care to say. Perhaps such judgements must, like tastes, be treated as data. The question is by what procedure they are used for the purpose of comparing, and choosing amongst, 'experiments' or courses of action.

There are, I think, two conceivable types of procedure. One consists in allowing all, or some large subset, of the hypotheses which the decision-maker has considered and has not absolutely excluded as impossible, to have some say in influencing his decision. This, because it consists in adding together contributions of stimulus from the whole array of non-excluded hypotheses, we may call the integrative solution. The other consists in carrying to its logical conclusion the idea that the hypotheses are rivals, and concentrating attention on those two or few of them which out-rival all the others in their power of stimulus. This I call the focus-values solution. Each of these two types of procedure can be illustrated by constructions using potential surprise. In defining the integrative solution we must first point out that, since we are concerned with rival, that is, mutually exclusive, hypotheses about a unique, non-divisible experiment, it will not do to integrate the area under any projection of the curve $\phi = \phi\{x, y(x)\}$. The reader will, I think, at once concede that if the members of some subset of hypotheses of, for example, gain, all carry equal degrees of potential surprise, only that member of the subset which speaks of the highest gain will be of any concern to the decision-maker. If so, we plainly must not add together the degrees ϕ of interestingness or stimulating power which the members of this subset can respectively claim when each is considered on its own; the powers of all are subsumed under that of the most powerful, just as the profile or silhouette of a file of soldiers standing one behind the other will be that of the tallest soldier. But it may then be tempting to suggest that we should integrate the area under a projection on the ϕy-plane of the twisted curve $\phi = \phi\{x, y(x)\}$. For in this projected curve, say $\phi = \phi_p(y)$, the values assumed by ϕ would depend on y only, and each element $\phi_p(y)\, dy$ of the area $\int_0^{\bar{y}} \phi_p(y)\, dy$ under the curve would correspond to a different value of y from that of any other element. However, this procedure also is logically indefensible. ϕ measures the degree of stimulus which each hypothesis considered by itself would be able to impart, and the hypotheses relate to a unique, non-divisible experiment and are mutually exclusive. To draw stimulus from the supposition that some one idea is true, and simultaneously to draw stimulus from the supposition that a second idea is true, when this second idea is a denial of the first, is rationally impossible. Before we can integrate, we must obtain a set of elements whose respective hypotheses are not mutually exclusive; whose hypotheses, that is to say, are such that we can assert the truth of any one without thereby denying the truth of the others. An 'integral' solution is possible, but not by means of the ϕ-surface; it requires a function of its own whose nature has been suggested to me by what I have heard from Mr Ralph Turvey about the work of Professor Ingvar Svennilson, with which I am not acquainted because of its being in Swedish. I gather that Professor Svennilson uses what is formally a frequency-ratio concept of probability, but perhaps he thinks of it as a subjective assigning of 'marks' to various hypotheses; for he is, I think, concerned with the case where the hypotheses are mutually exclusive. The essence of Professor Svennilson's construction, as Mr Turvey has described that construction to me, is that each of the additive terms, after the first, is the difference between one hypothetical gain and the next larger hypothetical gain (when the hypotheses are arranged in order of the size of gain they respectively speak of), each such difference being reduced, before the summation is made, to that amount which, if expected with certainty, would be equivalent to it. The summation of such terms is logically perfectly legitimate, if we are satisfied with a probability concept which is formally that of frequency-ratio but must essentially be something quite different because it is being used in a context where frequency-ratio is meaningless. Whether such summation is psychologically a good approximation to the truth is a quite different question, and whether it is a methodologically convenient and manageable hypothesis, and whether it promises to be fruitfully suggestive, are yet other questions.

Whatever answers we give to these three latter questions, it is interesting to consider whether an analogous construction is possible with potential surprise instead of frequency-ratio probability.

I do not know whether Professor Svennilson supposes the decision-maker to include hypotheses of *loss* amongst his set of hypothetical outcomes, but we shall certainly do so, and our 'integrative' solution must, like the focus-values solution, provide us with two magnitudes, one representing the influence on him of the hypotheses of gain and the other that of the hypotheses of loss. Since both magnitudes will be obtained by the same kind of procedure, we need only consider, say, the 'gain' side. In constructing our set of additive terms (from which we can if we like proceed by a limiting process to an integral) we must, of course, observe the rule that no two or more terms must be hypotheses carrying the same degree of potential surprise; that out of any such subset of hypotheses, only the largest gain must be included. Thus our first term will be one corresponding to the upper extreme $x = x_u$ of the inner range. We may allow ourselves, perhaps, to identify this term with $\phi(x_u, 0)$, but thereafter we must put the ϕ-surface quite out of mind. The mental process we attribute to the decision-maker if we adopt the integrative solution, indeed, the very shape of his mind, differs entirely from what is implied by the focus-values solution. Under the integrative solution we are to suppose that as he passes in review larger and larger hypotheses of gain, the decision-maker draws from the excess of each such value of x over its predecessor, after making allowance for the increasing degrees of potential surprise associated with each successive difference, an additive contribution to the total stimulus that he derives from the 'gain' hypotheses as a whole. I do not think this conception contains any formal logical self-contradiction, but it does seem to me an unnatural and difficult mental feat. If there is no logical self-contradiction in adding, in this special way, contributions of mental stimulus derived from mutually exclusive hypotheses, it is none the less, I think, a highly artificial and psychologically unreal supposition. People who have never asked themselves how frequency-ratio probability can possibly have any relevance or meaning for the analysis of uncertainty (i.e. ignorance) about the outcome of a non-divisible isolated experiment, are predisposed towards some sort of additive solution, because it is by an additive procedure that we reach knowledge of the outcome of a divisible experiment. If, for the analysis of choice amongst non-divisible real-life experiments (i.e. choice amongst courses of action whose outcome cannot be known in advance), we discard the notion of frequency-ratio probability, ought we not also to discard our predisposition towards additive solutions and start afresh with an open mind? The notion that the power, effectiveness or significance of some set of elements can depend, not in any sense on their sum, but on the power and effect of the most powerful amongst them, is not after all so recondite. The difficulty of climbing a particular crag may consist in the cumulative exhaustion involved in overcoming a succession of difficulties; but often it will depend, instead, on the question whether the greatest of the individual difficulties can be overcome. The degree of discomfort and irritation caused by a noise, to a person trying to concentrate, will by no means be doubled if a second source of identical noise comes into play; if one man's hammer can stop you from being able to think, a second man's hammer will make no difference. But my belief in the focus-values solution, as opposed to the integrative solution, depends really on how I conceive the nature of expectation itself, as an act of creative imagination and not of 'rational' calculation; for calculation is impossible when the data are incomplete, and in face of ignorance, rationality is a mere pretence.

VII

THREE VERSIONS OF THE ϕ-SURFACE: SOME NOTES FOR A COMPARISON*

Two variants of the ϕ-surface have been proposed as alternatives to my own, one of them by Mr J. Mars, of Manchester University, and the other by Mr H. G. Johnson, of King's College, Cambridge. The modifications suggested by Mr Mars are in a sense more considerable than those of Mr Johnson. In his article† Mr Mars ostensibly retains the gambler indifference-map which is an essential part of my own scheme; but, in fact, if we accept his formulation of the ϕ-surface idea, the gambler indifference-map can be dispensed with. (I am not willing thus to dispense with it.) In my own scheme the ϕ-surface serves purely to locate the standardized focus-values of a venture. Once these have been determined, we can forget ϕ and use the standardized focus-values of x, numbers standing simply for amounts of money, as coordinates to plot a point on the gambler indifference-map. The shape of the latter is not formally and rigidly related to that of the ϕ-surface, though it may well be psychologically so related. By abandoning, or drastically circumscribing the role of, the gambler indifference-map, Mr Mars loses an essential 'degree of freedom' which my system possesses. He assumes that we can measure ϕ in units which will allow us, treating ϕ as negative for losses and positive for gains, to obtain an algebraic sum of the two values of ϕ, one at the focus-gain (primary or standardized; ϕ is the same at both) and the other at the focus-loss. This algebraic sum is then a measure of the attractiveness of the venture, and can be compared with measures similarly obtained for other ventures. If this procedure were accept-able there would plainly be no need for a gambler indifference-map. But the procedure is not acceptable, for it means that, when a scale for ϕ is given and a particular form is specified for the ϕ-surface with respect to that scale (that is to say, when for each point (x, y) the value $\phi = \phi(x, y)$ is a known number to be measured off on a known scale), the shape of every gambler indifference-curve is thereby also specified and, in consequence, the shapes of the gambler indifference-curves are not independent of each other, they have no freedom to

* *Review of Economic Studies*, vol. xviii (2) (1950–1), pp. 119–22.
† 'A study in expectations: reflections on Shackle's *Expectation in Economics*, Part I', *Yorkshire Bulletin of Economic and Social Research*, July 1950, pp. 63–98.

express that aspect of the individual's temperament which it is the purpose of the gambler indifference-map to express. In Mr Mars's variant the rigid connection between the shape of the ϕ-surface and that of each gambler indifference-curve, and the resulting rigid connection between the shapes of the gambler indifference-curves themselves, works out as follows:

Fig. VII 1 shows the profile of the ϕ-surface* at $y = 0$, that is, the curve $\phi = \phi(x, 0)$ in which the ϕ-surface meets a vertical wall erected

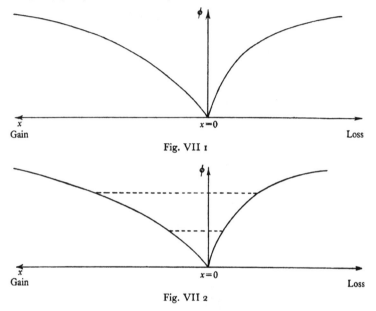

Fig. VII 1

Fig. VII 2

along the line $y = 0$ (the curve in which the ϕ-surface meets the ϕx-plane). The origin indifference-curve of the gambler indifference-map† can be obtained from this profile, on Mr Mars's interpretation, by supposing a straight line, coinciding initially with the x-axis, to be translated up the ϕ-axis, remaining always in the ϕx-plane and

---

* To simplify the particular demonstration which follows I have drawn this diagram according to the same convention as that used in *Expectation in Economics*, whereby ϕ increases in one and the same sense of its axis whether it arises from gain or loss (from positive or negative x), and not according to Mr Mars's scheme (see his Diagram X), where $\phi(x, y)$ is treated as negative if x is negative. The relative advantages of these two arrangements, as they appear to me, are discussed below. Figs. VII 1, VII 2 and VII 3 are all drawn as if the positive y-axis stood up perpendicularly from the paper towards the viewer.

† See *Expectation in Economics*, p. 30.

parallel to the x-axis. At successive stages of this translation we measure the distance, from the vertical line $x = 0$, $y = 0$ (that is, the ϕ-axis) of the points where the translated line cuts the profile (see Fig. VII 2). Each pair of such distances gives us the coordinates of a point of the origin indifference-curve, when the meaning of the ϕ-surface and of the gambler indifference-map are those ascribed to them by Mr Mars. To obtain another indifference-curve we select some particular value, say $x = c$, for the standardized focus-gain, and

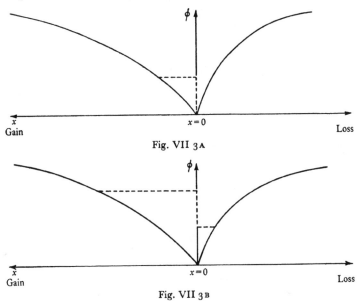

Fig. VII 3A

Fig. VII 3B

consider (instead of the straight line coinciding initially with the x-axis) a curve of 'crank-handle' form:
consisting of two horizontal straight rays connected by a vertical 'step', the height of this step being such that, when the lower horizontal segment or ray coincides with the 'loss' ray of the x-axis and the step itself is at $x = 0$, the intersection of the upper horizontal ray of the crank-curve with the profile $\phi = \phi(x, 0)$ is at a distance c from the vertical line $x = 0$, $y = 0$. We then translate the crank-curve
upwards (so that the 'step' slides up the line $x = 0$, $y = 0$) and plot on the plane of the gambler indifference-map the points representing the pairs of distances from the vertical line $x = 0$, $y = 0$ of the intersections of the crank-curve with the profile (see Figs. VII 3A, B). In Mr Mars's formulation the gambler indifference-map must be

thought of as the projection of the contour-lines of an actual surface on whose vertical dimension we mark off the algebraic sum of the values of ϕ, negative and positive respectively, at the focus-values of x. The height of the 'step' represents such an algebraic sum, and as we translate the crank-curve up the ϕ-axis, we can measure those pairs of values of x, one negative and one positive value, which if they were standardized focus-values would all represent the same net attractiveness of a venture, so that this set of pairs, or points, would trace the appropriate contour on the gambler indifference-map. It is thus plain that the shape of every gambler indifference-curve will be governed by that of the ϕ-surface, and that the shapes of the gambler indifference-curves will be rigidly related to each other. No such rigid connection is implied by my own conception of the ϕ-surface and the gambler indifference-map, and the latter is free to reflect a different aspect of the individual's attitude to uncertainty from that reflected by the ϕ-surface.

While I cannot accept Mr Mars's suggestions for revising my conception of the ϕ-surface and gambler indifference-map, I should like now to touch on an interesting point which he makes, and which I think must have been suggested to him by his way of drawing the ϕ-surface, viz. with a negative as well as a positive ϕ-axis, so that when x is negative $\phi(x, y)$ is measured downwards instead of upwards from the xy-plane. With this arrangement, and treating, as he does, ϕ as measurable, Mr Mars has produced in his Diagram X a presentation* which (when imagined as a three-dimensional model) has an undeniable aesthetic attraction; the bold sweep of the curve, which is the form taken in his version by the profile of the ϕ-surface, has its fascination; it is a pity that to make the ϕ-surface self-sufficient in this way entails, as in my view it does, a sacrifice of flexibility and power. Now if, in Mr Mars's version illustrated in his Diagram X, we consider successive profiles obtained by making vertical sections in planes parallel to the ϕx-plane and located at successively higher values of y (potential surprise), these profiles will resemble in general character the one located at $y = 0$, but their respective slopes at any one value of x will be successively less steep. All these profiles will pass through the y-axis, the line $\phi = 0$, $x = 0$, at some positive slope $\dfrac{\partial \phi}{\partial x} > 0$, while we shall have also $\dfrac{\partial(\partial \phi/\partial x)}{\partial y} < 0$, and the surface will thus have, as it were, a 'ploughshare' form, a clockwise twist as we go from lower to higher values of y. This contrasts, as Mr Mars has pointed out, with the assumption implicit in Figs. II 3, II 4, etc., of

* Mars, op. cit. p. 87.

Expectation in Economics (first edition), that at rather high values of y and low numerical values of x we shall have $\phi = 0$. Through this assumption my diagrams show the two sloping sheets of the ϕ-surface separated from each other, except at the point $x = 0$, $y = 0$, by a V-shaped flat region of the xy-plane over all of which $\phi = 0$. The meaning of the assumption is that very small imagined gains or losses, associated with very high potential surprise, will have no power to interest the enterpriser and will, therefore, be 'subliminal'. The influence that a particular choice of geometrical symbolism can have on one's thinking is here strikingly illustrated, for while in my own diagrams my own assumption appears, I think, quite natural, the case would be quite otherwise if my assumption were incorporated in Mr Mars's diagrams. There it would break the smooth downward sweep of all the profiles except that at $y = 0$, and would thus, according to my feeling, appear 'unnatural'. In Mr Mars's diagrams the assumption would be represented by a platform between two cliffs, one above and one below it, while in my diagrams it is simply the flat floor of a valley from which the sloping sides rise on either side. As to which assumption is the more realistic, it is for others to judge; the point is not of great importance.

I turn now to Mr H. G. Johnson's version of the ϕ-surface, and here again I incline to think that aesthetic considerations have played some part. Mr Johnson has actually constructed in wood a physical representation of his variant, and has written an explanatory article with diagrams and a photograph.* At a first glance, Mr Johnson's version appears simpler than my own, and has a quasi-symmetry which, even apart from the pedagogic advantages claimed for the model, is undeniably attractive. A more important characteristic is that this variant gives us a certain extra scope, in that it allows us, if we wish, to assume that ϕ is an increasing, instead of a decreasing, function of potential surprise, over some range of x, without having to resort to any odd-looking or complicated form for the ϕ-surface. I am doubtful whether such an assumption would ever be appropriate, but the possibility of pointing to the parts of the model relevant to such an assumption, and asking why the potential surprise curve avoids them, might be valuable didactically. At any rate, the inclusion (and the possibility of including) of these regions is as justifiable and useful as the inclusion, in a Cartesian diagram, of all four quadrants when perhaps only one or two are going to be assigned a role and meaning in the particular argument.

* 'A three-dimensional model of the Shackle ϕ-surface', by H. G. Johnson, *Review of Economic Studies*, vol. XVIII (2) (1950–1), no. 46, p. 115.

VIII

THE ECONOMIST'S VIEW OF PROFIT*

The word 'profit' occurs in economic theory in two quite distinct contexts. For the earliest economists a question of prime interest was what principle determines the proportions in which the aggregate income of a national or world economic system is shared out amongst those whose collaborative effort produces this income. For modern economists the question what makes the size of this income or its speed of growth go up and down is also fascinating. In the answers they have proposed to each of these questions economists have used the word profit, but they have sometimes greatly confused themselves by supposing that they were using it in the same sense for both these purposes. A theory of profit must embrace both uses of the word and show the relation between them; but it must avoid suggesting that the two meanings can for the economist's ordinary purposes be amalgamated into one. The difference between the two meanings belongs to the essential nature of things, and to ignore it is to treat life as something different from what it is.

Any product which is brought to its final usable condition today, any product which today appears for the first time on the shop counter or in the showroom window, has in one sense been in process of manufacture since men first began to make tools. For the tools that were used yesterday in putting the finishing touches to this product or transporting it to the retail shop were made with other tools, and these with still earlier existing tools, and so on. For two reasons, however, we can ignore all of these stages in the preparations which have made possible the selling of this product to a customer today, except those of the last few months or years. First, any tool or machine contributes to the making of hundreds or thousands of other tools or machines, and so when we look back to see how much of the work that the world did on this day last year, or the year before that, or a hundred years ago, was effectively leading up to our act of sale today, we see what the mathematicians call a rapidly convergent infinite series where only the first few terms are large enough to matter. And secondly, it is clear that it is only in the later stages of the process, where steel which could have been used to make any kind of tool whatever had become specialized into a loom and that

* *The Company Accountant*, new series, no. 26 (1953), pp. 8–13.

loom had woven cloth of a particular kind, that the resources which were put into the process were *committed* to the particular kind of end-product which is displayed in the showroom today.

But though the time-intervals which must elapse between the committing of resources to the production of a more or less completely specified end-product are finite and in effect are only periods of months or a few years, yet these intervals inescapably exist, and their existence is a vital consideration for the economic theorist. For at that point of time when the decision is taken to commit some resources to a particular line of production, it is in the nature of things impossible for anyone to know precisely and for certain what will be the market exchange value of the end-product at that future date when it will be ready. This situation is part of the essence of things. It may be slightly concealed by some of our institutional arrangements, but it cannot be abolished by them. You may object that the manufacturer of a commodity often fixes the price at which he will sell it. But this, of course, does not compel the customer to buy it at that price, and you as accountants will be conscious of the possibility that goods may stand in the books of the firm at prices at which it may later prove impossible to sell them. Again it may be pointed out that many goods are bespoke by the customer and the price settled before the greater part of the total expense is made. But this merely transfers the uncertainty to the customer. A ship-owner may find, for example, that when his new ship is delivered he has paid much more for it than the price at which orders are being currently accepted for similar ships. Lastly you may perhaps ask 'What of a completely planned economic system, where all production is undertaken in conformity with a centrally constructed plan which embraces every economic aspect of life and looks many years ahead?' It is still, fortunately, impossible to plan human feelings and aspirations, it is impossible to plan imagination and invention and fashion and politics. In spite of all the plans, a product which we start to make today can fit well or ill into the situation which will exist when it is ready. To abolish the market and prevent the registering of a market price does not abolish the difference between a product which exactly fills the bill and one which has to a greater or lesser degree missed its mark because those who designed it did not have second sight or superhuman luck. In all production, because it takes time, there is an ineradicable uncertainty. The answer can never be known in advance to the question: 'When this product will be finished, will its production turn out to have been worth while?'

If it is of the essence of human life that today's productive commitment of resources must aim at a market located in the future and even many years ahead, so that there can be no knowing today whether this use of the resources will turn out to have been, according to the market verdict of that future day, a good use or a regrettable one, it follows that someone today, at the moment of committing the resources, must be prepared to accept for better or worse the consequences of this commitment whatever they shall turn out to be, and without knowing what they will turn out to be. Thus one economic role which somebody must perform is that of bearing uncertainty, both in its subjective aspect of experiencing feelings and in its objective aspect of reaping factual consequences, and in both of its phases, first the interval between the moment of committing oneself to a course of action and the moment of learning the result, and secondly, the time after the result is known. There is a second economic role with which we are concerned, distinct from the bearing of uncertainty about the outcome of a course of action once that course has been embarked on; this second role is the actual deciding upon one course of action out of many that are open and whose respective consequences are, in strictness, unknown. The relation between these two roles and the degree to which under modern institutional arrangements they can be and are separated and performed by different persons is a complex and subtle question. But there can surely be no question that the two roles are intimately connected, that the decision-maker inevitably has a large personal stake, of reputation as well as material gain, in the success of his decisions, and that the uncertainty-bearer will be unwilling to forgo all part in shaping the decisions. Thus we can at first assume that the two roles are inseparably fused into a single economic function.

Uncertainty is inherent in production, but it does not follow that all who take part in it need bear uncertainty; those who wish can contract out of uncertainty. Let us assume that money is regarded by everyone as an unchanging standard of value. Then if, amongst all those who intend to contribute the services of themselves or of their property to the making of some exchangeable thing, some agree to accept from the others a stated money payment and to surrender to these others all their rights in the product, we can say that at the date when these contracts are made the planned operation has two quite different meanings for the two groups of producers. To one group it means an income of known size, for the other group it means the unknown difference between the total of the contractual payments and the price for which the product will exchange. Let us treat this second group as a single person and call him the enterpriser, and let us ascribe to him both of the two roles I discussed just now, that of decision-maker and that of uncertainty-bearer. Then what induces him to venture on production is something essentially different in character from what induces the recipients of contractual incomes to furnish their services. The total of these contractual incomes is a known single number of pounds sterling. But the enterpriser's inducement cannot, in its essential nature, be represented by a single number, for if it could, if, that is to say, we supposed him from the very beginning of his mental process of decision to have in mind only one such number, we should have to regard him as being in effect certain that this number of pounds would turn out to be the actual profit. Thus, then, it seems that we must think of the enterpriser, in his general or typical situation, as having in mind a number of different hypotheses about the number of pounds of profit or of loss that will result from his venture of production. If so, how can he ever decide whether or not this venture is worth while? According to one hypothesis, it will result in an actual loss; according to another, it will give him a large profit. How can this conflict be resolved; how can he extract from the perhaps wide variety of conjectures that he entertains, some simplified and condensed representation of his total feeling about the venture?

Economic theorists have, I think, suggested three distinct types of answer to this question, two of which we may perhaps call the rough-and-ready and the mathematical solutions. The first of these consists of supposing the enterpriser to say himself 'The best guess I can make is that the profit will be such and such. But to be on the safe side let us call it so and so much less than that.' This sort of answer raises many questions in a critical mind. Just what is meant by a 'best guess'? Which side is the 'safe' side? Why should it be necessary to reduce the best guess rather than increase it? And so on. When pressed, the 'rough-and-ready' theorist will perhaps tell you that in statistical terms the 'best guess' can be thought of as the *mode*, that is, the estimate which, if the venture were repeated many times or were treated as one of a large class of similar ventures, would most often come true. This is, I think, an answer which earns good marks; but not for the 'rough-and-ready' theory. For this answer carries us straight on to the ground of the probability theorist, who may or may not agree with this particular solution, but will certainly prefer it to the rough-and-ready formulation. The mathematical probability theorist has, however, a more sophisticated solution of his own to propose, to explain which he gives us a brief lecture on the principles of games of chance.

'If', says the mathematician, 'you throw a pair of symmetrical dice a great many times, you will find that the sum of the numbers on the two upper faces of the dice comes, in about $\frac{6}{36}$ of all cases, to seven. In about $\frac{4}{36}$ of all cases it comes to six, and in about $\frac{5}{36}$ of all cases to *five*; and so on. For each of the possible numbers from 2 to 12 which can turn up, we can obtain a frequency-ratio, that is to say, the proportion of throws in which this particular number will turn up. It will be plain to you (continues the mathematician) that if we add up all the frequency-ratios they must by definition come to unity. And furthermore, if we assume that, say, a five represents a profit of £1000, a six represents a profit of £2000, while a two represents a loss of £500, and so on, we can actually work out to a close approximation, on which we can rely, the total profit to be obtained by making, say, one thousand throws. To do this, we simply multiply the frequency-ratio of each contingent profit by the amount of that profit and by one thousand, and add together all the answers. The result is what is called the mathematical expectation.'

This impressive name may mislead us into thinking that the mathematician has performed a miracle, has got something out of his calculating machine that he did not put into it, and has changed the enterpriser's situation from essential uncertainty to certainty. But he has not. He has only shown how a set of data in a form which conceals some implicit knowledge can be made to yield this knowledge up. The frequency-ratios which describe the behaviour of a pair of dice or of a business environment are in just as full a sense knowledge about these systems as the length, breadth and depth of a box are knowledge about the box. And just as the length of the box tells us nothing about the individual fibres of which the box is made up, so the frequency-ratios tell us nothing about the individual throws of the dice, or the individual and particular business ventures, that compose the total experiment involving very many throws or ventures, which experiment is the thing that the frequency-ratios describe. It is exceedingly important to be clear about this matter. We have two entirely distinct ideas. First there are the individual throws of the dice or the individual business ventures or decisions on a given occasion to produce a given product. About each one of these considered separately as a unique individual case, frequency-ratios can tell us nothing. For plainly there is no 'frequency' about an individual case in the strict sense of this word. (We can compare this idea, that frequency-ratios are irrelevant and meaningless for individual cases, to the idea that if we know only that a given road goes from Manchester to Leeds, we still know nothing at all about the compass-bearing of any particular short segment of this road.) Secondly, there is the large class or collection of individual throws or ventures, all taken together as one whole and treated as a unity. It is some characteristics of this whole series of throws that can properly be described by a set of frequency-ratios. Thus the relevance and validity of the mathematicians' method of mathematical expectation turns entirely on the question whether there are to be a great number of ventures or acts of production which are similar, in the appropriate sense, to each other and to the members of a past series from whose results the frequency-ratios can be obtained, or whether we are concerned with a business venture which is unique.

The table of the relative frequencies of the various contingent results of some type of operation or venture is often displayed graphically as a frequency-curve, and the meaning which the possible shapes of such a curve are sometimes said to have for the business man illustrates the confusion into which we can be drawn by failing to distinguish the individual, indivisible instance from the whole series of instances. Such a curve may be comparatively wide and flat, and so indicate that perhaps large losses and large profits are both fairly frequent with the given type of venture, or it may be rather narrow-based and high, indicating that the great majority of results are rather closely clustered about one value, for example, zero. The same given mathematical expectation can be yielded by two curves of widely differing shape. If the business man is genuinely concerned with a large number of ventures all considered as constituting a single whole, how can it matter to him whether the frequency-table of the results of these ventures has a high or low dispersion? Yet it is sometimes claimed that a high dispersion, a wide flat curve, is equivalent to a high 'riskiness' in the type of venture considered. For this conflict there are, I think, two possible explanations. First, if the individual ventures are to be undertaken one after another, then a high dispersion corresponds to a highly fluctuating series of results of these ventures. And a connection is possible between the frequent occurrence of large losses, alternating with, and compensated for, by large profits, and danger to the firm. For the losses when they occur may endanger the firm's cash position or its solvency, even though they will shortly be reversed. But secondly, there is the possibility that in equating a high dispersion with a high 'riskiness', some writers are making an unconsciousness and non-legitimate transition from consideration of the series of ventures collectively as a whole to consideration of each individual venture by itself. If curve A has a broader base than curve *B*, this means that ventures of the type belonging to curve *A* *can* yield larger losses, and larger profits, than those of the type belonging to curve *B*. But this has nothing to do with *frequency*. It is a fact better stated in a different form, and this is a matter to which I shall return.

We ought next to ask: Over how much of the whole field of business operations can we look on decisions as having to be taken repeatedly in nearly the same circumstances, so that probability calculations, at least in a rough intuitive form, can be applied to them, and over what part of the field are decisions in some sense unique, each of them a case peculiar to itself? A proper discussion of this would take far too long for this essay, and I must be content to show that at least one extremely important type of business action involves non-repetitive decisions.

An experiment can be logically incapable of being repeated even once, for its very performance may irrevocably alter the circumstances in which it was made. A military commander cannot decide his tactics on the reckoning that if they fail once they may succeed another time; for if he loses the battle there will be no other time, and, indeed, whether he wins or loses, the result of the battle will so radically alter the political and military background, morale, resources and objectives, that there cannot be another battle which could be looked on as a repetition of the first in similar circumstances. Somewhat the same can be said of an election campaign fought on a particular 'platform'; and in former times an adventure of geographical exploration was likely to alter once for all the setting of such expeditions. But there is a less dramatic and more usual reason why a particular 'experiment' must be looked on as unique for the particular person or firm who contemplates making it. This is, that the resources at his command are limited, and if he loses them he cannot try again. For a business man, the possibility of a crippling loss of capital implies a large-scale operation, and perhaps we can say, typically either the founding of a new enterprise or a large extension of plant for an existing one. It is, indeed, in the field of investment-decisions (in the economist's sense of the word 'investment'), that personal uniqueness of the occasion mainly occurs. A man does not have to decide every month or every year whether or not it will pay to build a new factory or order a new ship; and even if by looking for several decades ahead he can see several dozens of such occasions, the remoteness in future time of some of these occasions prevents them from serving the purpose of repetitions of the 'experiment' he is about to make now; for the 'present value' of a given sum of money due to be paid or received in twenty or thirty years' time, when discounted at ordinary interest-rates, is of course but a fraction of its nominal amount.

There is thus, I contend, at any rate one highly important class of business decisions where considerations of relative frequency are not to the point and where calculation of a mathematical expectation is perhaps not possible and in any case not meaningful. The enterpriser must surely attack such problems by a different line of thought.

Coming, some years ago, to the conclusions I have mentioned about the relevance of numerical probability concepts for the analysis of true uncertainty, I sought to devise some alternative approach. The idea from which I started was that the confused and slender evidence as to what will be the future consequences of given present actions, which experience affords us, is much better adapted to the negative task of rejecting some imagined consequences as implausible or impossible, than to that of selecting particular hypothetical con-sequences as worthy of positive belief in varying degree. Hypotheses that require, as we say, a stretch of the imagination, that seem to require the breaking down of some obstacle that appears at present solid and invincible, that seem extravagant and to partake of fantasy, we find it possible to set aside. But this leaves us, in general, with a wide range of hypotheses, concerning the outcome of any particular course of action, on which we might now embark, all of which we feel to be equally and perfectly plausible or credible. Of each one of these hypotheses it is true that, if we were to remain in our present state of mind, with the same 'dossier' of evidence and the same interpretation of it, until the moment when the actual outcome will declare itself, we should not be in the least *surprised* by the coming true of this hypothesis.

Now if several hypotheses are all regarded as perfectly plausible, in the sense that no one of them would cause the least surprise if, without our changing our opinions in the meantime, it came true, it is surely meaningless to say that we have any positive confidence in the truth of any one of them. To have a degree of positive confidence in any one hypothesis is surely to regard all the rivals of this hypo-thesis, which are incompatible with it, as in some degree suspect or unacceptable, as strained and implausible. Then if in fact several hypotheses, concerning some one question, are all regarded as perfectly plausible, no one of them can claim any degree of our positive belief or confidence. But simply to label all the hypotheses which are regarded as perfectly plausible with a ticket saying that the confidence or positive belief in them is zero, would serve no purpose, for all these hypotheses would then find themselves in the same category, in this respect, as all those which had been set aside as more or less implausible. Thus I was led to turn upside down the orthodox approach, in which we think of the various hypotheses as claiming various degrees of belief, or confidence, or probability, and to think instead in terms of disbelief. And to suggest the very special character of this measure, with details of which I need not trouble you, and to avoid the confusing overtones of suggestion which more familiar words might carry, I called this measure, in accordance with that way of looking at the matter which I outlined a moment ago, potential surprise.

Disbelief in a hypothesis, even when it amounts only to a moderate scepticism and is by no means absolute, must surely tend to weaken the power of that hypothesis to stimulate and arrest the attention of the person who entertains it, whether the content or 'face-value' of the hypothesis is in itself good or bad. But when that content is good, the hypothesis will surely have more stimulating power the better the content is; and again if the content is disagreeable in itself, it will hold the individual's attention more strongly, the worse it is. Thus it seems that there are two influences at work in determining the power of fascination, as it were, exercised by any hypothesis of a given profit or a given loss on the mind of the enterpriser. First, this power will be less, the higher the degree of scepticism or *potential surprise* he associates with it. And secondly, this power will be greater, the higher the degree of success or of misfortune represented by the content of the hypothesis.

Regarding the first of these influences we can surely say that when the degree of scepticism attached to a hypothesis amounts to absolute disbelief and rejection, when the hypothesis is altogether excluded as impossible, this will reduce its practical interest to nil. Thus it follows that if there is indeed a considerable range of both profits and losses which the enterpriser looks on as 'perfectly possible', as entirely plausible suggestions of the outcome of his venture, he will find at first as he passes these suggestions in review, moving outwards in one direction or the other away from a zero hypothetical profit, that the interest and stimulation of these hypotheses for a while increases; but eventually when that range is reached where he begins to attach increasing scepticism to these ideas, there will come a point where some particular hypothesis, amongst those of positive profit, exceeds all the others in its power to focus the enterpriser's attention; and again on the 'loss' side, there will be some hypothetical amount of loss which will gain most attention. I have used advisedly the expression 'focusing of attention', for it seems to me that when the occasion of choosing one course of action out of several possible ones is an isolated or virtually unique occasion, the appropriate question for the enterpriser to ask himself is 'What is the best that I can hope for, and what is the worst that I need fear, if I decide on this particular course of action?' The respective answers to these questions are given, I suggest, by the two hypotheses, one of gain and one of loss, which are the 'most interesting' or 'most arresting' in the sense I have just defined.

I have traded upon your patience with what I am afraid must appear a most esoteric and tedious argument. I wanted to contrast the subjective and psychological emphasis of the approach which I am suggesting, with the objective and arithmetical preoccupations of orthodoxy. But now let us move faster. If the enterpriser can indeed arrive, for each of the projects he is comparing, at two figures representing respectively 'the most that he stands to gain' and 'the most that he stands to lose' by this venture, there are various ways in which we could imagine him to use such pairs of figures as a basis of choice between the projects. For example, he might have in mind an upper limit for the loss he is prepared to contemplate, and so choose from amongst all the projects which do not threaten a greater possible loss than this, the one which promises the highest figure as its 'possible gain'. The losses and gains in question might be thought of not as absolute amounts but as proportions of the amount to be invested in the venture. Or more generally we can imagine a table arranged as follows. In a column at the left would be written a series of hypothetical losses going up in size from one to another by equal steps. In a row opposite the smallest of these hypothetical losses there would be a series of gains also going up by equal steps. In a row opposite the next larger 'loss' figure there would again be a row of hypotheses of profit, but these would not increase by equal steps but by such steps as would make the pair of figures, the loss given in row 2 and the profit named in row 2 and, say, column M, neither more nor less desirable in the view of the particular individual than the combination of the loss in row 1 and the profit in row 1 and column M. And so on. Thus by running a pencil down any given profit column, and taking each figure in it in association with the loss figure at the beginning of the same row, we should get a succession of pairs of figures, a gain and a loss, between which pairs the enterpriser would be indifferent. On such an *indifference-table*, to move from left to right (no matter which row we start at nor which we end at) would be to move to successively more desired positions. Such a table (differing, in general, in its actual figures from one person to another) would reflect the particular enterpriser's temperament and an aspect of the inherent shape, so to speak, of his mind, so that his motive for preferring venture A to venture B would be represented by the more rightward position of A when the two ventures were roughly located on the table. Or we can say that, with such a table before him describing the mind of a particular enterpriser, an independent observer who was informed of the actual amounts of the focus-gain and focus-loss which this enterpriser had assigned to each of the ventures, would be able, by roughly placing each of them in its appropriate place on the table, to tell which was preferred by seeing which lay furthest to the right.

One conclusion at least which is of some concern to the theoretician emerges from this construction. When the outcomes of alternative ventures are uncertain (that is, are felt by the particular individual to be unknown to him) we can no longer say that the enterpriser will seek to 'maximize profit'. A civil servant might perhaps amend the proposition by saying that the enterpriser will seek to maximize profit 'having regard to the possible loss'. But this makes all the difference in the world.

The economist is sometimes accused of studying an artificial world of his own invention which is utterly unlike reality. This charge mistakes the purpose of theory, which is to render reality intelligible by radically simplifying it. The theoretician selects from the immensely rich and complex mass of phenomena some few features that particularly strike him. He may choose those particular features because he suspects that they spring directly from the essence of the business, or because they readily suggest an analogy with some other, perhaps mechanical or biological, system which is familiar to him and which he therefore 'understands'. Or perhaps the selection is made on unconscious aesthetic grounds. In any case, there is extremely drastic selection and rejection; masses of observed things are thrown away as the mere dross of the theory-building process, as not merely useless but, for the purpose in hand, a positive encumbrance, debris which must be pushed aside. The next step is to give to those features which are retained an exactness of description which fits them for use as structural elements in a deductive system. Such a system is merely an assemblage of sentences or propositions falling into two sets. One of these sets, the initial propositions or axioms, are chosen by the two criteria, first, that they must all be mutually consistent and non-contradictory, and secondly, that they should each reflect an aspect of reality. What the axioms say explicitly is the mere embryo of their full purport. This implicit content must lastly be brought to view by logical inference from the axioms, a process which adds, alters and creates nothing in itself but merely displays what has been already created by the definition of concepts and the choice of axioms. The purposes of this deductive stage in the process are, first, to enable us to see clearly and more fully what our theory is, and secondly, to compare it afresh with the results of observation, which can now confront it at a vastly increased number of points.

Because a theory is built up from a few elements withdrawn or abstracted from the proliferating jungle of events, we call it an abstract system. Is it justice that this term should carry, as it seems to do, a faint pejorative echo?

Now the great 'subjective revolution' which economic theory underwent in the early 1870's left us, as one of its results, with a theoretical model where abstraction and the 'tidying up' process had been carried to a quite extreme degree, in the interests of properly displaying, and establishing the validity of, an idea which remains and will always remain one of the greatest discoveries of economics: the idea of the all-pervasive interdependence of economic affairs. In this model what was chiefly left out was *time* in all significant and interesting aspects. And a discussion of human affairs in abstraction from time is perhaps rather like an analysis of language in abstraction from meaning. However, this latter exercise would be quite strictly a study of nonsense, and the General Equilibrium model invented by one of the greatest of all economists, Léon Walras of the University of Lausanne, is very far from nonsense.

The theory of general static equilibrium shows us a state of ultimate and timeless adjustment maintained (if the use of this word does not involve a contradiction) by the freely competitive self-interest of the individual suppliers of productive services, these services being such as contribute technically and essentially to the actual production, transport and sale of goods. In such a state each worker, each acre of ground, and each machine will earn per day that amount by which the withdrawal of one such productive unit (the quantity engaged of each other type of resources remaining unchanged) would reduce the daily output of the system as a whole. And the total of all the payments to the suppliers of productive services, when they are determined on this principle, will exactly exhaust their total product.

We can perhaps epitomize the character and spirit of this model by saying that it represented a predictable, impersonal and frictionless machine like the solar system. Or, more briefly still, it was inhuman. And profit, I think we can say, depends essentially on those very characteristics of the real economic world which are thus lacking from the general equilibrium model. Profit depends on the radical and inherent unpredictability of human affairs; on men's power and ambition to *alter* their economic environment and not be content merely to respond to it; and on the fact that all economic adjustments to changed governing circumstances take time. One of the forms taken by the business man's endeavour to control his environment is his effort to bring into his situation some element of monopoly. This word is for the economic theorist a technical term with a precise meaning, and its utterance by him does not in itself convey any sense of condemnation. Shakespeare had a complete and absolute monopoly of Shakespeare's plays, and if in the days of James I you had wished to commission a new Shakespeare play, only Shakespeare could have supplied it. If you wish for a new sculpture by Jacob Epstein, it is to him you must go, and only Norman Hartnell can design for you a dress by Norman Hartnell. All these are instances of the monopoly of a product which is in some more or less essential way bound to a particular producer. Every creative artist and every craftsman has a natural and unbreakable monopoly of his own products, and, so, in a less conspicuous and important way, but no less genuinely, the personal bents and special capacities of the members of a firm, the shape of its organization, and the moral weight of its traditions and history, may leave their mark on its products so that these are not fully imitable by others. But having achieved this, it is natural that, for example, Rolls-Royce should wish to associate their name in the public mind with the excellence and individuality of their motor-cars. To do this they resort to advertising. And from this it is but a short step for any firm to reverse the process and to advertise in order to create, rather than merely call attention to, the individuality of their products. Now a product which has its own special features and qualities, whether these be 'real' and objective or exist merely in people's minds, will gather to itself a circle of buyers to whom these qualities specially appeal, and who will consequently be willing to pay a little more for this product than for another which objectively is just as good. But a producer who can raise his price without losing all his customers is in some degree a monopolist. And if the proportionate increase in his price is larger than the consequent proportionate decrease in the physical quantity of his sales, his net revenue will be increased. And this is monopoly profit.

To attempt to set out the arguments by which economists have sought to condemn or to defend the supposed practices of monopolists or of 'monopolistic competitors' would require a book, and they are quite irrelevant to my purpose, which is to assign some meanings to the word profit. Now I have been suggesting that we do not need this word until we come to a model of the economic system where time and uncertainty are essential elements. Yet monopoly can be introduced as an element of a 'timeless' model. Nevertheless, far more useful and realistic insights into the practices and consequences of monopolistic competition can be gained by studying them in an 'expectational' than in a timeless model. When business men are asked whether it must not always be their object to set their output week by week at such a level as will maximize their profit for that week, even if a larger output would still cover costs, they answer, that they are not so foolish and short-sighted as to offend their customers and spoil their market for the future by wringing extra profit out of a temporary shortage. And so it is clear that the advantages which a business man can draw from elements of monopoly in his situation depend, like those he can get from improvements of organization or of productive technique, the application of new scientific discoveries or the invention of new products, on his power of imagination, on his luck and skill in forming expectations as the basis of far-looking plans. And this brings me round full-circle to the distinction with which I began: the distinction, as I can now express it, between profit as a subject of expectation, of conjecture, and of many mutually incompatible hypotheses, and profit as a fact recorded in the books of the accountant. These two things are, of course, related. Expectations must be constructed from experience. But realized and recorded profit is only one ingredient, perhaps not even the most important one, out of which expectations of profit are cooked up. Abstraction is essential to all theory and all understanding. But there is a point beyond which simplification is achieved only at the expense of something essential in the phenomena; and no theory which wipes out the distinction between past and future can have any useful bearing on the nature and role of profit.

IX

THE NATURE AND ROLE OF PROFIT*

What part, if any, can the word 'profit' usefully play in economic theory and analysis? Is there some notion, essential or valuable to economic theory, for which the customary content of the word profit, in everyday language and in the literature, makes it the most suitable name? If so, how can we most usefully define profit and what will then be its place in the structure of theory?

Those services of men, and of their possessions, which contribute to the creation of any object, event or state of affairs (any product) must for the most part be rendered some time before that product can emerge. It is of the nature and essence of human life that there can be no knowing in advance what will be the exchange value (in money or anything else) of the product at the date when it will be ready. Thus, in general, in the nature of things the contributors of productive services would have to render them without knowing, exactly and with a feeling of certainty, what they would get in exchange, were it not for the arrangements by which they can contract out of this uncertainty. The uncertainty concerning the exchange value which the product will have when it emerges ready for use cannot be abolished, it can only be shifted. Some customary or institutional arrangements shift this uncertainty to the buyers, who contract, in advance of those stages of production which account for most of the cost, and thus in advance of the irrevocable steering of productive services into the particular product, to buy the product at a specified price when it shall be ready, thus exposing themselves to the possibility that at the future moment when the product shall emerge its spot price will turn out to be lower, or higher, than the

---

* *Metroeconomica*, vol. III (1951), pp. 101–7. This essay makes no pretence of offering a complete theory of profit, but aims merely to emphasize the essential and radical difference of nature between profit in the *ex ante* sense of something imagined or expected, a whole bundle of mutually inconsistent pictures with varying degrees of credence, or even several and various such bundles existing simultaneously in the minds of different people, and on the other hand profit in the *ex post* sense of a unique, actual and recorded past event. The stimulus to write this essay came from reading the exceedingly interesting and penetrating 'Comment' by Mr J. A. Stockfisch in the *American Economic Review* for March 1951, part of a symposium which began with Professor J. Fred Weston's article called 'An uncertainty theory of profit' in the December *Review*.

price they have contracted to pay. But more usually the uncertainty rests with the body of producers taken as a whole, and is shifted only within that body.

For simplicity let us assume that all parties take money as their standard of value, so that when a person buys an object which he feels certain he will later sell for no more nor less money than he gave for it, his act of purchase yields him, in his subjective reckoning, no *ex ante* loss or gain. If, then amongst all those who intend to contribute to the making of some exchangeable thing, some agree to accept from the others a stated money payment and to surrender all their rights in the product, we can say that at the date when such contracts are made the production plan of the product (the product as yet existing only as an idea, intention, or plan) has a significance derived from two quite distinct elements. First there is the total contractual payment to some of the producers. This is a scalar quantity. Secondly, there is the unknown difference between the contractual payment and the price for which the product will exchange. This difference is a bundle of pairs of quantities; if we like, of points or vectors. In each of these pairs of numbers (the numbers being ordered or labelled within each pair so that we can refer to the first numbers of the pairs and their second numbers) the first number is a hypothesis concerning the difference that will emerge between the exchange value of the product and the total contractual rewards; the second number is an index of the place occupied by this hypothesis on some scale of belief in the mind of some individual.

It will be noticed that hitherto from the beginning our wording has been carefully chosen to make it clear that we are speaking of thoughts which look forward from the individual's 'present moment' (his viewpoint) rather than backward. This does not mean that we prejudge the question whether the word 'profit' is best used exclusively in connection with thoughts about the future, and not in connection with knowledge of the past; but it does mean that the distinction between past and future is absolutely vital and essential, and that if we allow the word profit a part to play in each connection it will necessarily have two quite distinct meanings. I shall indeed maintain that we need two different words. Let us first think of the futurewards or *ex ante* context.

Those who accept contractual incomes give in exchange a promise to render certain specified services or performances, and having made their contracts they have no further interest or concern in the outcome of the whole venture of production and sale, except in so far as they may fear default on their contracts. By their degree of willingness or otherwise to make contracts to render various sorts of service for the purpose of producing various sorts of product, those who contemplate accepting contractual incomes can in some degree influence the choice of product and methods of production, but the ultimate decision what to produce, and how, must evidently rest with those who forgo contractual rewards and accept the outcome in ignorance of what it will be. Can the criterion, by which these owners of the equity will shape their decisions, be suitably described as maximizing something, and, if so, what do they seek to maximize?

We have suggested that the equity-owner, whom we will call the enterpriser, has in mind concerning the difference that will emerge between his contractual outgoings and the exchange value of the product a number of hypotheses, to each of which he assigns some degree of belief or of doubt. We have formalized this suggestion by saying that the difference is represented in his mind by a bundle of pairs of numbers. This bundle, taken as one whole, can in any one of various ways be assigned a valuation, a scalar magnitude, and we can then suppose him to decide upon the character, quantity and method of obtaining his product with a view to maximizing this scalar. But a procedure of this general kind is not the only model we can construct of his process of choosing amongst the entire range of possible products and methods which presents itself to him, and I think that some light can be thrown on the nature of profit, or on the question how best to define profit or separate its various appropriate meanings, by using my own apparatus of potential surprise function, ϕ-surface, and gambler indifference-map.

When the enterpriser buys productive services or materials and embarks on the making of a product for future sale, his act is formally indistinguishable from any other act of investment, as economists understand this word, and we can suppose him to obtain for each possible product, by which I mean each hypothetical quantity of each hypothetical good that he has in mind, a pair of standardized focus-outcomes in the manner, and having the meaning, described in *Expectation in Economics*. When these pairs, that is, these points, are plotted on the enterpriser's gambler indifference-map, some will lie on higher and some on lower indifference-curves, and that point which lies on an indifference-curve higher than those containing any of the other points will stand in some definite relation to those other indifference-curves and also especially to the origin indifference-curve. It is these relations that we wish to study.

By *project* let us mean any proposed transformation or series of transformations, to occur or begin at some stated date, of the enterpriser's whole collection of resources (including the 'identity trans-formation' which leaves the collection unchanged). Thus a project is some plan which says what shall be done with every part of the enterpriser's whole fortune. When the enterpriser has determined for any such project a standardized focus-gain and a standardized focus-loss, he can by using these as coordinates find a point on his gambler indifference-map corresponding to that project. If this point is the origin of the map, the project is such as virtually to relieve him of any fear of loss and deny him hope of gain (its potential surprise curve must be T-shaped or V-shaped, touching the line of zero-potential surprise at only one point, namely, the point of zero hypo-thetical gain and loss). We are assuming (see above, p. 95) that everybody takes money as the standard of value,* so that one project which would correspond to the origin of the gambler indifference-map would be the holding of the enterpriser's entire fortune, that is, the total market value of the collection of resources that he owns, in the form of money. The kind of projects which concern us are those according to which the enterpriser would produce in a particular way a particular quantity of a particular product, using the whole or some part of his fortune for his purpose and, we may assume for sim-plicity and convenience, leaving the rest in the form of money. The origin indifference-curve, OS in Fig. IX 1, is the set of all points which each represent a project that the enterpriser regards as neither more nor less desirable than the combined avoidance of all fear of loss and all hope of gain. At any point on the origin indifference-curve, that is to say, the fear of loss is exactly compensated by the hope of gain.

Suppose, then, that the enterpriser has in mind a project which he assigns to the point R in Fig. IX 1, a project which has, for him, a standardized focus-loss represented by the distance OP and a standardized focus-gain represented by the distance PR which is the sum of the distance PQ from the horizontal axis to the origin in-difference-curve and the distance QR from the origin indifference-curve to the point representing the project. What is the interpretation of this picture in terms of the ordinary associations of the word 'profit' and the propositions about it?

Is profit 'the compensation for uncertainty-bearing?' There are two meanings to be distinguished here. In school a promised prize acts as an incentive to all the pupils, but only one eventually receives the prize itself. The incentive is a hope, some imagined event which is also in some sense and degree believed in. The event itself is plainly something utterly different in nature from the set of mutually con-

* That is to say, everybody is completely subject to the 'money illusion'.

tradictory imagined events, one for each pupil. There is here an illuminating parallel for our question about profit. A necessary condition, in order that a decision involving a fear of loss may be taken, is that there should be some other feeling capable of counteracting or overcoming this fear; there must be a hope of gain. When 'profit' means something which can compensate or counteract in the enterpriser's mind the discouraging influence of the idea or fear of loss, the word 'profit' is being used in an *ex ante* sense, standing for some-

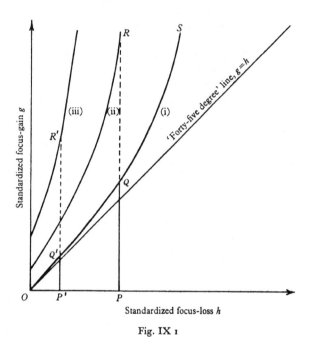

Fig. IX 1

thing imagined, an idea, not a recorded actuality. 'Profit' in the sense of an actual, recorded, past outcome of some course of action which has been actually followed can influence the enterpriser in two ways, both of them entirely distinct from the direct influence of expectations. It can influence his *subsequent* decisions indirectly, by helping to shape or determine his expectations of the outcome of hypothetical courses of future action; and it can change his actual stock of means of action, the size of his fortune. Plainly we cannot say that actually received, *ex post*, profit compensates or counteracts loss in his decision-making process. If actually received profit is, with a slight change of wording, 'the reward of uncertainty-bearing', this must be in some quite different sense.

Which part of Fig. IX 1 represents what just counteracts the fear of loss involved in the project corresponding to point R? Not the whole of the standardized focus-gain PR is needed, only that part represented by the distance PQ, that is, the height of the origin indifference-curve above the horizontal axis at the appropriate standardized focus-loss. The rest of PR must be interpreted in some other way.

Suppose that the enterpriser has in mind several projects all represented by points above and to the left of the origin indifference-curve. According to the meaning of the gambler indifference-map he will then choose that one which lies on the highest indifference-curve. Thus we may be tempted to say that a part such as QR of a standardized focus-gain is the component of 'profit' which by its variations between one project and another selects one of them as the most attractive. But this evidently does not mean that choice will fall on that project which has the greatest excess QR of the standardized focus-gain PR over the portion PQ which just compensates the standardized focus-loss. In Fig. IX 1 the project represented by the point R' lies on a higher indifference-curve than that represented by R, and will be preferred; but the distance $Q'R'$ is less than QR. Thus to say simply 'The enterpriser in choosing amongst projects seeks to maximize profit' can be misleading. Profit in the *ex ante* sense, whatever simplifying interpretation we suppose the enterpriser to make of the complex structure of expectations in his mind, by its nature involves uncertainty, and a two-dimensional entity seems the simplest which can preserve the essence of this fact.

Let us turn to the *ex post* context. The actual, recorded outcome of a course of action cannot possibly, in logic, be what counteracted or cancelled out, in the enterpriser's mind while he was making his decision before he embarked on the venture, his fear that this course of action might yield a loss. In any context where we make a meaningful distinction between past and future, the latter being essentially unknown, it is logically nonsensical to say that the quantity of resources devoted to a particular venture or project is a function of the *ex post* outcome of that venture. When all is past we can perhaps say that if the quantity or kind of resources devoted to a particular attempt had been different the outcome would have been different, but it can never be legitimate or meaningful to speak of the plan of action as depending in any sense on the actual outcome. If we write a functional connection $U = U(S)$ between outcome U and plan S, and if we insist on 'reading this from right to left' as well as from left to right, we are merely saying that when all is past and the outcome known, the plan which led to this outcome can be deduced. (This will evidently not in general be true, for the correspondence between plan and outcome, the latter crudely summarized in money, will seldom or never be bi-unique.) It is only in a static analysis, the description of a situation which is essentially timeless, that a single concept of 'profit' could ever be enough. Otherwise there must be at least two kinds of profit, two meanings entirely distinct and different in character. One of them is things imagined, a whole set of hypotheses each with a second dimension representing in some way the degree of belief, and perhaps with a third magnitude representing the degree of interestingness or power of stimulus. The other is simply a scalar magnitude recorded as the actual past outcome. This latter acts both as a judgement on the plan and as part-determinator of the means available for future plans. But on what does it pass judgement?

It seems very difficult to maintain that the outcome of any single decision, on evidence arising from that outcome alone, can ever be ascribed in definite proportions to the wisdom of the decision or to its good fortune, to ability or luck. For, however wisely the enterpriser interprets all the information available to him, however reasonably or with whatever imaginative power and insight he chooses the assumptions with which he must necessarily supplement that information, the factors hidden from him and perhaps from all men may utterly confound his hopes. Even if a man were ever to possess information complete in fact about all the factors which would determine the outcome of some proposed course of action, how could he know that this information was indeed complete? If we are to decompose *ex post* profit into a component due to skill and a component due to luck, this must be done on the basis of prior assessment of the skill of the enterpriser concerned, on the basis of a past record.

The beauty and cogency, in its proper context of assumptions, of the marginal productivity theory of the sharing of the product has tempted writers to ask: 'Is *profit* the payment for some productive service, or the reward of some factor of production for its part in the productive process, and if so, what service and what factor does profit reward?' I have tried to show in this essay that any such question is doubly ambiguous. Are we speaking of a world without uncertainty and therefore without any meaningful distinction between past and future, or are we speaking of the real world of uncertain expectation, of doubts, fears and hopes where the future is created in various shapes by men's imagination? A failure, in this latter case, to distinguish between expectation and actuality, between 'profit' in the sense of a hypothesis contending with other hypotheses in the mind of the enterpriser during his process of decision, and 'profit' in the sense of a unique, recorded outcome, is surely a logical blunder of the grossest and most catastrophic kind.

PART II

ON INTEREST-RATES

X

THE NATURE OF INTEREST-RATES*

The question what is the nature of interest, what psychological, institutional or technological realities it manifests and corresponds to, is surely the first one we must answer in seeking to know how interest-rates are determined. The time-preference hypothesis had all the incisive formal brilliance characteristic of marginal value analysis in general, but it belonged to that world of thought which virtually ignored *uncertainty*; which assumed that men choose between alternative trains of consequences each known in its entirety through all relevant future time. The liquidity-preference hypothesis utterly transformed the matter. Now M. Pierre Massé in an article which, I think, deserves very high praise: 'La Théorie générale de J. M. Keynes et le problème de l'intérêt' (*Revue d'Économie Politique* (1948)), seems to wish to synthesize the two views. I differ from him on two counts. First, the language of probability theory seems to me wholly unsuited to the analysis of uncertainty. But that is not the point here. M. Massé's contention that the propensity to save has, after all, a direct bearing on the interest-rate impelled me to try to re-think the theory of the nature and determination of interest-rates from fundamental considerations. This essay is an attempt to express the main outline of the result. Full development and the pursuit of all the questions this topic raises would occupy a whole book.

I wish to express my warm gratitude to Messrs Pember and Boyle, of Princes Street, E.C., for giving me access to their records of security prices and yields, and especially to Mr F. R. Althaus of that firm, to whose most kindly helpfulness and illuminating comment I am greatly indebted.

Concerning a stock of wealth, there are two kinds of decisions which its administrator must constantly be taking:

First, in what proportions it shall be composed of various things.

Second, how fast he shall augment or diminish it.

I shall describe some simple assumptions and my grounds for believing them true enough to be interesting and useful; and then show what formal criteria, on those assumptions, are logically appropriate to the decisions. Having arrived at the principles on

* *Oxford Economic Papers*, new series, vol. 1 (1949), pp. 99–120.

which the individual decision-maker* will administer his wealth, I shall consider what will happen when the many simultaneous individual decisions are acted upon or attempted. The conclusions thus reached will necessarily include a theory of the determination of the system of interest-rates.

My basic assumptions in brief are that an individual likes to possess things, the more the better; and likes to consume things, the more, in a given time, the better; and that he cannot both eat his cake and have it (but I think this notion needs special analysis to make it precise, and this I have attempted). Also that an individual's judgement as to how much wealth is represented by a given collection of things depends on his system of expectations, a system in which different hypotheses are given different degrees of influence on his decisions according both to the content and to the plausibility of each; and that it is the amount of his wealth thus reckoned that he will seek to maximize in choosing at each instant the proportionate composition of the collection; that hopes and fears thus play a central role in his personal relative valuation of different assets, and therefore in determining exactly what degree and direction of pressure on the market where the interest-rate is determined is contributed at any instant by each individual.

Why should a man accumulate or keep in being a stock of wealth? The feelings afforded by the possession of such a stock are essentially, I think, the feelings of security, power and freedom; in a word, the feeling of independence. Those three things are in a large measure all aspects of the same thing, for full freedom requires a degree of security from the consequences of other people's decisions, and also some power to execute one's own ideas. All this it is convenient to label with the one term *possessor-satisfaction*. Possessor-satisfaction is to be thought of as an instantaneous *intensity* which will be greater in that one of two otherwise identical personal situations in which the person's stock of wealth, by his own reckoning, is the greater.

A stock of wealth can consist of concrete objects (or systems of objects), or of abstract, generalized claims. Of the latter there are two kinds, dated and undated. *Undated* claims include banknotes and coin, credit balances at the bank, and unused permission to overdraw. All these I shall comprehend in the term money, but instead of speaking of a 'quantity of money' I shall often speak for the sake of vividness of a 'number of banknotes'. *Dated* claims are promises to pay stated numbers of banknotes at stated dates. For

---

* In the notion 'individual decision-maker' I include one who directs an enterprise as well as one merely concerned with his personal fortune.

theoretical purposes I shall refer to all such promises as 'bonds'. All concrete objects which embody wealth I shall call 'equipment'.

A stock of wealth, then, consists of banknotes, bonds and equipment. An object belonging to any of these three classes of objects I shall call an asset. The quantity of equipment comprised in any particular stock can be positive or zero, the quantity of bonds and that of banknotes can be positive, zero or negative. Since the market valuation (in banknotes) of any asset is merely a weighted average of personal valuations, any decision-maker's personal valuation of any asset except a banknote can differ from the market valuation. Finding himself at any instant in possession of a *given* collection of assets, a decision-maker will exchange some of his assets for others so as to get that collection of assets to which he assigns the highest personal valuation amongst all those collections whose market valuation is equal to that of his given collection. For thus he will maximize his possessor-satisfaction.

Ready money, banknotes in hand or available at the bank, is in ordinary circumstances the most reassuring form of wealth. Its power to discharge debts and contracts stated in terms of money is secure against market-value changes. Its equivalent in real goods (i.e. in a well-assorted bundle of many varieties of real goods) is felt to be more dependably stable than that of systems of concrete, specialized property or shares in them. It is available without delay. The man who has decided to keep in hand such-and-such a number of banknotes knows that, until he changes that decision, he will have that number of banknotes at his command for use at any instant, without need to know in advance when that instant will be. A bond is a claim to receive stated quantities of banknotes at stated future dates. If therefore deferment was of no account, a bond (given perfect trust in the honesty and solvency of the debtor) would be valued at just the sum of these quantities of banknotes. When there is a free market in bonds, the creditor can escape from the fixity of these dates of receiving payment, and can look on the bond as a source of banknotes available, by sale of the bond, whenever he may need them; but only at the cost of not knowing in advance how many banknotes he will receive. A man who accepts a bond in exchange for banknotes is therefore exchanging a known for an unknown quantity of banknotes. (For let us remember that by banknotes we mean money in readiness. When we ask, concerning a bond: What does this bond represent in money available instantly at an unforeseen instant, as banknotes themselves are available? the answer is: an unknown number of banknotes.) He will not make this exchange unless he has grounds for hoping that the unknown quantity will prove to be larger than the known; and amongst these grounds he will virtually always require (when considering whether or not to buy an existing bond or to allow a borrower to create a new one) that the quantities of banknotes due from the debtor shall add up to a total larger, by an amount depending on circumstances which we must analyse, than the amount he pays for the bond. The appropriate measure of this premium is the *yield*, defined as follows: Suppose that Q_k is the number of banknotes due from the debtor at a date of k time-units' futurity, such payments being due at the dates for which $k = 1, 2, \ldots$, up to L. Then if P is the number of banknotes paid at the present instant for the bond, and if r is such that

$$P = \frac{Q_1}{1+r} + \frac{Q_2}{(1+r)^2} + \ldots + \frac{Q_L}{(1+r)^L}, \quad \text{or} \quad P = \sum_{k=1}^{L} \frac{Q_k}{(1+r)^k},$$

r per time-unit is the yield of the bond at the present instant. The payments Q may be all equal and may stretch indefinitely into the future, being terminable only by the debtor buying back the bond at whatever may then be its market price. Or there may be a terminating series of equal payments with a final larger payment representing 'repayment of principal'. The equal payments in either case are conventionally known as 'interest payments'. But there is no reason in theory why the payments should not be all unequal, and even irregularly spaced in time, provided the dates and amounts are specified at the outset; the yield as defined above still measures the compensation offered to the buyer of the bond for accepting its terms. In actuality there are at all times on the market fixed-interest securities offering a great variety of time-schedules of payments. Some are due for completion of payments by the debtor within a few months (treasury or other bills) or a few years (redeemable government securities which are approaching the latest date for 'repayment of principal'); and the length of time over which future payments will stretch ranges up to perhaps forty years for the 'longest' redeemable gilt-edged. Lastly, there are the 'irredeemables', the holders of which are promised only an indefinite series of equal 'interest' payments until the securities shall be bought in by the Treasury at an unspecified date. In the rest of the formally theoretical part of this paper I shall assume, for the sake of simplicity and vivid presentation of main ideas, that only one type of fixed-interest securities exists, viz. irredeemable securities issued either by the Government or by individual enterprises. I shall suppose that these are issued in equal nominal units each called a 'bond'.

The hazard accepted by the buyer of a bond is that its market price in banknotes may fall after he has bought it. Even if he should not be compelled to sell the bond while its market price is low, still the fall must in some sense be regarded as the lender's loss, since if he had waited he could now have had the bond, as in fact he has, and also that number of banknotes by which its price has fallen; but these he has lost. This hazard has of course its counterpart in that the price of the bond may rise. It is the net effect of these two hazards, on the mind of a potential holder of the bond, which must be compensated by the yield.

Let us summarize our comparison of the characters of bonds and of banknotes. Dated claims, just like undated money, are abstract, generalized purchasing power, but they do not, as undated money does, combine certainty of amount with freedom of date of spending. If the holder of dated claims could feel certain that he would need banknotes in just those numbers at just those dates when they are due from the debtor (or at any rate, no sooner), those dated claims would represent a *known* number of banknotes. (But he cannot be justified in feeling certain of this.) Under all other circumstances dated claims represent an unknown number of banknotes. For this hazard the compensation, which induces people to hold some dated money, is pure interest as measured by the yield.*

A piece of concrete equipment resembles a bond in being valued for the sake of instalments of money to be received at dates in the future. The difference is that with concrete equipment the sizes of the instalments which will accrue at particular dates are not trusted promises but mere conjectures. This set of conjectures can be described, and a value in terms of banknotes in hand assigned to it, in various ways. For example, a single number can be assigned to each future date as the number of banknotes expected to be earned by the equipment in the unit interval ending at that date, and this number can then be multiplied by a coefficient to allow for the doubt in the owner's or potential owner's mind concerning the suitability of that number. The result will be a set of numbers (one for each relevant future date) each of which can be treated as though that number of banknotes were certain to be received at the date to which it belongs, and the piece of equipment will then be valued, by the individual in whose mind this process of conjecture and allowance for doubt has gone on, as though it were a bond promising those numbers of banknotes.

* Compensation for any doubt which there may be concerning the honesty or solvency of the debtor I do not regard as pure interest. Most of the 'interest' exacted by a moneylender is not 'pure interest' in my sense.

A collection of given quantities of banknotes, bonds and various systems of equipment (or shares in their equity) will have at any instant a market value and also a personal valuation assigned by the individual administrator of this collection, both these valuations being expressed as a number of banknotes. This personal valuation must not only take account of the administrator's system of expectations, in which rival hypotheses count for more or less with him according both to the content and to the plausibility (in his own view) of each, but must also take account of his own attitude to this state of uncertainty, the gratification or distress it causes him. Now it would be possible for him to turn the whole collection into banknotes at its market valuation, and there would then, of course, be no difference between personal and market value. To depart somewhat from this state of affairs by parting with some banknotes in exchange for bonds may give him a collection with a higher personal valuation. It may even be that, amongst all the different collections containing only banknotes and bonds, which he could obtain at the current market price of bonds, the one consisting wholly of bonds will have the highest personal valuation. It is evident, however, that the price of bonds cannot remain at a level which makes this true of all individuals. Except in so far as bonds are bought from the banking system, the banknotes paid for them remain in the possession of some individuals (those who sold the bonds), and the price of bonds must accordingly rise to a level where some individuals cannot increase their personal valuations of their own collections of assets by parting with banknotes in exchange for bonds, but will be content to retain the banknotes. Can we explain on reasonable grounds why there should always be some level (varying of course with circumstances) at which the price of bonds will satisfy this condition? The higher the market value of a bond, the less plausible (other circumstances given) is the hypothesis that the next movement of that price will be a further appreciable rise. But only an individual with whom this hypothesis carries some weight will value bonds higher than their immediate market price. Must we then suppose that some individuals will at any instant hold nothing but bonds, others nothing but banknotes? No. For let us look at the matter thus.*

* The analysis which here follows is an outline sketch, adapted to the very small space which can be spared for it in this essay, of a much more fully worked version first presented in my article 'An analysis of speculative choice', *Economica*, vol. XII (1945), p. 10, and in a further improved form in *Expectation in Economics*. For the sake of extreme brevity I have here laid aside the precisely defined concepts of my full technique and have adopted fresh terms for the roughly indicated ideas which take the place of the exact ones.

We have supposed that any uncertain outcome, such as the immediately future behaviour of the price of bonds, is represented in an individual's mind by a set of rival hypotheses to each of which he attaches some greater or lesser degree of importance according both to its content* and to the plausibility he concedes to it. Let us suppose, then, that embracing in one glance all the hypotheses of loss from the holding of a single bond, through a fall in the market value

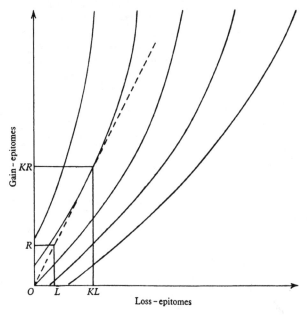

Fig. X 1

of bonds greater than is made up for by future interest payments, he can select some one amount of loss (say, *L* pounds) which sums up for him the whole of this part of his system of expectations; and let us call this amount of loss his *loss-epitome* for one bond; and that, similarly, he can find some one amount of gain (say, *R* pounds) which represents for him the whole of the other part of his system of expectations, including any payments due from the debtor within the time interval over which he looks ahead; and let us call this his *gain-epitome* for one bond. And in a Cartesian diagram (see Fig. X 1) let the abscissa measure losses and the ordinate measure gains, so that

* The proposition that it contains, without regard to the plausibility, in the given circumstances, of this proposition.

the loss and gain potentialities of a single bond, as seen by our individual wealth administrator in the circumstances of some one historical instant, will be represented by a point with abscissa L and ordinate R. The loss-epitome of a holding of N bonds will evidently be an abscissa NL, and its gain-epitome an ordinate NR. Now every point in the plane of our diagram* will represent some conceivable combination of loss-epitome and gain-epitome, a combination which could become actual in appropriate circumstances for some particular individual with some particular holding of bonds. Selecting any one such point, we can discover all those other points which represent situations neither more nor less agreeable to the individual, and join all these points by an indifference-curve, which, unlike the indifference-curves of value theory, will evidently have a positive slope. All points in the relevant quadrant of the plane will lie on one or other such curve, and if curve A (say) lies above and to the left of curve B, every point on curve A will represent a situation preferred to every situation represented by a point on curve B.

The indifference-curves will evidently slope up from left to right, but what will be their shape? A loss which is large in relation to his total wealth may appear to the individual a disastrous contingency, the fear of which can by no means be neutralized by an equally vivid hope of an equally large gain. But when contingent loss and contingent gain are both small in relation to his total wealth, equality between them may represent a situation neither preferred to nor rejected in favour of *zero* loss and gain, this latter being the situation secured by a decision to hold banknotes only and represented by the origin of the diagram. Thus it seems plausible that the particular indifference-curve which passes through the origin will have an increasing slope, equal to unity near the origin and becoming steadily steeper; and that the shapes of all the other indifference-curves will somewhat resemble it.

In our diagram the point (L, R) represents the subjective uncertainty-situation at a particular historical instant of an individual who then possesses *one* bond, perhaps some banknotes, but no equipment. This point (L, R) will be the same no matter how many or few banknotes he possesses in addition to his one bond; for the holding of banknotes cannot give rise to either loss or gain in terms of banknotes. The point with abscissa NL and ordinate NR will represent the situation he secures by holding N bonds,† and again it will be

---

* That is, in its relevant (upper right-hand) quadrant.

† N being thought of as a variable, no particular point (NL, NR) is marked on Fig. X 1.

unaffected by the number of banknotes he also possesses. Thus if, expressing the market value of his stock of wealth (whatever its actual composition) as so many banknotes, the individual imagines himself to carry through a process of successive exchanges of banknotes for bonds, this process will carry his situation along a straight line of slope R/L passing through the origin. If this line has a slope greater than the slope, at the origin, of the indifference-curve which passes through the origin, and the slopes of all indifference-curves increase from left to right, then the straight line will have somewhere a point of tangency with an indifference-curve. That point (if his wealth is enough to carry him so far along the straight line) will represent the situation preferred by the individual to all others which he can attain, and will determine the preferred composition of his stock of wealth: so many bonds, so many banknotes.* The amount of his wealth (at a given market price of bonds) will determine how far along the straight line he can go; if he cannot reach a point of tangency with an indifference-curve, he will have to be content with the highest curve encountered by that segment (of the straight line) over which he is free to move.

In the preceding analysis we have assumed that in deciding on the composition of his stock of wealth the administrator limits himself to a choice amongst combinations in various proportions of banknotes and bonds, and excludes from it equipment or equities. (Though we did this for analytical convenience, such a limitation is often compulsory for a trustee.) If we now relax this assumption, there are two alternative ways in which we can suppose the administrator to choose the composition of his stock of wealth when equipment of any number of different kinds, each signifying for him particular possibilities of gain and loss, can be included in it. We could suppose him to use a mental process equivalent to an elaborated version of the gain-and-loss indifference-diagram described above. Instead of an opportunity-curve consisting of a single straight-line segment whose end-points represent respectively the holding of his whole fortune in banknotes or in bonds, and whose intermediate points each represent some combination of banknotes and bonds, we have then in addition a swarm of points each representing the holding of his whole fortune in the form of shares in some concrete enterprise. On the diagram a point can then be found corresponding to any proportionate combination of any number of different assets, and the preferred combination can be determined as before. This analysis I have worked

---

* In Fig. X 1 the point of tangency is shown as corresponding to a holding of K banknotes.

out in detail elsewhere.* But for our present purpose another treatment is more directly illuminating. We suppose the individual to divide future time into unit intervals and to assign to the end-date of each such interval a single number to represent his 'best guess' as to the net† earnings of any enterprise or piece of equipment in that interval, and then to multiply each such number by a coefficient to allow for his doubt of the appropriateness of that number. The coefficient will take account not only of his uncertainty itself regarding the size of the instalment, but also of his attitude to that uncertainty, and the result will be a series of numbers, one for each relevant future date, which series will be on the same footing as the payments promised by a bond. This series of dated, uncertainty-adjusted instalments, and the market-price of the equipment, will together make possible the calculation of an exact analogue of the yield of a bond. This analogue or something closely resembling it has received from various writers a number of different names, such as 'rate of return over cost' (Irving Fisher) and 'marginal efficiency of capital' (Lord Keynes). Not all of these writers have sufficiently emphasized the need to allow for the individual's uncertainty and his attitude to uncertainty before calculating this measure, and before stating the proposition that equipment of each different kind will tend to be produced at a time-rate such that, in the given conditions of its production prevailing at any instant, the cost per unit will be pushed up to such a level as to make the marginal efficiency equal to the yield of bonds. It will be evident, I think, that the marginal efficiency of a piece or system of equipment is subjective and perhaps will not be set at the same figure by any two individuals who form an opinion on it. The marginal efficiency referred to in the above-mentioned proposition must be that of the *most sanguine* individual whose circumstances, in particular his command of wealth and his *expertise* in the line of production concerned, imply that he is potentially in the market for such equipment.

In so far as the purpose of the coefficients of allowance for doubt is to allow for the individual's liking or aversion for uncertainty, the scaling-down effected by them may, it seems plain, have to be comparatively severe when a large fraction of his total stock of wealth is embodied in one kind of equipment; for then his position may be more vulnerable to hazards whose importance per unit of equipment

---

* In 'An analysis of speculative choice', *Economica*, vol. XII (1945), p. 10, and in an improved and developed version, Chapter IV of *Expectation in Economics*.

† By *net* earnings I mean sales proceeds of product less expenses of operating the equipment.

is given. Thus for a given individual with given expectations there is likely to be some relation, between the quantity he possesses of any particular kind of equipment and the size of his total of wealth, which will make the marginal efficiency of that equipment equal to the yield of bonds. In order to adjust his actual situation to meet that condition, he may need to increase or decrease his holding of that kind of equipment. Moreover, he may even need to hold a negative stock of bonds: to become a borrower. This latter is the position sought by an enterprise when it issues debentures in order to hold a larger quantity of equipment than can be bought out of the equity capital alone. But the larger the ratio of the enterprise's debt to its assets, the larger will be the ratio of the periodic payments due on that debt to the earnings that can reasonably be expected from its real equipment, and the smaller the decline in its rate of profit which will compel it to default on those payments.* Thus there is plainly a point beyond which the buying of further equipment with borrowed money will reduce the administrator's subjective marginal efficiency judgement of this equipment below the interest-rate (yield) at which he can borrow. This idea can be very conveniently shown on the uncertainty indifference-map. The point representing the holding of a negative stock of bonds (the situation of an enterpriser who has become a net borrower in order to hold more equipment) can be constructed from the point which would represent the holding of the same equipment with a zero stock of bonds (i.e. without borrowing) by increasing the loss-epitome, and decreasing the gain-epitome, of this latter situation by the amount which the borrower is bound to repay (making due discounting allowance for the date of repayment).

I turn now to the second kind of decision which the wealth administrator must take: how fast to augment or diminish his stock of wealth. Here we wish to know two things: first, on what formal principles, and by reference (in applying those principles) to what empirical facts will he decide; and secondly, whether and by what mechanism the simultaneous decisions in this matter of all individual wealth administrators considered together will affect the interest-rate (the system of rates).

May we not say that the possession of a stock of wealth gives its possessor (through whatever psychic mechanism) some experience whose intensity would be somewhat increased by the addition of one

* This is Mr Kalecki's *principle of increasing risk*, which I should formulate by saying that the pace of growth of an enterprise's total assets must not too greatly exceed the pace of ploughing back of undistributed profits or raising of *equity* capital.

banknote's worth to the stock, and increased again, but by a slightly smaller amount, by the addition of a second banknote's worth, and so on? Let us call this experience *possessor-satisfaction*. But what do we mean here by possession? We do not merely mean 'having possessed *until* the present instant'. For possessor-satisfaction to be yielded there must also be the intention that possession shall continue for some time into the future. For how long? The word 'decision' plainly covers a considerable range of meaning, from mere intellectual recognition of the superiority of some one line of action over others, to an actual mustering of moral, mental and bodily forces for the beginning of its execution. But properly used it must always, I think, include the idea of mentally committing oneself, so that the immediate stage of the line of action decided on is treated and felt as an accomplished act. For each particular person in any given field of action this 'immediate' stage will have, more or less consciously, some particular extension from the 'present instant' (when the decision is taken) into future time. Let us call this time-interval the *decision-interval*. It seems to me reasonable to say that the decision-interval is the least interval for which possession must be intended to last in order that it may generate possessor-satisfaction, and also the longest interval for which 'intention' means something that can generate such a feeling. The decision-interval is thus a means of dividing a stock of wealth into two portions: that portion from which the owner can, at the given historical instant, derive possessor-satisfaction, and that portion from which he cannot derive possessor-satisfaction because he has decided to delete it from his stock within the decision-interval. He will, of course, require any assets thus dispensed with to yield satisfaction in another way: they will be exchanged for 'food and drink', which he can consume and thus derive *consumer-satisfaction*.*

If the wealth administrator believes that during the decision-interval some number N of banknotes will accrue to him as income, he may decide to spend a portion $(N-A)$ of these during the decision-interval on 'food and drink' and add the remainder, A, to his stock of wealth. Then by definition of the interval, this addition will be looked upon by him as something accomplished, which will therefore augment his intensity of possesor-satisfaction. In effect, we need make no theoretical distinction between the cases where N is zero,

---

* I use the expression 'food and drink', here and hereafter, as a more vivid substitute for 'consumption-goods'. I hope that such avoidance of words whose impact on our minds has been dulled by continual and various use may make the argument more readable.

so that any spending on consumption must actually reduce the stock of wealth below its level at the instant of decision, and the case where N is positive. The wealth administrator, according to this view, will have in mind the size that his stock of wealth will have at the *end* of the decision-interval. Any consumption he decides to make within the interval will reduce that size below what it could otherwise have been. If this reduction is by B banknotes, we may reasonably assume that the greater is B, the more intense will be his consumer-satisfaction and the greater also will be his corresponding *loss* of intensity of possessor-satisfaction; but that the greater B is, the smaller will be the increment in his intensity of consumer-satisfaction, and the larger will be the decrement of his intensity of possessor-satisfaction, resulting from a change of decision from B to $(B+1)$. Then his combined intensity of possessor- and consumer-satisfaction will be maximized if he so chooses B that a change of decision from B to $(B+1)$ will increase his consumer-satisfaction by no more nor no less than it reduces his possessor-satisfaction.

We have answered the question: On what formal principles will the individual decide how fast to augment or diminish his stock of wealth? We can now pass to the study of a *system* comprising a number of such individual decision-makers, and having also a banking system, but no taxation. There is a formidable difficulty. Hitherto we have been concerned with the thoughts occurring in one decision-maker's mind at an instant or, perhaps we should say, in a very short interval whose length can be neglected. We have spoken as though in reaching his decisions he knew how many banknotes would accrue to him as income in the decision-interval, and at what price he could sell or buy a given quantity of bonds. In a realistic model we cannot assume these things known to him when he takes his decisions, for they depend on the simultaneous decisions of other people. Nevertheless, something may perhaps be learnt from a model in which the individual does in effect base his decisions on known income and known terms of borrowing and lending (i.e. known terms of sale and purchase of bonds). Let us suppose that at the beginning of each 'week' every decision-maker (whether on his own behalf or as head of an enterprise) must send in to a central office a schedule in the form of a square array, each column of which is headed with a number representing a hypothesis as to the aggregate income of all decision-makers in the system for that week (the hypotheses covering a suitable range from low to high), and each row of which is labelled with a number representing a hypothesis as to the yield of bonds in that week. Any number inserted in a row and in a column of this array will stand for the individual's conditional promise to spend during the week, either on 'food and drink' or else on equipment for a net enlargement or improvement of his productive facilities, or on some combination of such consumption and net investment, that number of banknotes. The conditions for each such promise are that the aggregate income and the yield of bonds should be those named at the head of the column and the end of the row in which the number stands. The sum of the numbers inserted in any one place in the array by all the individuals who together compose the system is then the sum of their conditional promises to make so much expenditure and therefore *ipso facto* to provide the system with just that much income. On a second table, with columns and rows similarly labelled, each decision-maker would insert, for each combination of interest-rate and aggregate income, the number of banknotes* he would in those circumstances wish to hold. It is a familiar and reasonable assumption that when a man's income is very low he will spend a high proportion, or even the whole of it, on 'food and drink'; when it is very high, he will spend a lower proportion on 'food and drink'. The reverse may be true of his outlay on equipment, but not, perhaps, to such a degree as to reverse the net effect. Taking, let us say, the top row of each of the first set of tables (and for the moment ignoring the other rows), the central office is therefore likely to find that the sum of all the figures entered under some one hypothetical figure of aggregate income is equal to that hypothetical figure. Then taking the second row of all the tables, the central office will again find some one column where the figures in the row and column in question add up (approximately) to the number at the head of the column. The ultimate result of such a study of the first set of tables will be a two-column schedule showing, for each hypothesis concerning the interest-rate, some one size of aggregate income. Turning then to the second set of tables, the central office will find, for each combination of a particular interest-rate and aggregate income, a particular total number of banknotes which the decision-makers, all taken together, wish in those circumstances to hold. Being informed by the monetary authority what total number of banknotes is to be allowed to be in the hands of the decision-makers, the central office will then inform each decision-maker what the aggregate income and the interest-rate for the coming 'week' will be, and he will then proceed to spend banknotes, on 'food and drink' and on extra equipment, to the amount which he promised that, in the circumstances now laid down,

---

* By banknotes I mean, as explained above, bank balances as well as physical notes.

he would do. The banking system will at the same time be instructed by the central office to buy bonds from, or sell bonds to, any decision-maker at the announced interest-rate. On the level of abstraction of this model, and if we think of a small (self-contained) community, it is perhaps not too difficult to suppose that each citizen, knowing the aggregate income, could estimate within a little his own share of it. Thus each in drawing up his *ex ante* schedules at the beginning of each 'week' (which would automatically become the effective decision-interval for everybody) would make his conditional promises with knowledge of the circumstances in which he would have to fulfil any one of them.

By this model, therefore, we avoid the difficulties raised for theory by the fact that in reality the incomes which individual decision-makers assume or expect in deciding how much to expand on consumption or net investment may add up to more, or less, than the total of those individual expenditures. Such a discrepancy between aggregate expected income and aggregate intended expenditure must mean that some individuals will find that their decisions have been based on wrong premises. The continuous emergence of such disappointments and the continuous efforts by individuals to adjust their resulting situations must affect the course of events; but in a first approximation we wish to avoid these complications.

In our model, aggregate income is composed exclusively and precisely of aggregate expenditure on consumption plus aggregate expenditure on net investment. Aggregate individual saving I define, as usual, as aggregate income less aggregate spending on consumption. Thus it follows that aggregate saving by all individual decision-makers taken together is identically equal to their aggregate net investment, and this is true *ex ante* as well as *ex post*. What, then, will be the effect of a general weakening or strengthening of the desire of individuals to consume out of given incomes? Can it affect the interest-rate? Can the interest-rate in changing have repercussions on the number of banknotes saved per unit of time? In short, is there even partial truth in the proposition that the interest-rate is what equates the aggregate saving-flow and the aggregate net investment-flow?

It is expenditure which, in our model and in other more nearly realistic ones, elicits and measures output. A decision not to spend a given number of banknotes is a signal to someone not to produce that number of banknotes' worth of output; in our model this signal is given and obeyed explicitly, exactly, and without time-lag. A general weakening of the desire of individuals to consume out of given incomes means that each will enter a smaller figure than hitherto in each column of his expenditure array, this smaller figure being composed of a smaller amount for consumption and an unchanged amount for net investment. That total of conditional promises to spend, which matches the heading of the column in which these promises stand, will then be found in a column headed with a smaller aggregate income than the one which formerly yielded the solution. Thus, as the outcome of the transformation or individual income-consumption functions to greater frugality, the aggregate income will be smaller, the pace of accumulation (i.e. the identically equal flows of aggregate saving and aggregate net investment) will be unchanged. Nothing will thus have happened to the saving-flow, and any effect there may be on the interest-rate cannot occur directly through that flow. But the smaller total value per unit of time of transactions in general, corresponding to the smaller aggregate income, will require a smaller stock of banknotes to handle it with a given degree of convenience. Out of a given total number of banknotes in existence, more will then have to be held by persons induced by a low interest-rate to prefer them to bonds. In this indirect manner the rate may; to some small extent, be affected.

So far in this paper I have been outlining a general and largely formal theory. Neglecting the plurality of interest-rates, the great variety of 'fixed-interest' securities ranging from treasury bills to Consols and extending to commercial debentures of lower credit standing, and neglecting also the variety of 'legal persons' who lend and borrow, as different in their needs and their legal obligations as private mortals of small wealth and institutional immortals of huge wealth such as banks and insurance companies and charity trust funds, I have been concerned only with the most fundamental questions: why there should be interest, what part of the essential character of economic life it symptomizes; and by what psychic mechanism we can suppose men to choose determinately between such contrasted satisfactions as consumption and accumulation (which turns out, however, to be of minor relevance for us), and between security on one hand or enlargement of hopes on the other, between cramping but protecting certainty and hazardous freedom to fear loss and hope for gain. But now I wish to turn to detail and to factual illustration.

If the yield of a bond* is that feature of it which affords a presumption that, when all is said and done, the total number of bank-

* It will be remembered that we are using 'bond' to mean any promise-to-pay by an undoubtedly sound debtor.

notes eventually received by the purchaser of the bond, whether by reselling it or by holding it until redemption, will turn out to be greater than the number he gave for it, then this yield will surely be smaller when the lender's hazard is confined within narrow limits. Now when a security is due to be redeemed (that is, a final payment equal, or about equal, to the amount originally lent is due to be made) quite soon, the holder of it, should he unexpectedly need ready money, will easily find a buyer who feels sure of being able to wait the short time until redemption; the shorter that time, the more numerous such willing buyers will be, the more eagerly they will compete with each other for a small but sure gain, and the nearer, therefore, the market-price of the security will be to the final 'redemption' payment. Thus the yield, we should expect, will be low. By contrast, when the series of payments still due from the debtor stretches over many future years, it becomes impossible to guess what the terms of borrowing and lending will be at such remote dates; so much can obviously happen in the meantime to upset all calculations based upon the present visible situation. Thus as we turn from treasury bills, and bonds already called for redemption within a few months or a year or so, to bonds whose remaining life is still several years, we should expect the yield to rise rapidly at first; a bond with a remaining life of four years will have a much higher yield than one of only six months. But the power of 'present' knowledge to penetrate the future does not even seem to us to be much (and surely is far less than our indolent and unimaginative natures incline to suppose it). Enough hazards can crowd themselves into a remaining bond-life of 5 or 10 years to make us care little about the additional ones belonging to a life of 20 or 30 years, and we should accordingly expect the rate at which yield increases with increase of bond-life to slacken rapidly beyond the earliest years.

But if differences in length of life account for relative bond yields, what accounts for their general level at any instant? The ultimate refuge from market uncertainties (unless faith in the value of money is lost in a galloping inflation) is money. Let us imagine two situations such that each individual attaches the same degrees of doubt or assurance to given hypotheses in the one situation as he does in the other (different individuals perhaps differing from each other very widely in both the one situation and in the other); two situations, that is to say, which are identical in regard to the state of mind, knowledge, set of hypotheses entertained with given degrees of uncertainty, and attitude to such uncertainty, of every individual; and let us suppose them also identical in regard to the quantity existing of each form of wealth, and its distribution; except that the quantity of money is much larger in situation B than in situation A. Then it is plausible that the relative scarcity, in situation A, of that form of wealth which gives shelter from whatever market uncertainties exist in the minds of the various individuals will make banknotes dear in terms of bonds in that situation; that is, the yield of bonds will be higher in situation A than in situation B. If the monetary authority could in reality effect a transition from A to B, could, that is to say, largely increase the number of banknotes in people's possession* without thereby changing their expectations, it is plain that the price of bonds in terms of banknotes could be raised, in other words the yield of bonds could be lowered. It is plain also that though in reality any act of largely increasing the quantity of money would inevitably change people's expectations, some changes of expectations are easily conceivable that would strongly assist the reduction of interest-rates. Indeed, in a 'cheap-money drive' nothing succeeds like success; for if once a consensus of market opinion can be swung, by words and deeds of the monetary authority or its masters, to the view that bond prices will go yet a little higher, the resulting preponderance of orders to buy will push them that little higher, and justify the suasion that induced the buying; and thus step by step the monetary authorities can drive bond prices up and up: *possunt quia posse videntur.*

How, then, are we to explain the ultimate failure of the attempt, begun in the autumn of 1945 and backed by all the resources of modern government used with complete determination, to drive down the long-term interest-rate from its starting-level of 3 % per annum to 2½ % or even lower, and to establish it there as a respected permanency? To understand this failure we must consider the nature of the temporary success that was achieved.

The rate of interest is, of all prices, the one most inseparably bound up by the logic of its very nature with expectation and uncertainty. These are, indeed, the main reason for its existence. This is true at all times, but nowadays for two reasons this 'dynamic' character of interest-rates has come to be able to dominate all other aspects completely: first, the disturbed and 'experimental' character of the times makes the possibility of dramatic changes more real and insistently present to people's minds; and, secondly, the scale and incidence of taxes in Britain to-day makes *capital gains* immensely more attractive than what is conventionally thought of as 'income' from securities. Capital gains are untaxed, so that while 'interest' payments of £1

* In the bank account or pocket.

a year can to a rich man be worth as little as 6*d.* a year tax free, a capital gain of £1 is worth £1. This factor of taxation immensely increases the sensitiveness of long-dated gilt-edged security values to uncertainty and suggestions of change in trend or policy. For a rise in the yield of irredeemable stocks from, say, 2½% per annum to 3¼% per annum, such as occurred in Consols between November 1946 and April 1948, implies a capital loss sufficient, with tax at 9*s.* in the £, to wipe out some 16 or 17 years' net income from 'interest' payments, and correspondingly more as surtax increases. This state of affairs must mean that for most owners or free administrators of wealth, other than 'immortal' institutions not subject to tax, the hope of capital gains and the fear of capital losses completely dominates their outlook to the exclusion of the question of yield.

In short, bond prices were able to go on getting higher and higher, bond yields correspondingly lower and lower, so long as enough people were able to believe that they would go on a little longer. But they could not stand still at an extreme level and stay there. Once the rise had been checked, the spell broken, fears of capital loss took the place of hopes of gain. A bond whose price is high and rising can look profitable; one whose price is high and not rising is a mere peril. The rout, once started by the fuel crisis, carried Treasury 2½% stock down from 100 to 83 in 9 months.

These ideas and facts are illustrated in the accompanying figures. In Fig. X 2 the quantity of money, defined as the total deposits of the London Clearing Banks plus estimated notes and coin in circulation with the public,* is shown as a heavy continuous line M; the 'notes and coin' component of the quantity of money is shown as a light continuous line n; and the yield of 2½% Consols is shown as a line of heavy dashes Y. In mid-1945 the quantity of money had been increasing (with only seasonal and other minor interruptions) ever since the beginning of the war; the yield of Consols had been rather steady for some years at a little over 3%. The 'cheap-money drive' began in September 1945, and between then and November 1946 the quantity of money was increased by some £650 million or 10%. Moreover, the whole of this increase was in deposits and none of it in notes and coin. If the latter (as seems likely) are a fairly constant proportion of the money required for convenience in handling transactions, all the extra money must have been held as an alternative to other ways of storing wealth. (Between February and December 1946 the quantity of money actually increased by £1000 million, but part of that increase is seasonal.) The yield of

* From *Monthly Digest of Statistics* (H.M.S.O. 1948).

$2\frac{1}{2}$ % Consols fell, between those dates, from 3 % per annum to $2\frac{1}{2}$ %. In the spring of 1947 the fuel crisis shook the belief in the Exchequer's power and willingness to go on supporting and shouldering up the bond market; failure of belief in a *continuing rise* meant, inevitably, a rush to get out of gilt-edged at the perilous heights they had reached. Although the quantity of money continued, though very gently, to *increase*, the yield of Consols sprang back within 6 or 7 months to 3 %, and in another 8 months to $3\frac{1}{4}$ %, higher than it had been when there was £1000 million less money. But is this perhaps true only of irredeemable stocks? Let us look at Figs. X 3, X 4 and X 5, plotted from data given in Table X 1.*

Table X 1. *Yield as a function of number of years to earliest redemption, at three dates*

			7 Sept. 1945		14 Nov. 1946		13 Aug. 1947	
			Years	Yield	Years	Yield	Years	Yield
Conversion	3%	48/53	2·5	2·020	1·3	1·380	0·5	1·130
Nat. War	$2\frac{1}{2}$%	49/51	3·9	2·016	2·7	1·390	2·0	2·070
Defence	3%	54/58	8·9	2·720	7·7	1·940	6·9	2·875
Nat. War	$2\frac{1}{2}$%	54/56	9·0	2·500	7·7	1·870	7·0	2·725
War Loan	3%	55/59	10·1	2·738	8·9	1·988	8·2	2·912
Savings	3%	55/65	10·0	2·880	8·8	2·042	8·0	2·980
Funding	$2\frac{1}{2}$%	56/61	10·6	2·742	9·4	1·921	8·7	2·920
Savings	3%	60/70	15·0	2·970	13·8	2·234	13·0	3·046
Savings	$2\frac{1}{2}$%	64/67	—	—	17·5	2·184	16·75	2·925
Savings	3%	65/75	20·0	3·012	18·8	2·300	18·0	3·046
Treasury	$2\frac{1}{2}$%	75 or after	—	—	—	2·500	—	3·075
Consols	$2\frac{1}{2}$%		—	2·830	—	2·525	—	3·029

In each of these charts the curve relates the yield of bonds to their remainder of life. By the remainder of life of a bond I mean the time which has still to elapse before the debtor's final payment. For irredeemable securities, viz. $2\frac{1}{2}$ % Consols and Treasury $2\frac{1}{2}$ % stock, this life has been conventionally taken as 50 years. To represent a zero life I have used treasury bills. The other securities for which points are plotted on these charts have each a range of dates within which 'repayment' will be made, instead of a single date. For all these the earliest date of the range has been taken.

As we should expect from the foregoing analysis of the nature of interest, the slope of the curve in each chart is steep near the origin

* I drew all these curves freehand. Any more elaborate procedure would, for my present purpose, have been a waste of effort.

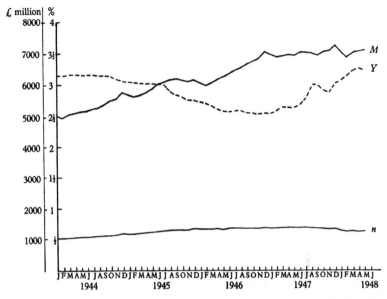

Fig. X 2. *M* is total deposits of London Clearing Banks plus notes and coin with the public. *Y* is yield of 2½% Consols. *n* is notes and coin with the public.

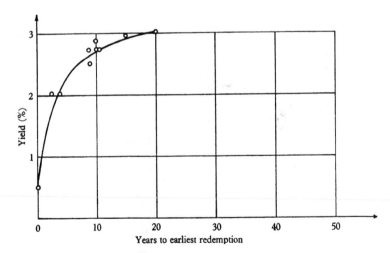

Fig. X 3. Yield as a function of remainder of life at 7 September 1945. Quantity of money: £6200 million.

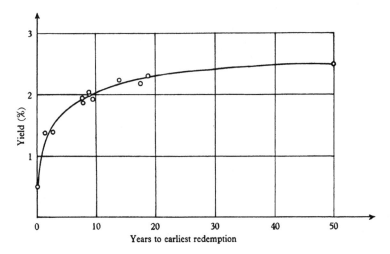

Fig. X 4. Yield as a function of remainder of life at 14 November 1946.
Quantity of money: £6850 million.

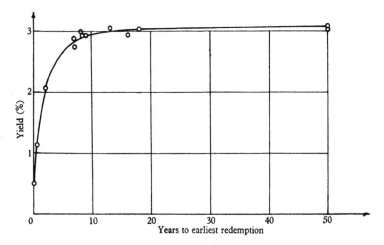

Fig. X 5. Yield as a function of remainder of life at 13 August 1947.
Quantity of money: £7000 million.

but becomes rapidly less steep* beyond 5 or 10 years. However, our main concern is a comparison of the shapes and positions of the curve at three different dates. Fig. X 3 shows yields at 7 September 1945, which I take as the start of the 'cheap-money drive'; Fig. X 4 shows how, by 14 November 1946, the whole curve had been pushed bodily downwards, and Fig. X 5 shows how by 13 August 1947, after the convertibility crisis, the curve had gone up again beyond its level at September 1945. In Fig. X 6 all three curves are plotted together for easy comparison.

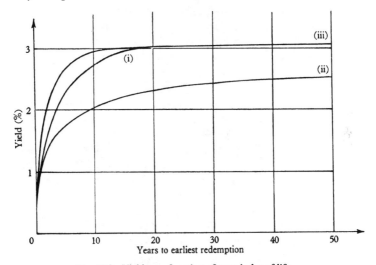

Fig. X 6. Yield as a function of remainder of life.

	(i)	(ii)	(iii)
Date	7 Sept. 1945	14 Nov. 1946	13 Aug. 1947
Quantity of money	£6200 m.	£6850 m.	£7000 m.

These violent movements ought to shock anyone who still believes that the rate of interest depends on the 'credit standing' of the government, or on the degree of thriftiness or extravagance of the people. They merely magnify and dramatize the fact that interest is a manifestation of uncertainty, and in highly uncertain times it will betray its nature by the scale and momentum of its changes.

* See p. 121 above.

XI

INTEREST-RATES AND THE PACE OF INVESTMENT*

It was until recent years an accepted doctrine that changes of interest-rates powerfully influence the pace at which enterprisers, all taken together, extend or improve their equipment. But this opinion has lately been challenged by the testimony of enterprisers themselves, given in response to systematic inquiry. Some simple developments of theory can, I think, resolve the apparent contradiction, and this it is the purpose of this essay to attempt.

The rationale of the doctrine is simple. A piece of equipment is bought because the buyer hopes that its use will at some future time bring in sums of money exceeding those which he will have concurrently to pay out in order to use the equipment, and that the net amounts by which the gross receipts exceed the associated outgoings will together be rather more than equal, when allowance has been made for their futurity, and for his doubt as to the correctness of his estimate of their size, to the immediate purchase price of the equipment. Let x years be the futurity of one such net amount or 'net return' whose size he estimates as c; and let $100r\%$ per annum be the rate of interest which can be had and must be paid on cash now lent for x years, where due payment of interest and principal is treated as certain. Then the equivalent in spot cash of a sum due in x years, if its size were known exactly and for certain to be c, would be $P = c(1+r)^{-x} = c\,e^{-\rho x}$. But in fact c is only an estimate or conjecture, and in order to allow for his doubt of its correctness the enterpriser must multiply it by a second coefficient. This doubt will differ in degree for different values of x, and the second coefficient must therefore be written $s = s(x)$. Thus the equivalent of c in cash free from doubt or deferment will be $p = cs(x)\,e^{-\rho x}$. Since the enterpriser need not run his plant at a loss, we can assume that c is non-negative for all x, and if we assume also that ρ stands at one and the same level for all x, we have for the value he sets on an instrument which he has in mind to buy

$$v = \int_0^\infty c(x)\,s(x)\,e^{-\rho x}\,dx.$$

* *Economic Journal*, vol. LVI (1946), pp. 1–17.

$c(x)$ may be looked upon, if we will, as that specific guess or estimate (regarding the size of the net return whose futurity is x) which has more to be said for it than any other guess in the light of the enterpriser's existing knowledge; this estimated size is then multiplied by a coefficient $s(x)$, which will usually be less than unity, to bring into the reckoning the enterpriser's awareness of the insufficiency of his knowledge. The distinction between these two influences on the size of the sum of money which, if it could be looked forward to with certainty, would be equivalent in the enterpriser's mind to his misty prospect of the net return which the instrument will yield at a date x years hence, is blurred and imprecise. Under which heading, for example, are we to put his general awareness of the inventiveness of mankind, which, though no smallest sign may yet appear of any invention which would render the proposed investment obsolete, yet warns him that this obsolescence is possible or even likely? It is on such ground as this that I prefer an altogether different construction, for which, however, I have not yet been able to obtain sufficient critical attention to justify its use here.

One further matter must detain us for a moment. We have spoken, by implication, of the coefficient $e^{-\rho x}$, by which each net return $c(x)$ is to be multiplied, as an allowance for 'futurity'. Below we shall sometimes call this allowance 'time-discounting' and refer to ρ as the rate of 'pure' interest. These phrases mean no more than that, because interest greater than zero can be obtained on loans which are regarded as free from risk of default, a future sum c is the equivalent of a present sum smaller than c, when the due receipt of both is *undoubted*. Since this reason for discounting given future sums is entirely independent of any question of doubt concerning the size of such sums, we need a term to distinguish the former reason, and accordingly use the phrases we have mentioned. Interest on loans free from risk of default is compensation for sacrifice of liquidity; compensation, that is to say, for accepting the possibility that the market value of the 'paper' received as evidence of the loan will fall, not through any fear of default, but through a change in the terms on which loans can be obtained. This is a risk of a sort entirely different from that concerning the eventual size of payments to be received in the future; and it is a matter with which we are not concerned, for our problem concerns the effects, and not the causes, of pure interest-rates.

Let u be the purchase price of an instrument of the kind the enterpriser has it in mind to buy, and y, which we will treat as continuously variable, be the quantity of such instruments ordered by all enterprisers in a unit of time. Then the conditions of production of such instruments being given, we have $u = u(y)$, and the pace of investment in instruments of this type, before allowance is made for concurrent depreciation of those already in existence, is $z = uy$ per unit of time. On account of their differing beliefs about the course of its future net returns (the form of $c = c(x)$), different enterprisers at any one time will assign different values to such an instrument. If these different valuations are arranged in descending sequence, it can plausibly be suggested that the orders placed for such instruments in any one unit of time will go so far down this list that the price u, which will be higher the larger the number y of orders concurrently placed, is just equal to the least sanguine valuation which actually yields an order. Let us then mean by v the least sanguine of current valuations which actually results in an order, and accordingly assume that at all times $u = v$. We can then write $y = y(v)$. We are now concerned with three elasticities:

that of v with respect to ρ, namely, $\eta_{v\rho} = \dfrac{dv}{d\rho} \dfrac{\rho}{v}$,

that of y with respect to $u = v$, namely, $\eta_{yv} = \dfrac{dy}{dv} \dfrac{v}{y}$,

that of $z = uy = vy$ with respect to ρ, namely, $\eta_{z\rho} = \dfrac{dz}{d\rho} \dfrac{\rho}{z} = \dfrac{d(vy)}{d\rho} \dfrac{\rho}{vy}$.

We have $\quad \dfrac{d(vy)}{d\rho} \dfrac{\rho}{vy} = \left(\dfrac{dv}{d\rho} y + \dfrac{dy}{d\rho} v \right) \dfrac{\rho}{vy} = \dfrac{dv}{d\rho} \dfrac{\rho}{v} + \dfrac{dy}{d\rho} \dfrac{\rho}{y} = \eta_{v\rho} + \eta_{y\rho}$

$$= \dfrac{dv}{d\rho} \dfrac{\rho}{v} + \dfrac{dy}{dv} \dfrac{v}{y} \cdot \dfrac{dv}{d\rho} \dfrac{\rho}{v} = \eta_{v\rho}(1 + \eta_{yv}).$$

If we prefer to define the pace of gross investment in instruments of a given kind as the *quantity* of them produced in a unit of time, rather than as the money-value of this quantity—that is to say, as y rather than as uy—then we have

$$\eta_{y\rho} = \dfrac{dy}{d\rho} \dfrac{\rho}{y} = \dfrac{dy}{dv} \dfrac{v}{y} \cdot \dfrac{dv}{d\rho} \dfrac{\rho}{v} = \eta_{yv} \eta_{v\rho}.$$

Thus under our assumptions the elasticity, with respect to the interest-rate, of the pace of gross investment in a given kind of instrument, whichever of the two definitions of this pace we adopt, is directly proportional to the elasticity, with respect to the interest-rate, of the least sanguine current valuation of such instruments which yields a decision to invest. Since, as we shall immediately show, a fall in the interest-rate will raise all valuations, some valuations which were previously extra-marginal—that is, lower down the list than the least sanguine one which yielded an order—may be raised above the margin, and the pace of gross investment in instruments of this type will thus be increased. Since the same will be true of instruments of all kinds, a fall in the rate of interest, not counteracted by any simultaneous other change, must be expected to increase the pace of gross investment in the system as a whole, and, if the only concurrent increase in the pace of depreciation of the whole existing capital equipment of the system is that arising from the increase of gross investment, there will also result an increase in the pace of net investment. It remains, in order to establish a presumption in favour of the doctrine that interest-rates influence the pace of investment, to show that they influence the values which are set on equipment. Let us suppose at first that an enterpriser treats the net amounts which will be earned by some instrument which he has it in mind to buy as known exactly and for certain; and see how under various assumptions as to the distribution over future time of these net amounts, the value which he sets upon the instrument will vary when the interest-rate is varied.

The simplest of these assumptions is that the instrument will yield its entire net return C at a single instant of a known futurity of x years. Then its value will be $v = C e^{-\rho x}$, and the proportionate change in this value due to a given proportionate change in ρ is

$$\frac{dv}{d\rho}\frac{\rho}{v} = -\rho x.$$

This elasticity increases numerically in direct proportion to the futurity x of the net return, and the proportion in question is itself equal to the interest-rate. In so far, therefore, as the expected net returns from a capital instrument are concentrated near some one future date, its value will be more sensitive to given proportionate changes in the interest-rate, the more distant the date, and the higher the interest-rate itself. A rather more realistic assumption is that the instrument will yield returns, net of all running expense including that for repairs and renewals sufficient to maintain it in perfect condition, at a constant time-rate for ever. Then if this time-rate is c we have

$$v = c \int_0^\infty e^{-\rho x}\, dx = \frac{c}{\rho},$$

so that if a new level of the interest-rate is $1/k$ times the old one, the new value of the instrument will be k times the old one. Could we, for example, reduce the appropriate interest-rate from 3 to 2 % per annum, the value of an instrument expected to yield uniform net returns in perpetuity would be multiplied by $\frac{3}{2}$, raised, that is to say, from $33c$ approximately or '33 years' purchase', to $50c$, or '50 years' purchase'. The supply-curve $y(u)$ of such instruments would have to be extremely inelastic (a condition quite the opposite of that which prevails in a slump) if such a rise of value were not to result in a large proportionate rise in the number of such instruments produced in a unit of time. For small changes we can express the matter in terms of elasticities. We have $\dfrac{dv}{d\rho} = -\dfrac{c}{\rho^2}$ and $\eta_{v\rho} = \dfrac{dv}{d\rho}\dfrac{\rho}{v} = -1$. The elasticity of the quantity of the instruments produced in a unit of time with respect to the interest-rate is $\eta_{y\rho} = \eta_{yv}\eta_{v\rho}$. Even, then, if η_{yv}, the elasticity of supply, is no more than $+1$, a given small proportionate change $\Delta\rho/\rho$ in the rate of interest will produce an equal proportionate change, of opposite sign, in the pace of price-deflated gross investment in the instruments.

Table XI 1

L	$\dfrac{\Delta v}{v_1}$ for $\Delta\rho = 0.03\text{–}0.04$ (1)	$\dfrac{\Delta v}{v_1}$ for $\Delta\rho = 0.02\text{–}0.03$ (2)	$\dfrac{\Delta v}{v_1}\bigg/\dfrac{\Delta\rho}{\rho_1}$ for $\Delta\rho = 0.03\text{–}0.04$ (3)	$\dfrac{\Delta v}{v_1}\bigg/\dfrac{\Delta\rho}{\rho_1}$ for $\Delta\rho = 0.02\text{–}0.03$ (4)
5	0·025	0·025	−0·10	−0·08
10	0·048	0·049	−0·19	−0·15
20	0·092	0·096	−0·37	−0·29
40	0·167	0·182	−0·67	−0·55
80	0·264	0·316	−1·06	−0·95

The most realistic simple assumption is, however, that the instrument is expected to yield uniform net returns for some finite number of years and then be abandoned. If the expected useful life is L we have

$$v = c\int_0^L e^{-\rho x}\,dx = \frac{c}{\rho}(1 - e^{-\rho L}).$$

In Table XI 1, column 1 shows $\Delta v/v_1$, where Δv is the difference $v_2 - v_1$ produced in v by a change from $\rho = 4\%$ per annum to $\rho = 3\%$ per annum, v_1 corresponds to the first and v_2 to the second of these values of ρ, and the useful life L is taken successively at 5, 10, 20, 40 and 80 years. Column 2 shows the same for an interest-rate changing from 3 to 2% per annum. Column 3 shows the quasi-elasticities $\dfrac{\Delta v}{v_1}\bigg/\dfrac{\Delta\rho}{\rho_1}$, where $\Delta\rho = \rho_2 - \rho_1$, $\rho_1 = 4\%$ per annum, $\rho_2 = 3\%$ per annum; and column 4 similarly corresponds to column 2.

In this table we see, for example, that a fall in the rate of interest from a level of 4 % per annum to one of 3 % per annum raises the value of the instrument, when this is expected to yield net returns of a constant amount per year for L years and afterwards nothing, by 5 % if L is 10, by 9 % if L is 20, by $16\frac{1}{2}$% if L is 40, and by $26\frac{1}{2}$% if L is 80. It is clear that the *percentage* by which the value of a durable instrument is raised by a given reduction of the interest-rate—that is, the sensitivity of the value to such changes—is a strongly increasing function of the expected revenue-earning life.

There is, then, a case for supposing that interest-rates should influence the pace of investment. Let us turn now to the testimony of enterprisers themselves.

A very full account of the method and results of the questionnaire inquiry, conducted by the Oxford Economists' Research Group in 1939, is given by Mr P. W. S. Andrews in *Oxford Economic Papers*, old series, no. 3 (1940), to which the reader is referred. The results are summarized thus by Professor R. S. Sayers in the same issue:

About one-quarter of the business men gave some answer to the questionnaire. Of those who replied, about three-quarters stated that the terms (in the broad sense) on which loans could be obtained had not affected their decisions to add to or maintain either fixed or working capital. One-quarter of those replying (about 6 % of those asked) gave some kind of affirmative answer.

In assessing the significance of these results [Mr Sayers proceeds] it is necessary to consider, first, whether the 25 % who replied constituted a fair sample, for our purpose, of the whole. Why, in fact, did the other 75% throw the questionnaire into the waste-paper basket?...My own guess is that most of the firms were, as a result of their own experience, not convinced that borrowing terms make much difference to their decisions. If this guess is the right one, we must obviously work on the assumption that the proportion of business men conscious of the effectiveness of borrowing terms must be much lower than one-quarter, though it may be rather more than 6 %.

What considerations can we have omitted from the theory stated above, to account for its leading to conclusions that the facts do not seem to support? A hint is provided by some of the comments which accompanied the business men's answers. The following comments of six of them seem specially illuminating:

A. Any profit or advantage expected from expenditure on plant or repairs, or from varying the quantity of stock* held, has greatly out-

* I.e. stock-piles of materials or products.

weighed the cost of borrowing or the income receivable by depositing surplus funds with bankers.

B. If the estimated advantage from a projected extension is jeopardized by a 1 % difference in interest, it hardly seems justifiable anyhow.

C. We are not generally affected by the cost of borrowing money and rates of interest, because we do not come to a decision to spend money on extensions unless or until we can see it will really be profitable to do so. The interest either paid on money borrowed on overdraft or earned as interest would generally speaking be small compared to the earning power on any such expenditure.

D. Difficult to imagine a position in which interest-rates could have any appreciable effect compared with taxation, on plans for extension. Have for some time been considering laying down small amount of extra plant, but the proposition, which includes a considerable risk, can be attractive only if 50 % return on capital value* is considered possible. Unless we get 33 %, any extension is out of the question.

E. If expenditure on new craft† were to be influenced by the cost of borrowing, the profit on the building project would be very much too low to render it a normal commercial risk.

F. Expenditure on plant extensions has been made only when the trend of business has shown this to be desirable. Question of financing, and rate of interest, has not affected it, as unless anticipated return were far in excess of such cost, the projects would not have proceeded to decision stage.

These comments all speak of an expected or estimated 'profit', 'return', or 'earning power' which must greatly exceed the cost of borrowing if the investment in question is to be made. The reason for this requirement appears in the references, in comments D and E, to 'risk'. We said at the beginning of this essay that an enterpriser must allow for his doubt concerning the correctness of his estimates of future net returns by multiplying each by a coefficient whose size will depend on the futurity of the net return in question; but we then, by assumption, excluded this doubt. Let us reintroduce into our expression for v a coefficient $s = s(x)$, and see what effect is produced by assigning different forms to this function. Let us first suppose this form to be such that s has the same value for all values of x; in other words, that the enterpriser makes the same allowance for doubt in regard to every instalment of net returns no matter what its futurity. In this case no difference whatever will be made to the sensitiveness of v with respect to ρ—that is, to the elasticity $\eta_{v\rho}$. For if

$$v = sc \int_0^L e^{-\rho x} dx,$$

* I.e. capital *cost*.   † Ships.

we have $\qquad \dfrac{dv}{d\rho}\dfrac{\rho}{v} = \{e^{-\rho L}(\rho L + 1) - 1\}/(1 - e^{-\rho L}),$

which is independent of s. It is not, then, a matter of indifference what form is assigned to $s = s(x)$, if we wish it to account for the meagreness of entrepreneurial reactions to the interest-rate. We may assume, perhaps, that $s < 1$ for all x; and let us put $s = 1/q$. Surely the allowance for doubt will be better able to reduce the leverage of the interest-rate, if q is relatively large for those instalments of net return whose present value (when no allowance is made for doubt) changes by the largest amount when the interest-rate changes? To discover some form of $s = s(x)$ which will make the allowance for doubt the solution of our paradox, we must discover which these instalments are.

When a reduction of the interest-rate raises the value of a capital-good whose earnings are expected to be uniform for a finite number of years and afterwards nothing, it is not the earnings of the nearest future years which contribute most to the total gain of value; nor is it always the most distant. Let u be the present value* of an element of net returns due at an instant x years hence, the size c of this element being treated as known for certain; and writing $u = u(\rho, x) = c e^{-\rho x}$ let us study the quantity $\dfrac{\partial(\partial u/\partial \rho)}{\partial x} = (\rho x - 1) c e^{-\rho x}$. $\dfrac{\partial u}{\partial \rho}$ will have a stationary value where $\dfrac{\partial(\partial u/\partial \rho)}{\partial x} = 0$, and the only finite solution of $(\rho x - 1) c e^{-\rho x} = 0$ is $x = 1/\rho$. We have also $\dfrac{\partial^2(\partial u/\partial \rho)}{\partial x^2} = \rho c e^{-\rho x}(2 - \rho x)$, which at $x = 1/\rho$ is positive. Thus $x = 1/\rho$ gives an extreme value of $\partial u/\partial \rho$ when $\partial u/\partial \rho$ is treated as a function of x, and as $\partial u/\partial \rho$ is everywhere negative this extreme value is a minimum, the point where the graph of the function, shown in Fig. XI 1, sags most deeply. If then, for example, $\rho = 0.03$ we shall find that the largest contribution to the total gain in value of the instrument, caused by a given (small) fall of ρ, is made by those instalments of net return which are due at dates of a futurity round about $x = 1/\rho = 33$ years; or if $\rho = 0.02$, by those of a futurity about $x = 50$ years. (See Table XI 2 and Fig. XI 1.)

The distribution of the total gain in the value of an instrument, due to a fall in the interest-rate, over the different periods in the assumed life of the instrument, is illustrated in Table XI 3, where,

---

* For the self-contained argument of this paragraph we are giving the letter u a meaning quite unconnected with that of the supply-price for which we used it on pp. 129, 130 above.

however, for sharper contrast we have used a large instead of a small change of ρ, with the consequence of displacing somewhat the date of maximum effect. We again consider the effect of pure time-discounting alone on the value of a prospective series of net returns whose sizes are taken as known for certain. Here column 1 shows the value, discounted to some one point of time standing for 'the present', of the assumed net earnings of an instrument in successive

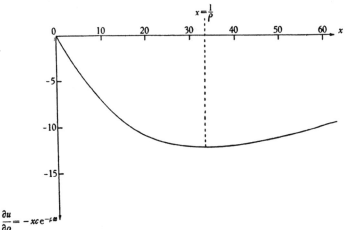

Fig. XI 1. Graph of $\partial u/\partial \rho = -xc\,e^{-\rho x}$ with $c=1$, $\rho=0.03$. When $u=c\,e^{-\rho x}$, $\partial u/\partial \rho$ has a minimum at $x=1/\rho$ and afterwards approaches zero asymptotically.

Table XI 2

$$\frac{\partial u}{\partial \rho} = -xc\,e^{-\rho x} \text{ with } c=1,\ \rho=0.03$$

x	$-xc\,e^{-\rho x}$	x	$-xc\,e^{-\rho x}$	x	$-xc\,e^{-\rho x}$	x	$-xc\,e^{-\rho x}$
0	0	15	-9.56	30	-12.20	45	-11.67
1	-0.97	16	-9.90	31	-12.23	46	-11.57
2	-1.88	17	-10.20	32	-12.25	47	-11.47
3	-2.73	18	-10.49	33	-12.26	48	-11.37
4	-3.55	19	-10.74	34	-12.26	49	-11.27
5	-4.30	20	-10.98	35	-12.25	50	-11.16
6	-5.00	21	-11.18	36	-12.22	51	—
7	-5.67	22	-11.37	37	-12.19	52	—
8	-6.29	23	-11.54	38	-12.15	53	—
9	-6.87	24	-11.68	39	-12.10	54	—
10	-7.41	25	-11.81	40	-12.05	55	—
11	-7.91	26	-11.92	41	-11.98	56	—
12	-8.37	27	-12.01	42	-11.91	57	—
13	-8.80	28	-12.09	43	-11.83	58	—
14	-9.20	29	-12.15	44	-11.75	59	—

future decades of its total life of 80 years, the time-rate of these earnings being supposed constant throughout and the rate of interest ρ being 4 % per annum. Each figure in this column, that is to say, is an evaluation of

$$v_m = c \int_A^B e^{-\rho x} dx = \frac{c}{\rho} (e^{-\rho A} - e^{-\rho B}),$$

where we put A successively equal to 0, 10, ..., 70 years, and B correspondingly equal to 10, 20, 30, ..., 80 years. Column 2 shows the same for $\rho = 2$ % per annum. Column 3 is a companion to column 1, and shows what percentage of the total value of the instrument is attributable to each future decade of its life, and column 4 is a similar companion to column 2. Column 5 shows the excess of each figure in column 2 over the corresponding figure in column 1; it shows, that is to say, that part of the total *gain* in the value of the instrument which is attributable to each decade of its life. Column 6 shows what percentage each figure in column 5 represents of the total of the figures in column 5—that is, what percentage of the total gain in value is attributable to each decade. In column 7 the figures in column 6 are cumulated, so that, for example, by looking at the figure in column 7 opposite decade 4, we can see what percentage of the total gain in value, due to a change from $\rho = 4$ % per annum to $\rho = 2$ % per annum, is attributable to the first half of the instrument's life.

Table XI 3

Decade	Present value, in terms of 'years' purchase', of net returns in each decade		Percentage of total value of instrument attributable to the net returns of each decade		Excess of column 2 over column 1	Percentage of the total *gain* in value attributable to each decade	Column 6 cumulated	
	$\rho = 0.04$	$\rho = 0.02$	$\rho = 0.04$	$\rho = 0.02$				
	(1)	(2)	(3)	(4)	(5)	(6)	(7)	
1	8·24	9·06	34·5	22·6	0·82	5·0	5·0	100·0
2	5·52	7·42	23·2	18·7	1·90	12·0	17·0	95·2
3	3·70	6·07	15·4	15·3	2·37	15·0	32·0	83·2
4	2·48	4·97	10·3	12·5	2·49	15·7	47·7	68·2
5	1·68	4·07	7·1	10·2	2·39	15·0	62·7	52·5
6	1·12	3·33	4·8	8·3	2·21	14·0	76·7	37·5
7	0·75	2·73	3·2	6·8	1·98	12·5	89·2	23·5
8	0·50	2·23	2·1	5·6	1·73	11·0	100·0	11·0
Total	24·00 (approx.)	40·00 (approx.)	100·0	100·0	16·00 (approx.)	100·0		

Now let us suppose that the instrument's life is of 40 instead of 80 years. The relevant figures from Table XI 3, columns 1, 2 and 5, are reproduced below as Table XI 4. Here the first two columns again show the present value in terms of 'years' purchase' of the earnings of each decade, for interest-rates respectively of 4 and 2 % per annum, while column 3 shows the excess of each figure in column 2 over the corresponding figure in column 1; it shows, that is to say, that part of the total gain in the value of the instrument which is attributable to each decade.

Table XI 4

Decade	Present value, in terms of 'years' purchase', of net returns in each decade		Excess of column 2 over column 1
	$\rho = 0.04$ (1)	$\rho = 0.02$ (2)	(3)
1	8·24	9·06	0·82
2	5·52	7·42	1·90
3	3·70	6·07	2·37
4	2·48	4·97	2·49
Totals	20·00 (approx.)	27·50 (approx.)	7·50 (approx.)

From this table it can be seen, for example, that when the value of the instrument is raised from 20 to 27·5 years' purchase, by means of a reduction of the interest-rate from 4 % per annum to 2 % per annum, two-thirds of this gain of 7·5 years' purchase is attributable to the more distant half of the intrument's life, the period *beginning* 20 years hence. Again, if we had considered a life of only three decades (neglecting the fourth row of the table), nearly half of the total gain of 5 years' purchase would have been attributable to the last third of the useful life.

Let us compare these results with those of Table XI 1. There we found that the value of an instrument is more sensitive to changes of interest-rates *the farther into the future its assumed revenue-earning career extends*. If this career is assumed to be very short—say of only 5 or 10 years—the value responds very little even to quite a large change in the interest-rate. But the length of this career is by no means a matter of mere physical durability. The most frequent reason for assuming *ex ante* that an instrument's useful life will be short is that its earning-power seems liable to vanish, at some unpredictable date, through inventions of new methods and changes of demand. If each future year is regarded as holding some given numerical chance of such a change, or as contributing something to a gradual change, then if we take in enough future years the obsolescence of the instrument by the end of that time becomes virtually certain. Alternatively, we can say that the more distant the future date we look at, the more worthless is any guess as to what the market and other conditions will then be, and the more worthless, therefore, and the more heavily to be discounted for doubt, is any guess as to the earnings at that time of any complex and specialized instrument. Thus a limit is set by uncertainty to the useful life which it is sensible to assume.

In accordance with this argument,* let us suppose that the impact (i.e. the reciprocal of s) of the enterpriser's allowance for doubt increases exponentially with the distance into the future of the date he has in mind, so that $s(x) = e^{-hx}$. This is not only reasonable *a priori*, but is in fact what every theorist does who speaks of a *marginal rate of risk* conceived as analogous to the rate of risk-free† interest, and often, indeed, added to the latter in order that the sum of these two rates may be equated to the marginal efficiency of capital under any of its synonyms.‡ Then writing $R = h + \rho$ we have

$$v = c\int_0^L s(x)\, e^{-\rho x}\, dx = c\int_0^L e^{-Rx}\, dx = \frac{c}{R}\left(1 - e^{-RL}\right).$$

An indication of the numerical value which, for illustration and experiment, may be assigned to R, is given us in one of the comments quoted above, where an enterpriser spoke (in comment D) of a proposition which could be attractive 'only if 50% return on capital value§ is considered possible. Unless we get 33% [the enterpriser proceeds] any extension is out of the question.' Let us suppose at first that, so far as physical durability is concerned, the net return c

---

* And with our suggestion that allowance for doubt will be most able to reduce the power of changes in interest-rates to stimulate or depress investment, if the impact of this allowance (supposing s to be less than 1 for all x) is heavy upon those instalments of return which, in case of a change of ρ, make the largest contribution to the increase or decrease of v.

† By 'risk-free' or 'pure' interest we mean interest free from risk of default, not free from the risks entailed by illiquidity (see p. 129 above).

‡ 'Rate of return over cost' (Irving Fisher); 'marginal efficiency of capital' (Lord Keynes); 'internal rate of return' (K. E. Boulding); 'prospective rate of profit' (M. Kalecki). All of these mean an exponent μ such that the value of the instrument, $v = \int_0^\infty c(x)\, e^{-\mu x}\, dx$, is equal to u its purchase price.

§ 'Capital cost' must be meant; but if we suppose this enterpriser's valuation to be the marginal one, it will be equal to capital cost.

is calculated after sufficient allowance for repairs and renewals to maintain the technical efficiency of the instrument indefinitely; and that the whole risk of obsolescence is allowed for in the component h of $R = h + \rho$. Taking the enterpriser's remarks to mean that the lower figure gave a value for the instrument which made it marginal in the circumstances of the case, we have as the value relevant to our elasticity calculations

$$v = c \int_0^\infty e^{-Rx} dx = \frac{c}{R} = \frac{c}{h + \rho},$$

so that

$$\eta_{v\rho} = \frac{dv}{d\rho} \frac{\rho}{v} = -\frac{\rho}{R},$$

and if, for example, $\rho = 0\cdot03$, then $\eta_{v\rho} = -0\cdot09$.

In this case, therefore, a change in risk-free interest-rate from, say, a level of 3 % per annum to one of 2 % per annum would raise the (formerly) marginal valuation of the instrument by about 3 %. Had there been no allowance for doubt (had the marginal rate of risk been zero), the percentage increase in v due to this fall in ρ would have been 50 %. It begins to be clear that we have obtained a solid clue to the meagre powers of the interest-rate as a stimulator of some forms of investment.

A marginal rate of risk as high as $h = R - \rho = 30$ % per annum may be exceptionally high. Moreover, it may be that the 'return on capital value' of 33 % should be interpreted not as R, but as c/v; for the former, even when considered as the magnitude which becomes equal to the marginal efficiency of capital when u is equal to v, is a rather sophisticated notion. So long as the useful life is taken as unlimited, R and c/v are the same; for if $v = c(1 - e^{-RL})/R$ so that $R = c(1 - e^{-RL})/v$, then $R \to c/v$ as $L \to \infty$.

An appreciable divergence appears between R and c/v when RL is small, for then the factor $(1 - e^{-RL})$ becomes appreciably less than 1. Thus for any given value of R a sufficiently small value of L will make $R \Big/ \dfrac{c}{v}$ small. But even if h is only 15 % per annum—that is, half what we have assumed above—so that $R = 18$ % per annum, the ratio $R \Big/ \dfrac{c}{v}$ is already 0·835 for L no greater than 10; and with so short a useful life as this, a change in the rate of pure interest from $\rho = 3$ % per annum to $\rho = 2$ % per annum, even with a zero marginal rate of risk, would change v by only 0·037 or, say, $3\frac{3}{4}$ %. Thus if the 'return on capital value' which an enterpriser takes as his minimum requirement is of the order of 10 or 15 % per annum, then whether this figure means R or c/v, the value of the instrument will be insensitive to even very large proportionate changes in the rate of pure interest; for if, on the ground of the absence of positive contrary signs, the revenue-earning life of the instrument is assumed to be long, allowance for doubt will render negligible the net returns of all but a few years immediately ahead; while if it is assumed to be short, the influence of the rate of pure interest is weak even without any allowance for doubt.

Table XI 5

5-year period	Present value, in terms of 'years' purchase', of the net returns in each 5-year period		Percentage of total value of instrument attributable to the net returns of each 5-year period	
	$R=33\%$ per annum (1)	$R=18\%$ per annum (2)	$R=33\%$ per annum (3)	$R=18\%$ per annum (4)
1	2·424	3·294	80·8	61·0
2	0·466	1·339	15·6	24·8
3	0·089	0·544	3·0	10·1
4	0·017	0·221	0·6	4·1
Total	2·996	5·398	100·0	100·0

This part of our argument is illustrated in Tables XI 5 and XI 6. In Table XI 5, column 1 shows the value, discounted both for deferment and doubt at a combined rate $R = h + \rho = 33\%$ per annum, of the net returns in successive future 5-year periods of the instrument's assumed useful life of 20 years, these net returns (which, in common with the useful life itself, are estimates made in the light of the knowledge available to the enterpriser at his 'present moment') being supposed constant throughout. Column 2 shows the same for $R = 18\%$ per annum. Column 3 is a companion to column 1 and shows what percentage of the total value of the instrument is attributable to each future 5-year period of its life, and column 4 is a similar companion to column 2. Table XI 5 uses 5-year periods, instead of the decades of Table XI 3, because with such numerically large exponents the present values of net returns decrease so rapidly with increasing futurity.

In Table XI 6, column 1 shows the percentages by which the value of an instrument, assumed to produce uniform net returns for 5, 10, 20 and 40 years respectively, is increased by a reduction of the rate of pure interest ρ from 3% per annum to 2% per annum when the marginal rate of risk h is 30% per annum; column 2 shows the same for $h = 15\%$ per annum, and column 3 the same for $h = 0$.

From Table XI 6 it will be seen that even with a marginal rate of risk as low, in comparison with those suggested in comment D, as 15% per annum, a reduction of the rate of pure interest by as much as one-third may increase the value of an instrument expected to be used for 40 years by only some 6%. If no allowance needed to be made for uncertainty, such a reduction of the rate of pure interest could increase the value of this instrument by 18%. Now, there must surely be at any time in the minds of the enterprisers a larger number of contingent investment plans each having a value lying within 18% of its cost than there are of such plans each having a value lying within 6% of its cost. If so, allowance for doubt, when this allowance takes the form and degree we have supposed, greatly reduces the sensitiveness of investment to given reductions of the rate of pure interest.

Table XI 6

$\Delta v = v_2 - v_1$, where v_1 corresponds to $\rho = 0.03$, v_2 corresponds to $\rho = 0.02$

L	$\Delta v/v_1$ for $h=0.30$ (1)	$\Delta v/v_1$ for $h=0.15$ (2)	$\Delta v/v_1$ for $h=0$ (3)
5	0.019	0.022	0.025
10	0.027	0.037	0.049
20	0.030	0.052	0.096
40	0.031	0.059	0.182

We have shown that allowance for the hazards which beset the prospective earning career of many forms of equipment can easily render ineffective, as a stimulator of investment in these forms of equipment, even a large proportionate change of the rate of pure interest. If the problem we are trying to solve is held to consist of the question 'What factor severely restricts the influence of interest-rates on the pace of investment?', we answer that this factor is the allowance for doubt. But if our problem is cast in the form 'Why is it that enterprisers deny, in the main, that interest-rate changes *have ever* affected their investment-decisions?', then there is an additional explanation. It is this latter question which is posed by the replies to the Oxford questionnaire.

When a man takes a decision on any matter whatever, he tacitly or unconsciously takes into account a great range of circumstances which are all relevant, in the sense that if any one of them were materially different his decision might be different. But a very large proportion of these circumstances are simply taken for granted, and conscious thought and attention are concentrated on those elements of the problem which are either incompletely and doubtfully known, or else which are liable to rapid change on a scale which affects the issue. The very fact that he is engaged in making a decision shows that something in the relevant circumstances has changed, and, before beginning his consideration of the issue, he must list in his mind all such changes which have occurred since the problem last occupied him. These will then seem to be the efficient causes of his decision. When he is afterwards asked how his decision was reached, he will make no reference to all those aspects which merely seemed to provide a stable frame for the play of the active factors; elements which, without necessarily remaining perfectly constant, had shown proportionate changes (on which the degree of contrast, and the power to attract attention, depend) too small to be noticed.

Let us call a reduction of an interest-rate from, for example, 4 % per annum to 3 % per annum (or from 5 to 4, or from 2 to 1), a *unit reduction* of the rate. Then the largest fall in the yield of British Consols which occurred between any two successive years in the period 1870–1913 was of 0·15 unit, while a fall, between two successive years, of 0·33 unit or more occurred only three times in the eighteen years 1919–36. Turning back to the case where L tends to infinity, so that

$$v = c \int_0^\infty e^{-Rx}\, dx = \frac{c}{R} \quad \text{and} \quad \eta_{v\rho} = -\frac{\rho}{R} = -\frac{\rho}{h+\rho},$$

let us again put $h = 0.30$, $\rho = 0.03$, $R = h + \rho = 0.33$; and in the light of the figures just given regarding historical speeds of change of ρ, let us consider a change in ρ of 0·33 unit—namely, from a level of $3\frac{1}{3}$ % per annum to one of 3 % per annum. This change in ρ will imply a change in R from $33\frac{1}{3}$ % per annum to 33 % per annum—that is, a proportionate change $\Delta R/R = 0.01$, and since $v = c/R$, such a change in ρ, the rate of pure interest, will raise the marginal valuation of the instrument by about one-hundredth. If the elasticity of supply of the instruments in question were as much as 5, still a drop from $3\frac{1}{3}$ % per annum to 3 % per annum in ρ, the rate of pure interest, would give a percentage increase in the pace of gross investment in such instruments of no more than

$$\frac{\Delta z}{z} = \eta_{z\rho} \frac{\Delta\rho}{\rho} = \eta_{v\rho}(1 + \eta_{yv}) \frac{\Delta\rho}{\rho} = -0.10 \times (1 + 5) \times -0.10$$
$$= 6\%,$$

or if we prefer price-deflated gross investment

$$\frac{\Delta y}{y} = \eta_{y\rho} \frac{\Delta\rho}{\rho} = \eta_{yv}\eta_{v\rho} \frac{\Delta\rho}{\rho} = 5 \times -0.10 \times -0.10$$
$$= 5\%.$$

But are not such calculations rather beside the point in such a case as this? Is it really to be supposed that an increase of 1 % in the estimated, or rather the conjectured, value of the instrument will strike out any spark of enthusiasm in the enterpriser's mind? Will he even trouble himself to revise his estimates at all on account of such changes as have ordinarily occurred in recent decades in the long-term rate of pure interest? And we must then ask: even if such an increase in value should be noticed, and even acted upon, by a few enterprisers, *how many* would there be, even over the whole range of industry, who had in mind at any one time a project which was sub-marginal *by only* 1 %?

To sum up—I have endeavoured to show:

(1) the rationale of the belief that interest-rate changes influence the pace of investment;

(2) that this influence must certainly be strong on the pace of investment in instruments of those kinds which men believe can be depended on to continue earning net returns for many decades after they are constructed;

(3) that the strength of the influence of interest-rates on the pace of investment in those kinds of equipment which are subject to the hazards of invention and fashion can be rendered negligible by an allowance, of a size such as enterprisers themselves imply that they adopt, for doubt concerning the correctness of the 'best guess' they can make, on available knowledge, as to the size of future net returns from such equipment; provided the *form* of this allowance is that of a rate used for discounting in the same manner as the interest-rate; or is some other strongly increasing function of futurity;

(4) that, historically, the movements of the long-term interest-rate in Britain have seldom been rapid or abrupt enough to constitute appreciable changes of circumstance, or to engage the enterprisers' conscious attention as such.

It may be well to repeat, in conclusion, that where, as with houses, doubt concerning future net returns is small, there is nothing in what we have said which contests the belief that the interest-rate can powerfully affect the demand-price and thus the pace of investment in a given type of instrument.

PART III

ON INVESTMENT AND
EMPLOYMENT

XII

THE MULTIPLIER IN CLOSED AND OPEN SYSTEMS*

Mr Keynes's multiplier theorem has two stages of elaboration. In the first it is an immediate inference from an assumption about the tastes of individuals in the choice between consuming and accumulating income. In the second, a further assumption is added about the change in the quantity of consumption goods produced in unit time, which will be induced by a change, realized or expected, in sales in unit time to consumers. This second assumption could take any one of many specific forms. Hitherto in expressing the multiplier principle authors have assumed *equality*. From the two assumptions together, the more immediate consequences of an attempt by entrepreneurs to change the aggregate speed of equipment-growth are deduced.

To predict what a consumer will do in face of a change in the set of market prices confronting him, we assume that certain tastes are an inherent part of his make-up. We are equally entitled to assume a certain quality of mind in the individual which, in the case of any change in his own income,† or his estimate of it, would dictate that in given circumstances some particular proportion of the increment should be spent on additional consumption, and the rest either allowed to constitute a continuing growth of his cash-holding or be continually exchanged for securities. In either case the non-spending of this latter part permits the accumulation of output, i.e. the growth of equipment, instead of requiring the consumption, i.e. current destruction, of output. Human nature is not so widely various but that, if the incomes of any considerable sample of the population are

---

* *Oxford Economic Papers*, old series, no. 2 (1939), pp. 135–44.

† The variables considered in this article are of dimension ux^{-1}, where u is either money value or physical quantity, and x is time. That is to say, each of these variables represents a speed (or *time-rate*) and is measured as so many units of money value per unit of time, or so many units of physical quantity per unit of time. The terms 'income', 'output', 'consumption', 'accumulation', 'growth of equipment', denote variables of this kind. I have used the words 'income', 'output' and 'consumption' without any explanatory phrase, in the belief that they will convey the above meaning without ambiguity. But I have written 'speed of accumulation' in order to avoid any confusion between a flow having a time-dimension, on the one hand, and a stock on the other.

increased, the resultant of these individual tastes in the matter of spending or not spending will be much the same as if the increases were enjoyed by any other sample of equal size. Thus we are entitled to think of the economy as a whole as having a certain inherent quality which we call its *propensity to consume*, and which implies that its aggregate spending per unit time on consumption can be regarded as a function of certain variables amongst which its aggregate income, or net output, is the most important.* We can take the partial derivative of aggregate consumption-spending per unit time with respect to aggregate income, and call this the economy's marginal propensity to consume. It is a reasonable assumption that this derivative will be greater than zero but less than unity; an individual who gets, for example, an increase of salary will both spend more and save more in each unit of time than he did before.†

This inherent behaviour-pattern of income-receivers is not capable by itself of explaining why an increase in the output of goods intended as additions to equipment should give rise to an increase in the output of goods intended to be consumed. From this inherent propensity we can only infer that if general output is increased, i.e. if the quantity, measured in value, of goods in general produced per unit time is increased, then the value of consumer-purchases in unit time will also increase in a certain proportion λ, less than unity, to the increase of general output. If a larger proportion than $1 - \lambda$ of the increment of general output is intended by entrepreneurs to constitute a growth of equipment, then stocks of goods ready for consumption will begin to be depleted. If entrepreneurs are induced by this to increase the output of consumption goods, then we have the second aspect of the multiplier principle, in which an extra assumption enables it to explain certain links in a process in time.

Let us illustrate these notions by a simplified model. Suppose that the economy produces only one kind of good, and that this can be either consumed or accumulated. The physical output of the economy

---

* The economy's aggregate consumption-spending in unit time is not in strictness a single-valued function of its aggregate income. For any given aggregate income the aggregate consumption is likely to be different with a different *distribution* of that income between the high and low income-brackets. It would be more correct, therefore, to say that aggregate consumption is a function of as many variables as there are individual incomes in the economy. If it is approximately true, however, that the distribution of each given aggregate of incomes is unique, i.e. if for each level of aggregate income there is only one set of individual incomes, the more compact statement involves no loss of accuracy.

† This is all that Keynes required to postulate to make the multiplier theorem valid.

at any moment is the physical quantity of this good produced in unit time at that moment. This output is evidently equal to the time-rate of consumption plus the time-rate of change of the accumulated stock. The level of output is the resultant of two sets of decisions. (1) Entrepreneurs decide what quantity of the good per unit time they wish to add to their accumulated stock; each makes a decision referring to his own stock, and the aggregation of these decisions gives the intended speed of growth I_e of stock as a whole, from the entrepreneurial side. (2) Income-creators, comprising entrepreneurs, workers and suppliers of all other means of production, decide each for himself what proportion of his share of output he will consume and what proportion he will allow to be accumulated. The proportion is a function of the absolute size of his share of output. Thus the proportion in which income-creators as such desire aggregate output to be divided between consumption and accumulation is a function of the level of aggregate output. For any given absolute level E of output, the desires of income-creators indicate a certain speed I_i of accumulation.* It is reasonable to assume that according to the resultant of the desires of income-creators $\Delta I_i / \Delta E < 1$.

There are two groups of possibilities: (1) the function $I_i = \phi(E)$ or its inverse $E = f(I_i)$, expressing the interdependence of output and accumulation according to the desires of income-creators, remains stable; (2) the form of the above function changes.

Under (1) a change in the level of output can emerge from either: (i) decisions by entrepreneurs, implying, if they are exactly realized, that accumulated stock will grow faster or slower in the immediately ensuing short interval of time than it has in the just completed short interval; (ii) a change in the aggregate of individual income-creators' estimates of their incomes (i.e. the absolute sizes of their shares of output), leading them to adjust their consumption to a different supposed level of aggregate output, which they believe to be the actual level.

In case (i) entrepreneurs will at first raise output to a level whose excess over the old level is equal to the difference which their intentions imply between the new and old speeds of growth of accumulated stock. But only a proportion $d\phi(E)/dE$ of this increment of output will actually constitute an increment of the speed of accumulation, for income-creators as such, to whom the extra output accrues and who have the disposal of it, will by hypothesis use part of it to

---

* The reader will understand that both I_e and I_i are *ex ante* concepts. That is, they express intentions or expectations, not the emergence of actual recordable values from moment to moment. They are therefore not necessarily equal.

raise their level of consumption. If entrepreneurs still desire to attain a speed of accumulation I_e, there must be a sufficient increase of aggregate output E to satisfy $E = f(I_i)$ when $I_i = I_e$. This process of adjustment may have effects on the expectations of entrepreneurs and lead to a further increase of I_e, and so on.

In case (ii) the reactions are much less predictable; the actual increase of the time-rate of consumption is likely to induce an increase of output sufficient at least to leave the actual time-rate of accumulation as high as it was initially. This may induce an increase of I_e with further reactions.

Under (2), if initially the speed of accumulation is I_1 and output $E = f(I_1)$, and the form of the latter function then changes to $F(I)$, where $F(I) > f(I)$, it seems likely that the impact effect will be a reduction of I to a level I_2 which satisfies $E = F(I_2)$ at an unchanged level of E. This will be followed by a growth of E as entrepreneurs try to restore the speed of accumulation to its initial level. Thus, after a time, E may stand at a level $E = F(I_1)$, that is, the new form of the function expressing income-creators' wishes will be in operation with the speed of accumulation back at its initial level. In this case, as with all others, further reactions through the effect on expectations and personal income estimates are likely to follow.

If we now remove the assumption that only one good is produced, output can no longer be measured in physical terms, but must be measured in value, and in a closed economy will have the two components: (1) net speed of improvement of equipment, i.e. the aggregate of those changes in unit time in individuals' valuations of their own plant and inventories, which are due to physical growth or improvement;* (2) value per unit time of consumer-purchases. No material difference is made to the theory. An increase in the output of goods intended to become net additions to equipment will induce an increase of consumer-spending, because the workers and entrepreneurs who produce this extra flow of additions to equipment will not wish to receive its value entirely in the form of accumulating wealth but partly in the form of consumption. Only that part of this flow of additions to equipment whose value they are willing to retain

---

* Thus if an individual's equipment consists exclusively of a stock of y units of some homogeneous material, each unit having a value x, the speed of change of the total value yx of his equipment will be $\dfrac{d(yx)}{dt} = x\dfrac{dy}{dt} + y\dfrac{dx}{dt}$. We define his contribution to the first component of the economy's output as equal to the first term $x\dfrac{dy}{dt}$, regarding the other as a windfall gain or loss on capital account.

unspent will constitute a net growth of the economy's equipment. The remainder will be offset by the depletion of stocks of ready consumers' goods.* Further successive increases of output, intended to arrest and make good this depletion, will each contribute only a part of itself for this purpose, since those who produce these extra flows will only accept part of their value in the form of accumulating wealth and will require in part to be paid with consumers' goods. Hence, the growth of equipment will not be accelerated by the amount intended until output has been increased more than was originally regarded as sufficient for this purpose.

How fast and how far will the level of aggregate output rise? We should like to know, for each level of output, by how much this level would be increased within each of a number of different periods, as a consequence of a given attempted increase of its first component. Perhaps entrepreneurs will go on increasing the economy's output up to the level where the growth of equipment has been accelerated to the extent which they initially intended. This is what writers on the multiplier principle have hitherto assumed. But it seems to be based on the implicit assumption that the process of adjusting aggregate output to this level will leave entrepreneurs' expectations of the future earnings of equipment unchanged. If when they initially decided to produce more additions to equipment per unit time they did not expect such a large increase of aggregate output (i.e. aggregate income), it seems likely that they will decide on a further acceleration of equipment-growth. But if their initial decisions were based on the expectation of a rapid growth of aggregate output, it is even possible that the actual increase will disappoint them. In short, the full elaboration of the multiplier principle involves a consideration of what will happen to the inducement to invest.

The length of time which must elapse after an attempt by entrepreneurs to effect a given acceleration of equipment-growth, before output as a whole reaches any given level, does not depend purely on how entrepreneurs respond to an increase of sales per unit time to consumers. The notion of an individual's propensity to consume means that the amount he now decides to spend on consumption in

* If such stocks are low there may be a tendency for prices of consumers' goods to be raised., As Keynes explained (*General Theory*, pp. 123, 124), this will change the value of the marginal propensity to consume, partly by causing individuals with *given* money incomes to postpone some consumption, partly by redistributing aggregate real income in favour of entrepreneurs whose individual marginal propensities to consume, in view of their large incomes, are below the average of all individuals.

a short interval stretching forward from the present moment is a function of the net output in this interval of himself and his property, according to his present expectations. If other people are intending to spend more in this interval than they did in the just-completed interval on such services as he or his property supply, his expectations may underestimate his income. When the interval in question has elapsed, he may become aware that his *ex ante* estimate fell short of what has actually accrued to him, and in such a case he may set his income estimate for the next ensuing interval higher than he did for the one which has just elapsed. But this process of successive adjustments of income estimates, in which each individual's income estimate made at one moment influences those which other individuals will make of their own incomes at subsequent moments, occupies time. For example, the impact on the earnings of companies of a change in the time-rate of spending of some individuals will only affect the spending of dividend-receivers after a considerable interval of time. Thus the successive adjustment of income expectations is a part of the explanation why an attempt to accelerate equipment-growth starts a process of continuing change occupying time.

The conception of the multiplier principle set out above in no way conflicts with Keynes's exposition.* The multiplier is the inverse of the ratio of an increment of the speed of equipment-growth to the accompanying increment of output, the time-interval of measurement being taken as short as we like. The two increments will in general both be smaller if we measure over a shorter interval, but there is no reason to expect that their ratio will be materially affected. The multiplier is therefore a ratio which has some particular value at every moment of time. A period of time must elapse between the moment when the output of goods not intended for immediate sale to consumers is increased, and the development of an equal acceleration of the net growth of equipment, with its corresponding increase of output as a whole.

The lag in the propagation of a stimulus to output as a whole arising from an attempt to accelerate the growth of equipment is not

---

* 'In general, however, we have to take account of the case where the initiative comes from an increase in the output of the capital-goods industries which was not fully foreseen. It is obvious that an initiative of this description only produces its full effect on employment over a period of time. I have found, however, in discussion that this obvious fact often gives rise to some confusion between the logical theory of the multiplier, which holds good continuously, without time-lag, at all moments of time, and the consequences of an expansion in the capital-goods industries which take gradual effect, subject to time-lag and only after an interval.' (*The General Theory of Employment, Interest and Money*, 1936, p. 122.)

the only important consequence of the fact that the income relevant to consumption-decisions is income *ex ante*, an estimate which is necessarily based on the previous, not the current, consumption-decisions of others. For this implies that the level which aggregate income will actually attain over a short interval stretching forward from the present moment, according to the estimate which it will be possible to make at the end of this interval, will depend largely on what individuals expect, at the beginning of the interval, that their incomes will be. Movements of output can be initiated by the adoption of sanguine or cautious expectations of their incomes by individuals.

In our simplified model above we have lastly considered a change in the form of the function expressing aggregate consumption as a function of aggregate income. Apart from the behaviour of the Stock Exchange, whose influence can be subsumed under the causes of changes in income-expectations, the most usual influence which might change the form of the function is perhaps the speed of change of income-expectations, i.e. the extent to which the expected income of one period differs from what was expected to be the income of the just-completed period. An individual cannot instantly adjust his consumption-scheme to a very large change in his income.

Hitherto we have considered a closed economy, in which net output has two components.* The output of an open economy has a third component, namely, the excess of the value of its exports over that of its imports (including in these categories services but not claims). That part of its exports to which there corresponds an equal value of imports is already comprised in our second component: for imports in themselves make possible consumption without either current production of goods or depletion of equipment, and if there were no exports at all, we should have to exclude from output (of the region being considered) an amount of consumption equal to the value of its imports. If the value of exports exceeds that of imports, then something is being produced in the region to which there corresponds neither consumption within the region nor growth of the equipment of the region. It will be shown, on the assumption that no part of this excess represents net payment of interest to foreigners, that this third component is entirely on the same footing as, and may be added to, our first component.

In the first place, this flow (the excess in unit time of exports over imports) satisfies the desire of some suppliers of productive services to receive the value of these services in the form of durable equipment

*Cf. p. 150 above.

or titles to the earnings of equipment, rather than in immediate consumption. Neglecting any effect on exchange-rates between currencies and the repercussions of that effect, let us consider what will happen in the following cases of a change in the value per unit time of goods and services exported, which is uncompensated by any change in the value per unit time of goods and services imported, or of a corresponding uncompensated change in the import-flow: (i) an increase in exports; (ii) a decrease in exports; (iii) an increase in imports; (iv) a decrease in imports. Let s be the excess of the value of what we export in unit time over the value of what we import in unit time.

(i) In so far as this increased excess of exports is not provided for by a diminution in the speed of growth of home equipment, extra workers, equipment and entrepreneurial services must be engaged in producing this extra flow of excess exports. The suppliers of these extra flows of productive services will wish to receive the value of them partly in consumption; but, by hypothesis, no part of their own output, nor imports corresponding to it, is available for them to consume. Until extra consumable output is forthcoming, they will cause a continuing shrinkage of stocks of ready consumables. The taking into employment of extra resources hitherto unemployed will only arrest this shrinkage to the extent that the newly employed workers and others are willing to be paid with claims on foreigners; to the extent that they demand consumption, they will consume the extra output which they themselves are producing. The extra force of labour and equipment taken into employment to provide the consumption, say A, demanded by the producers of the extra unbalanced exports, must therefore be of such a size that the part of their payment which they are willing to receive in the form of claims on assets abroad is equal to A. The multiplier principle works in exactly the same way when the increment of unconsumed* output goes abroad as when it stays at home.

(ii) In so far as the output Δs which foreigners have ceased to buy does not continue to be produced as an addition to home equipment, total output† will be reduced by some amount $k_R \Delta s$, where k_R corresponds to, but is not necessarily equal to, the ratio of the increment of total output which would be associated with an increment Δs of the unconsumed component of output. For, if when total output is high, the economy's marginal propensity to consume is low, this means that its members all taken together are not very eager, in case of an increase of that output, to add to their consumption. Ac-

---

* I.e. not consumed at home.   † I.e. of the open economy.

cordingly they will be correspondingly less reluctant, if their total output be slightly reduced when it is at a high level, to reduce their consumption. Thus, if at high levels of total output an increment ΔI of the non-consumed component will be associated with an increment $\Delta C = (k-1)\,\Delta I$ of the consumed component, then a decrement ΔI will be associated with a decrement $\Delta C = (k_R - 1)\,\Delta I$, where $k_R > k$.*

When the economy's output is high we should therefore expect the reduction of output associated with a given decrease of the export surplus to be numerically larger than the increment of output associated, at the same high level of output, with an equal *increase* of the export surplus. Correspondingly, when total output is low, and the economy's marginal propensity to consume consequently high, any increment of output will consist largely in extra consumption, any decrement of output will consist largely in a decrement of net equipment-growth.

(iii) A decrease of the quantity consumed per unit time of home-produced goods, associated with an equal increase of the quantity consumed per unit time of imports, in so far as it results in a decrease in the output of goods intended for home consumption, and not in a piling-up of stocks of these goods, is exactly on the same footing as case (ii), and the 'reverse-multiplier' effect will work in the same way.

(iv) A decrease of the import-flow, not associated with a decrease either of the export-flow *or* of consumption, implies an increase of the non-consumed component of output which will develop according to the multiplier principle as depletion of stocks of ready consumables is arrested by an increase of output.

The main points put forward are thus as follows:

(1) It is entirely untrue that the multiplier principle involves any confusion between *ex post* and *ex ante* concepts.

(2) The multiplier itself is a ratio obtained immediately from the marginal propensity to consume. By itself this ratio cannot tell us how fast or by how much the level of output will change as a consequence of an attempt to change the speed of growth of equipment. For this we need also to know what will happen to the inducement to invest as output (i.e. aggregate income) begins to change.

(3) The consumption per unit time which an individual decides on is a function of his income *ex ante*. His expectations may be sanguine or cautious. If a large proportion of individuals are sanguine or cautious in their income-expectations, the level of aggregate income

---

* See G. L. S. Shackle, *Expectations, Investment, and Income* (Oxford, 1938), Chapter VII.

actually emerging, i.e. aggregate income *ex post*, will move in the direction tending to justify these expectations. Hence income-expectations are capable of initiating a process of growth or decline of output.

(4) The form of the function connecting an individual's consumption-spending with his income may become different immediately after a very large, swift and unexpected change in his income, and will only gradually be restored to the form applicable to gradual changes of his income.

(5) In an open economy, the excess of the value of exports of goods and services over that of imports of goods and services is on the same footing with regard to the propensity to consume as that part of home output which constitutes a net growth of home equipment.

(6) At any one level of output the proportions in which a marginal increment of output will be distributed between consumption and accumulation are likely to be different from those in which a marginal decrement of output will be distributed between reduced consumption and reduced speed of accumulation.

XIII

TWENTY YEARS ON: A SURVEY OF THE THEORY OF THE MULTIPLIER*

It is now twenty years since the doctrine of the multiplier was first precisely and explicitly set forth. In his famous article, one of the great landmarks of economics and of the *Economic Journal*, which published it in 1931, Mr Richard Kahn made (I give his own words) 'no claims of originality'. It is, I think, only on a very narrow and impoverished definition of originality that this disclaimer can be accepted. Important advances in any branch of knowledge are almost necessarily founded on pre-existing, though perhaps vaguely formulated, ideas. The originality of those who make such advances consists in the power to imagine new structures composed of old ideas whose connectibility has not been recognized; and in the effort of mind by which they bring vague ideas to a sharp focus and give them precise expression. The idea that if out of a large pool of unemployed men, by a conscious and deliberate act, 100 were drawn and given employment, so that a new steady stream of wages and profits, flowing directly from their activity, was added to the national income, further men might as a consequence, on certain assumptions, be spontaneously drawn from the pool and also given employment, had for long been vaguely mooted when Mr Kahn wrote. Professor Austin Robinson may not have been the only one who, already in the early 1920's, had in conversation wondered why 'if someone spent an extra pound, it did not put everyone into employment'. In 1929 Lord Keynes had based a plea for public works on† an argument which groped for the multiplier analysis but failed to seize it. Under what assumptions the engagement of the first 100 men would of itself cause still others to be engaged; what determined how many these others would be; whether, or in what circumstances, the consequence of 'artificially' providing employment for some of the unemployed would cause a steep or unlimited rise of prices; and how, and with what consequences, the employment of the extra men could be financed were questions that no one, until Mr Kahn's article appeared, had been able to answer. Mr Kahn's achievement, and that of Mr Meade, whose contribution Mr Kahn acknowledges on

* *Economic Journal*, vol. LXI (1951), pp. 241–60.

† Lord Keynes and Sir Hubert Henderson were joint authors of the Liberal pamphlet *Can Lloyd George Do It?*

his first page,* was to provide precise and sharp-edged tools by which all these matters could be dissected and an insight gained into the nature of the whole process. To have disentangled successfully so subtle, complex and elusive a skein of vague interrogatives, which till then had been felt rather than thought, makes Mr Kahn's article on 'The relation of home investment to unemployment' one of the most original contributions of the last fifty years. Indeed, the strongest impression that a reader gets, on re-reading the article after the two decades and the cataclysm of events and ideas that have intervened, is of its modernness and failure to grow obsolete. There is only one section, I think, that could nowadays be omitted without any loss except that of historical perspective, and that is Section IX, where Mr Kahn sought to translate his results into the language of the *Treatise on Money*. But that section gives me a pretext for beginning this survey with a glance at that whole body of interpenetrating theoretical contributions (not confined in their scope to the multiplier principle itself) to which the article belongs, some of them preceding and some following it, and together showing how a mountain was moved by the combined tunnellings of several theorists, none of whom at the time could see where he was going or realize the extent of the landscape that would be revealed.

The *Treatise on Money*, as Mrs Joan Robinson pointed out in one of the contributions† I have spoken of, aimed in the first place at explaining the general level of prices, because changes in this level were thought to govern profits, and these in their turn to induce or discourage productive activity and the giving of employment. The explanation of the price-level of goods in general (as distinct from the relative prices of particular goods, which was the subject-matter of marginal utility theory) was sought in those days in the Quantity Theory of Money, and it was the failure of Lord Keynes's titanic efforts to wrest and hammer that theory into an instrument fit for his purpose that really cleared the way for the invention, by himself and others, of something radically different and superior.

A main element in this new invention was the (short-period) supply-curve of consumption-goods in general,‡ which we find in

* *Economic Journal*, vol. XLI (1931), p. 187, n.1. Mr Kahn says that the second half of his article was 'fundamentally based' on unpublished work by Mr J. E. Meade. Mr Meade's contribution was the equality, *ex post*, of saving and investment. See below, pp. 159, 160.

† Joan Robinson, 'The theory of money and the analysis of output', *Review of Economic Studies*, vol. I (1933), p. 22.

‡ The short-period supply-curve of investment-goods in general, which by the positive slope that it must evidently have beyond some particular output, explains

the literature for the first time, so far as I know, in Mr Kahn's article. By that simple device Mr Kahn solved the problem of whether and when a policy of public works would cause 'inflation', would raise prices, and when not. For if the supply-curve is flat in some neighbourhood of the prevailing situation, that is to say, if 'goods in general' are in perfectly elastic supply, even in the short-period, how can an increase in their output, from whatever source may come the causal increase in demand, be accompanied by a rise of prices? Now the supply-curve of an individual good had been a familiar tool for many decades, and Marshall had shown that when the marginal cost of production of a commodity is uniform for all levels of output, price will not be altered by a strengthening* of demand. How had this idea escaped application to the case of general output? Simply because all economists had till then been taught from the beginning of their studies that economics is the science of the best adaptation of scarce means to rival ends. The supply of a single good could be elastic in response to price, because a strengthening of demand would enable its producers to bid resources away from other lines of production. But how could the supply of all goods at once be elastic? Even the existence of millions of unemployed did not at first bring home to economists the realization that, in a depression, physical means of production are not scarce.

Three at least of the tributary streams of thought which, gaining limpidity upon their way, flowed ultimately into the *General Theory*, had their source in Mr Kahn's article. The second of these was the *ex post* equality of saving and investment. In the article this appeared as Mr Meade's relation. There we have already the explicit statement that a programme of public works (or any other net addition to the investment-flow) will finance itself:

The argument will apply [Mr Kahn says in his opening sections] to any net increase in the rate of home investment...it will be demonstrated... that, *pari passu* with the building of roads, funds are released from various sources at precisely the rate that is required to pay the cost of the roads.

how the marginal efficiency of capital can be supposed to respond immediately to changes in the interest-rate, had appeared in a diagram of Mr Meade's *The Rate of Interest in a Progressive State* in 1933. This book is another piece of the literature that future archaeologists of thought will find embedded in the foundation-stone of the *General Theory*. The idea of a supply-schedule of investment goods had however been used in 1926 in one of the great classics of economic literature, Professor Sir Dennis Robertson's *Banking Policy and the Price Level*.

* Here I use the expression *strengthening* of demand, as I have for many years, as a short synonym for *upward shift of the demand-curve*.

Mr Meade's relation was the following:

Cost of investment
= saving on the dole + increase in excess of imports over exports
+ increase in unspent profits − diminution in rate of saving
due to rise in prices.

Reading this formula, one has the curious feeling that Mr Kahn and Mr Meade were like two men who have struggled to the top of a mountain pass, only to collapse exhausted without glancing at the prospect they have opened up. It speaks of 'unspent profits' and of a 'rate of saving' as though of two distinct things. To distinguish two different influences or tendencies working on a single magnitude is, of course, perfectly legitimate; but had they chanced to begin with a closed system, as would perhaps have been logically better though less practically relevant and interesting; and had they gone down still further towards basic essentials by assuming away the dole; then would they not have made it clear that their remaining two items amounted simply to the net change in the aggregate rate of saving of all people taken together, whether profit-receivers or wage-earners? It was left for Professor Jens Warming of Copenhagen, in a very remarkable article* which has not received, I think, the recognition due to it, to press home the essential point:

He who saves passively fails to employ, for example, tailors; if then some other person borrows the money and employs engineers, there is equilibrium between the positive and the negative side of the saving. But if neither tailors nor engineers are employed, it is likely that *somebody else will save less*† and thus counterbalance the original saving.

And again: 'When nothing is invested, no net saving can exist.' And

When a house is built, somebody's property must have increased in value to an equal extent during the same time; either the owner's property or his creditors'; that means, somebody must have saved.

The fact that net investment can only increase by a given amount if income increases sufficiently for the saving done out of the extra income to be equal to the extra net investment is, of course, only another way of expressing the multiplier principle. That principle,

* 'International difficulties arising out of the financing of public works during a depression', *Economic Journal*, vol. XLII (1932), p. 211.
† Italics in the original.

explicitly formulated, is the third of the tributary streams I have referred to, and to it we can now turn in earnest.

Mr Kahn did not, I think, set himself consciously to add a new tool to the economic analyst's outfit, but rather to work out the principles for solving a practical problem. This he thought of as essentially a problem in 'comparative statics', a problem involving the comparison of two states of affairs, each of which is thought of as persisting unchanged through time, except for the transition from one to the other, which transition is not itself the object of attention, and plays a merely formal part in the analysis.

If, then, in a closed system, two such states differ in the pace of net investment, that is, in the net time-rate at which the equipment (the houses, shops, schools, factories, transport systems, farms, etc.) of the system as a whole is being improved or extended, to what extent will they differ in total net time-rate of production of all goods whether for consumption or for extending equipment? We may consider, if we like, two countries, each isolated from all others, similar, at the moment when we observe them, in regard to the numbers, tastes and abilities of their populations, and in their material possessions and equipment, but differing in that in one of them net investment is running at £1000 million a year while in the other it is running at £1050 million a year. What difference between their respective national incomes will be associated with this difference of £50 million a year between their respective time-rates of net investment, that is, of net growth of equipment? To ask for the ratio of these two differences, the difference of incomes in relation to the difference of investment-speeds is to put the question in the form in which it has become familiar to us in the literature subsequent to Mr Kahn's article, and especially in the work of Lord Keynes, who named this ratio the multiplier. Mr Kahn's own original question, however, was not in terms of value-streams, income and net investment, but in terms of employment. The difference between these two questions, or forms of what is essentially the same question, can be compared to the difference between the two questions: How many kilowatts of electric current are being used at some given moment to light a certain room? and: How many electric-light bulbs are in operation at that moment in that room? Mr Kahn wrote:

The increased employment that is required in connection actually with the increased investment will be described as the 'primary' employment....To meet the increased expenditure of wages and profits that is associated with the primary employment, the production of consumption-goods is increased. Here again wages and profits are increased, and the effect will be passed on, though with diminished intensity. And so on *ad infinitum*. The total employment that is set up in this way in the production of consumption-goods will be termed the 'secondary' employment.

Mr Kahn's definitions of primary and secondary employment give us, as the definition of what Lord Keynes afterwards called the 'employment multiplier', the ratio:

$$\frac{\text{primary employment} + \text{secondary employment}}{\text{primary employment}}.$$

The relation between the *investment-multiplier*, which compares income measured in money-units of changeable purchasing-power with investment measured in those same units, and the *employment-multiplier* just defined, is explained by Lord Keynes in Chapter 10 of the *General Theory*. The possibility of an appreciable difference in their numerical values arises from the possibility that, in the initial state of affairs, the elasticity of supply of investment-goods in general may differ from that of consumption-goods in general, and from the possibility that the ratio of the investment-stream to the stream of output as a whole, in the initial state of affairs, may be widely different from that of the 'marginal' or incremental streams with which the multiplier principle is explicitly concerned. For if we imagine a supply-curve of investment-goods and a supply-curve of consumption-goods, any 'initial situation' will be represented by two points, one on each of these curves. The shapes of the curves, the location on them of the initial points and the respective distances of the mutually associated movements along them which occur when there is a transition to a larger investment-stream may be such that a smaller or larger proportion of, say, the incremental investment-stream is accounted for by a rise of prices than is the case with the incremental consumption-goods stream. For if the supply-curves are taken to be short-period supply-curves, in the sense that greater output can be obtained only by applying more labour to a given outfit of equipment, and if as may then reasonably be supposed the curves are upward-sloping,* and if price is proportional to the wages-cost of the marginal unit of output, then plainly, for each of the two kinds of output, money-value of output will rise in a larger ratio than will the numbers of those employed in making that output. But the ratio between the increments of employment in making the two kinds of goods need by no means be the same as the ratio between the increments of money-value of the two kinds of output. Thus we have the

* So that greater outputs are associated with higher prices.

possibility of a difference between the investment-multiplier and the employment-multiplier.

The true importance of Mr Kahn's article consists in the central and fundamental contribution it made to the *General Theory*; and the interpenetration of his and Lord Keynes's thinking is apparent in details which assume a sudden historic significance when we re-read the article and the *General Theory* side-by-side. Such, for instance, are the assumption* that 'money-wages are not raised as a consequence of the reduction in unemployment', and the definition† of involuntary unemployment as a state of affairs where the elasticity of supply of labour in terms of *money*-wages is infinite. The proximate *purpose* of the article, however, was to explode the objections currently raised against public works as a cure for unemployment, and much of its space was in consequence taken up with matters which lie somewhat outside our theme. That purpose gives the article some of its modernity: for those objections rose partly from a fear (astounding though it seems, when we compare 1931 with 1951) that public works would have inflationary effects; and Mr Kahn was at pains to point out that the price-effects could not be serious unless employment was so much increased as to bring us on to a steeply rising part of the supply-curve of consumption-goods. For his formula he assumed, indeed, that consumables as well as labour were in perfectly elastic supply with respect to their money prices. Let us do so at first.

Out of the total stream of extra wages, profits, etc., generated in a closed system through the employment of one thousand extra men on net investment, let k be the proportion spent on consumption-goods. Consumption-goods being, we have assumed, in perfectly elastic supply, an extra flow of them, corresponding in amount at unchanged prices to the extra spending, will be provided through the employment at unchanged money wage-rates (labour also being in perfectly elastic supply) of k thousand further men. The consumption-spending of these latter will call for the engagement of k^2 thousand still further men and so on. When all is said, the placing in employment of one thousand extra men on net investment will have required the placing in employment of $k + k^2 + k^3 + \ldots$ thousand extra men on making consumption goods, so that altogether the numbers of extra men placed in employment will be $1 + k + k^2 + k^3 + \ldots$ thousand.

Provided k is less than unity, this series converges to $\frac{1}{1-k}$, and this is the *employment-multiplier*. The assumptions of perfect elasticity of supply of both labour and consumables here ensure (less restrictive

* Kahn, op. cit. p. 175. † Keynes, op. cit. p. 15.

assumptions could equally ensure it) that the employment-multiplier and the investment-multiplier are numerically equal; indeed, the former has been obtained by what is in effect a calculation of the latter.

This is the bare bones of the multiplier principle. Its simplicity and 'obviousness' are illusory. As soon as we begin to ask how far in the analysis of practical affairs and concrete situations it will carry us; how it can be statistically tested and measured; what the relaxation of simplifying assumptions involves; and what are the deeper parameters of the system which ultimately determine the ratio; we are confronted with a list of exceedingly subtle and intricate questions, which a great many authors have spent much time and labour in seeking to unravel. These questions are, I think, as follows:

(1) The ratio k measures a characteristic of the body of consumers all taken together as one whole. But decisions about spending income on consumption are taken by individuals,* and behind k, the *propensity to consume* of the whole system, there must lie the individual propensities. By ascribing to any individual some propensity to consume we mean that out of a given income, or a given small increment of a given income, in given circumstances, he will decide to spend such-and-such a proportion on consumption-goods. What, then, is this 'given' income on which his decision is based? Is it the wages or profits he actually received in the just-elapsed unit time-interval? But in that case does he never make any concession to his hopes and fears regarding the next and other future intervals? Is it the wages or profits he expects to receive in the interval on whose threshold he stands? But if so, in what sense is this income 'given'? And above all, what happens if his expectations are disappointed; if he receives more or less than the amount which his spending-decision assumed? What if the simultaneous income-estimates of many or most individuals are pervaded by an inherent bias, changing in direction with change of external circumstances? My estimated income no doubt governs my spending, but will not the spending of others influence my future estimations of my income? What part should such considerations play in the theory of the business-cycle?

(2) Assuming, however, that we can answer question (1), either by resort to the argument of 'large numbers' (which, however, can scarcely be legitimate when we consider that individuals must inevitably be influenced in forming their income-expectations by many factors in common) or in some other way, how do we aggregate the

* Within the meaning of 'individual' we can include 'the members of a household in consultation with each other'.

individual propensities into the propensity to consume of the whole body of consumers? It must plainly be by a weighted average using the sizes of the individual incomes as weights. The *distribution*, therefore, of a given aggregate income affects the proportions in which it will be divided between consumption-spending and other disposal, and we have to ask in what contexts it will be legitimate to assume that any given aggregate will be composed of a unique set of individual incomes. There are evidently important contexts in which it will *not* be safe to say that because, in two situations, aggregate income is the same, therefore aggregate consumption-spending will be the same in both.

(3) But again, does the proportion of his income that an individual decides to spend on consumption really depend so predominantly on the size of that income that other influences can be neglected? Quite apart from the possibility of change in such circumstances as the numbers of his dependents, regarding which, for the system as a whole, it *will* be legitimate in a reasonably short period to resort to 'large numbers', there are elements that can change too rapidly to be excluded by any shortening of the period, without rendering the multiplier useless for any practical analysis. Such is the market-value of a person's Stock Exchange securities. When Consols drop 10, 20 or 30 points in a few months or a year or two, this must surely affect the readiness to spend of those who held them; and here any 'large numbers' argument is plainly out of the question. Change in the level of income (whatever means we adopt to make 'income' an operational concept for our purpose) may be so great and so rapid that consumption habits and legal commitments cannot be at once adjusted. Do we, in fact, need a 'consumption-function' including some other independent variables besides income?

(4) By his direct and practical approach Mr Kahn avoided entanglement in a question which has since been much debated: is there what Lord Keynes calls a 'logical theory of the multiplier, which holds good continuously, without time-lag, at all moments of time',* or must we think of the multiplier doctrine as describing a process which advances stage by stage in a temporal succession and requires an appreciable time-interval for its full working out? Lord Keynes's answer, and the one for which I shall argue below, is that there is no conflict between these two conceptions. The issue can be evaded by saying explicitly, as I did above, that we are studying a question in comparative statics; and this is, I think, what Mr Kahn in effect does.† But comparative statics is a fragile and limited tool,

* Keynes, op. cit. p. 122.   † Kahn, op. cit. p. 183, n. 2.

and the character of the temporal process is quite fundamental if the multiplier is to be invoked in business-cycle theory.

(5) But the great temporal process relevant to business-cycle theory involves far more than the pure multiplier principle. If the pace of net investment in the system proximately governs the system's aggregate income, does not aggregate income, by its size and especially by its changes, react upon net investment? It is in this context that the multiplier idea acquires all its power and all its difficulty. How, if we wish to *measure* the multiplier, are we to sort out the various time-lags? How can we know, when income and net investment have both increased between two dates, how many times during that interval the shuttle of mutual influence has flown to and fro? Which increment of income are we to link, as regards date and therefore size, with which increment of net investment, and which increment of net investment are we to link with which increment, or which acceleration of growth, of income? Are not the 'distributed lags' involved likely, indeed, to be so complicated and so much interwoven as to render impossible the statistical measurement of the multiplier from time-series? Does this objection apply only to the comparison of momentary states at dates not widely separated? Would it perhaps be safe to compare the averages of a five- or ten-year period with an equal period twenty or fifty years later? Here there are other well-recognized troubles; the longer the time, the more restive and uncontrollable become the impounded 'other things'.

(6) Time-series, however, are not the only statistical means available. Family-budget data collected all at the same date from families in a ladder of income-brackets have also been used, and have given results different from those obtained from time-series for the same country.* How can such differences be reconciled?

(7) Discussion has nearly always tacitly assumed that the propensity to *reduce* consumption in face of a *decrease* in income is equal to the propensity to increase consumption in face of an increase in income. But what of habits, commitments and the time required to adjust plans to a new situation? When income falls after a very short stay at a higher level, will the reaction be the same as when it falls from a level it has held for a long time?

By a person's *propensity to consume* we mean a schedule assigning to each hypothetical level of his income the corresponding level of his

* See William Fellner, *Monetary Policy and Full Employment* (University of California Press, 1946), and James S. Duesenberry, *Income, Saving and the Theory of Consumer Behaviour* (Harvard University Press, 1949).

consumption-spending. As a tool of comparative statics this notion offers no difficulty: one state of affairs which we suppose the person concerned to look on as unchanging in past and future is compared with another such state, these states being alternative hypotheses not temporally related to each other; the question whether we mean by the person's income his experienced income of the immediate past or his expected income of the immediate future does not arise, since they are equal. As soon as we allow him to suppose, on 31 December, that the number of shillings that will compose his January income can differ from the number that composed his December income we have to ask whether the number of shillings that, on 31 December, he decides to spend in January on consumption will be related in his mind to the number he did receive in December or to the number he expects to receive in January. Although we speak here of a finite interval, choosing a month because months have names, what is really in question is a pair of time-rates each expressed as so-and-so many shillings per unit of time. Surely the income-magnitude most relevant for deciding on a time-rate of consumption-spending will be the magnitude concerning identically the same time-interval. When the econometrician introduces 'lagged' income into his consumption-function what he is really concerned with is either pace of change of income or else a stock of wealth accumulated over time. Both of these may be highly relevant, but the propensity to consume is itself a relation between the two rates of flow, not between one of these rates and the acceleration of the other, nor between one rate and an integral over time of the other. To the first part of question (1), then, I suggest we must answer that intended consumption-spending, in so far as it depends on income, is proximately a function of expected income.

Supposing the viewpoint or 'present moment' to be at 31 December, let us add together for all individuals the number of shillings that each expects to receive as income in January, and call this the aggregate expected income, Y_A, of the economy for January. Individual propensities to consume being given, there will correspond to this aggregate Y_A a determinate number $C_A = C_A(Y_A)$ of shillings which the individuals all taken together will decide, at 31 December, to spend on consumption during January. If in a closed system the aggregate realized income Y_P of any month is equal to the number C_P of shillings actually spent on consumption in that month plus the net number E_P of shillings-worth by which enterprisers all taken together have in that month augmented or improved their equipment, and if for our immediately future month of January we assume that consumption-intentions will be successfully executed so that $C_P = C_A$, and also assume that realized net investment E_P will prove equal to intended net investment E_A, and if we take the latter as given, then there will be some level C_S of consumption-spending which will just bring realized aggregate income Y_P to equality with expected aggregate income Y_A. Now if C_A is greater than C_S, Y_P will be greater than Y_A, and it is plainly likely that on 31 January expected incomes for February will be set higher than they would otherwise have been, and probably at a higher time-rate than those expected on 31 December for January. A cumulative process in which Y_P is larger month by month can thus be easily imagined to start. If C_A is less than C_S the consequence could correspondingly be a cumulative process of contraction. In either case we should, of course, have to make some assumption about the reaction of net investment to the successive changes of Y_P and C_P, and the most obvious one is that its reactions would be such at first as to reinforce the cumulative expansion or contraction of economic activity. Plainly an unlimited variety of models could be constructed by varying and adding to the assumptions about the effects of expectations on decisions and of outcomes of these decisions on subsequent expectations, regarding both consumption and investment, but that is outside the scope of this survey. In answer to the second part of question (1) we can surely say that the propensity to consume ought to have an important place in any business-cycle theory.

Before we consider what the assumptions of the foregoing argument involve, let us notice what it is that the satisfying of the condition $C_A = C_S$ ensures. It ensures that in the aggregate income expectations will not be disappointed. It does not ensure that individual income-expectations will be fulfilled, and it is evidently conceivable that equality between C_A and C_S will come about by the offsetting of unpleasant against pleasant surprises. If the group of individuals who experience larger incomes than they had expected are on the whole more sensitive to such surprises, or operate on a larger scale, than those who experience unpleasant surprises, then a cumulative expansion may be started even when $C_A = C_S$; and vice versa. Nor does the satisfying of that condition ensure that January's realized income will correspond to full employment or to any other particular level of employment. It means merely that relations amongst the triad of aggregate *ex ante* variables, intended net investment E_A, intended consumption-spending C_A and expected income Y_A, are in harmony such that $Y_A = C_A + E_A$, and thus, since on our assumptions there is an identical equality $Y_P \equiv C_A + E_A$, that $Y_P = Y_A$. There is no reasonable apologetic for the assumption of identical equality $Y_A \equiv C_A + E_A$, for no individual can know the intentions of all other individuals, and $Y_A \equiv C_A + E_A$ would require all individuals to harmonize their plans in advance in a Hayekian equilibrium.* In a system where we do not abstract from uncertainty there is no guarantee that when the doings of January are looked back on from 31 January the record will show that the realized ratio C_P/Y_P of consumption-spending to incomes has turned out equal to the propensity to consume C_A/Y_A. Some critics have said that the use made of propensity to consume in the *General Theory* confuses *ex post* with *ex ante* concepts. This has justice only in the sense that Lord Keynes does not discuss the possibility that C_P/Y_P may not equal C_A/Y_A; that, in fact, he keeps within the frame of comparative statics. An argument in terms of comparative statics cannot indicate the possibilities discussed above, for by its nature it cannot distinguish meaningfully between past and future, between expectations and intentions on the one hand and outcomes on the other hand.

Now the foregoing argument will not be interesting and significant unless we use *income* to mean the value of net output. Net investment must therefore comprise not only the net growth and improvement of durable equipment but also changes in inventories. And we have assumed that the amount of net investment intended, at 31 December, to be done during January will at 31 January have been actually done, and that intended consumption-spending for January will likewise be exactly carried out. We are thus assuming that producers either correctly foresee the consumption-spending of January or that they respond to it with negligible time-lag; and in the latter case, that they adjust any change of consumable output to exact equality with the change in consumption-spending. Neither of these two main assumptions is realistic, and we must seek some more plausible account of the process of reaction. This brings us to question (4).

The view of the multiplier mechanism as a process requiring time to reach its full effect, and the view of it as an expression of tastes, or potential reactions, existing at an instant, are not in conflict. The multiplier process can be looked at as something recorded or as something foreseen, it can be looked at *ex post* or *ex ante*, but the instantaneous multiplier is necessarily *ex ante* and, since it can involve the expectations or potential reactions of different combinations of groups of people, it is not unique.

There are, I think, at least two concepts of the instantaneous and two of the process multiplier. The income-receivers' instantaneous

* See F. A. Hayek, 'Economics and knowledge', *Economica*, vol. IV (1937), p. 33.

ex ante multiplier is connected with the marginal propensity to consume, which is a relation between *ex ante* magnitudes, by a trivial manipulation. If ΔY_A is the difference between two hypothetical levels of Y_A the aggregate of the incomes expected by income-receivers, and if ΔC_A is the difference between the respective corresponding levels of their aggregate intended consumption-spending, then since we have identically $\Delta Y_A \equiv \Delta C_A + \Delta[Y_A - C_A]$, that is,

$$\frac{\Delta Y_A}{\Delta[Y_A - C_A]} \equiv \frac{1}{1 - \dfrac{\Delta C_A}{\Delta Y_A}},$$

and since we assume that C_A is a function of Y_A, we have

$$\frac{\Delta Y_A}{\Delta[Y_A - C_A]} \equiv \frac{1}{1 - \dfrac{\Delta C_A(Y_A)}{\Delta Y_A}},$$

or in words: the ratio of the difference between two levels of the aggregate of the incomes expected by income-receivers to the difference between the corresponding levels of their aggregate intended accumulation is the reciprocal of the excess of unity over their marginal propensity to consume. If in this identity we replace $\Delta[Y_A - C_A]$ by ΔE_A the difference between two hypothetical levels of the aggregate of enterprisers' intentions for net investment, the identity becomes a conditional equation

$$\frac{\Delta Y_A}{\Delta E_A} = \frac{1}{1 - \dfrac{\Delta C_A(Y_A)}{\Delta Y_A}},$$

which expresses the condition of *multiplier equilibrium*, that is to say, the harmony, on the macro-economic level, of the expectations and intentions of income-disposers as such with the net-investment intentions of enterprisers.* The reader will perceive that while $\dfrac{\Delta C_A(Y_A)}{\Delta Y_A}$ expresses a functional connection, viz. the marginal propensity to consume, the expression $\dfrac{\Delta Y_A}{\Delta E_A}$ is not, in the foregoing equation of multiplier equilibrium, a function but a mere fraction; we cannot regard enterprisers' intentions as depending on income-disposers' (simultaneously-held) expectations; we cannot, that is to say, meaningfully write $E_A \equiv E_A(Y_A)$.

* See G. L. S. Shackle, 'The multiplier in closed and open systems', *Oxford Economic Papers*, old series, no. 2 (1939), pp. 135–44, reprinted as Chapter XII above.

Of the two process multipliers, one, the *ex post* multiplier, is the ratio of a recorded difference of income levels to the associated difference of net investment levels. If the latter difference is regarded as in any sense the proximate cause of the former, it must surely be accepted that there is *some* conceptual lag greater than zero, however short it may be, between the occurrence of the two changes. Otherwise we should have to admit that the proximate cause was really not the occurrence of a change of level of net investment but the expectation of this change. To say this, however, is not to grant what some writers have contended or implicitly assumed, viz. that the infinite convergent series $1 + k + k^2 + ...$, referred to on p. 163 above, represents a temporal sequence of stages with a lapse of one 'income receipt interval' (e.g. if all income-receivers were paid weekly, one week) between the attainment of one stage and the attainment of the next. For a man who has been unemployed and is re-engaged on a Monday will not wait until Saturday before he increases his consumption. Knowing that he is now in work, the local shopkeepers will give him some extension of credit. Their own incomes will thus increase before the re-employed man gets his first pay-packet, for it is the act of rendering service which creates income for the shopkeeper at the moment when he performs this service; the settling of his account is merely, as Professor Boulding has explained,* the exchange of one asset (debts receivable) for another (cash). The pace at which the multiplier can run through the terms of the infinite series depends ultimately on the speed with which knowledge or belief can be created and propagated. A group of income-receivers whose output (and therefore income, in the true sense*) increases know of this from the moment of its occurrence, and are likely to act accordingly; those immediately affected by those actions may, indeed, take some little time to appraise the increase in their own incomes (again in the relevant sense, of an increase in the instantaneous time-rate of output, or of input into the general productive machine), but they certainly need not wait for the lapse of an entire 'income-period'.

A sophisticated observer who sees net investment increase may express the consequence he expects from it as an *ex ante* process-multiplier. No further elaboration here is needed.

Although Lord Keynes did not distinguish between *ex ante* and *ex post* multipliers, he did distinguish between an instantaneous and a process multiplier, and explained the relation between them.† Let

* K. E. Boulding, *A Reconstruction of Economics* (New York. John Wiley and Sons, 1950).　　　　　　† Keynes, op. cit. pp. 122–5.

me try to express the substance of those pages within the framework developed above. Net investment actually effected in January, E_P, depends on the intentions in mind at 31 December not only of enterprisers but also of consumers. If the intentions of enterprisers on 31 December regarding the quantity which they will produce during January of each kind of good (whether they mean it to count as part of consumption or as part of net investment), and their intentions regarding the price to be charged for each kind of good, and the intentions of income-receivers regarding the number of shillings they will spend on consumption during January, are all executed according to plan, then net investment *ex post*, E_P, will come out as the resultant of all these sets of decisions and need by no means be equal to E_A. But if it is smaller than E_A this fact (since consumers do not buy looms or locomotives) will largely reflect a shrinkage in inventories of finished consumers' goods. When on 31 January the enterprisers note this reduction they will presumably set their planned output of consumables for February at a time-rate intended to meet consumption-spending (for which they will assume a higher time-rate than they did for January) and to begin to restore, or more than restore, inventories to their former level. Having under-estimated, on 31 December, the quantities that consumers would buy at the prices set for January, the enterprisers may decide on 31 January to raise prices for February above their January levels. This may shift downwards individual schedules of propensity to consume. So far as Y_A (expressed as a time-rate) is higher for February than for January, as is likely, this increase may well be due mainly to the raising of enterprisers' expected incomes, which, so far as they fall in upper-income brackets, may be subject to less-than-average marginal propensity to consume. All these effects will in themselves tend to bring about, in some subsequent month, a harmony between expected and realized magnitudes, making $E_P = E_A$ and $Y_P = Y_A$. But in suggesting that such forces would in fact rapidly restore such harmony, or that they might even keep it continually in being, Lord Keynes was leaning heavily on his 'comparative statics' framework and entirely neglecting induced investment, which in the most recent Trade Cycle theory, that of Professor J. R. Hicks, is the intimate partner of the multiplier in the mechanism of fluctuation.

In his *Contribution to the Theory of the Trade Cycle*,* Professor Hicks says in the opening paragraphs of his analysis: 'We cannot avoid

* It is hardly necessary to recall that this book, as Professor Hicks amply acknowledges, draws much inspiration from Mr Harrod's work on Dynamics.

taking a hand in the prodigious controversy about the process of adjustment implied in the multiplier theory. For our "dynamic" programme makes it quite impossible for us to allow any looseness of thought on this crucial matter.' In spirit and fundamental method, Professor Hicks's theory belongs to the same family as those of Frisch, Tinbergen, Kalecki and the econometric school in general; but he, even more than they, will admit no element into the design which could interfere with the machine-like precision of its working; its structure and causal connections, that is to say, are formal and mechanical and make no explicit reference to any psychological links in the chain of stimulus and reaction. The word 'expectation' occurs, I think, only once in the whole book, the notion of *ex ante* magnitudes is held throughout at arm's length, and we find in consequence, as we should expect, that consumption-spending is made to depend on past rather than contemporaneous income: 'People earn their incomes and *then* spend them.' (Italics in the original.)

There can be no reasonable quarrel with the building of a trade-cycle theory on these behaviouristic lines. This kind of building brings 'dynamics' on to the same austere epistemological footing as the most modern of value theory, and it is indeed unavoidable if we are to have a clear-cut pattern of movement derived with rigorous logic from simple premises. But we ought not to forget the wealth of possibilities which are deliberately jettisoned when we use a non-expectational multiplier. As I once tried to show,* a complete theory of the trade cycle, in which we need no special and extraneous explanations of the turning points but derive the whole fluctuation by an expectation-reaction pattern, can be built around the multiplier and a more general and less artificially mechanical concept of induced investment. Such a scheme may have some advantages in simplicity as well as in explanatory power over the rigidly 'econometric' model. These remarks are not meant as a criticism of Professor Hicks's brilliant construction. Nor do I intend as a criticism of it the following remark, which I think has no practical relevance, but serves to show the surprising results (which might in other cases be important) obtainable by handling our systems in full abstraction. Let U_t and V_t be two flows such that when we look at the recorded outcomes of any period t from a viewpoint at the end of that period, U_t and V_t add up to the income Y_t of that period. And let U_t be a linear increasing function of the income Y_{t-1} of the preceding period: we have

$$U_t + V_t = Y_t \text{ and } U_t = f(Y_{t-1}), \quad \text{so that} \quad V_t = Y_t - f(Y_{t-1}).$$

* G. L. S. Shackle, *Expectations, Investment and Income* (Oxford, 1938).

Then if

$$Y_{t-1} < Y_t \text{ we have } f(Y_{t-1}) < f(Y_t) \quad \text{and so} \quad V_t > \{Y_t - f(Y_t)\}.$$

Professor Hicks assigns names to these variables as follows: U is consumption, V is 'accounting' (or *ex post*) saving, the actually recorded difference between consumption-spending and income in any period, and $\{Y_t - f(Y_t)\}$ is the saving 'proper' to period t according to the *consumption-function* $U = f(Y)$. On the above assumptions, then, actual saving will be greater than 'proper' saving whenever income is increasing. Now let us switch round the names, and say that U is saving, V is 'accounting' (or *ex post*) consumption, and $\{Y_t - f(Y_t)\}$ is the consumption 'proper' to the period, according to the *saving-function* $U = f(Y)$. It will follow that actual consumption will be greater than 'proper' consumption whenever income is increasing. There is a perfect formal symmetry between the two sets of assumptions. Why, then, must we say that Professor Hicks is justified in choosing consumption, rather than saving, as the variable which is the subject of active and conscious decision, while saving is the residual? It is surely because some people do not know what their incomes of the current period are* and consequently cannot choose how much they will save out of the income of that period; for *saving* is what becomes of income when nothing is done about that income. If the size of income is not known, one cannot know how much to 'do' about it (how much to spend) in order to make saving come out

* If the institutional framework were such that the size of all incomes of January became known to their recipients during January (if we had not to accept the fact that, for example, profits, partly earned during January, may not be 'ascertained' and published until many months later) it would be easy to suppose that people explicitly decide their saving of January as a function of their incomes of December, and put the appropriate number of shillings in the money-box during the course of January, spending all the rest, whether much or little, as it comes in.

The contrast between the results of the two alternative assumptions can be illustrated as follows:

I. When *saving* is the residual and consumption $U_t = \frac{2}{3} Y_{t-1}$ we might have

Period	Income	Consumption	'Accounting' saving	'Proper' saving
$t-1$	12	—	—	—
t	24	8	16	8

II. When *consumption* is the residual and saving $U_t = \frac{1}{3} Y_{t-1}$ we should then have

Period	Income	Saving	'Accounting' consumption	'Proper' consumption
$t-1$	12	—	—	—
t	24	4	20	16

at a desired level. But one *can*, without knowing the size of one's income, control and consciously decide the size of one's consumption-spending. Professor Hicks is justified, but only by an argument which invokes ignorance of the size of one's current income, an ignorance which, along with all other kinds of uncertainty, is rigidly denied any mention in his book or place in his construction.

The question whether the multiplier applicable to a *decrement* from a given level of individual or aggregate income is equal to the multiplier applicable to an *increment* to that same level was first asked, I think, in Chapter VII of my *Expectations, Investment and Income*. The answer there suggested, that a high propensity to save out of an increment reflects a greater concern, at the given level of income, with extra saving than with extra consumption, and that this will be reflected in a tendency to preserve saving rather than consumption in case of a decrement of income, so that most of the latter will consist of decreased consumption (whereas most of the corresponding increment would consist of increased saving) is superficially the opposite of that given recently by Professor Duesenberry in his book referred to above. But Professor Duesenberry's entirely different argument is dynamic while mine is static; he refers to the difficulty of rapidly adjusting consumption plans and commitments to a change of income, and so concludes that at first a decrement will be met mostly by decreased saving. This is, I think, a realistic view.

It is time to conclude. Only a book in itself could pretend to survey in detail the ever-growing literature of the multiplier, or even to give a reasonably comprehensive list of writers who have contributed to it. I have, therefore, deliberately refrained from any such attempt. The names mentioned here are those of the pioneers only, those who actually brought the multiplier idea into being or watched at close range its early infancy; together with the names of Mr Harrod and Professor Hicks, who may, perhaps, stand representative of the multitude of its later guardians. My purpose has been to commemorate the laying twenty years ago, by Mr Kahn and his co-adjutors, of the foundations on which so important a part of the modern theory of employment rests.

XIV

MYRDAL'S ANALYSIS OF MONETARY EQUILIBRIUM*

In the ten years preceding the outbreak of war in 1939, monetary theory and dynamic economics were immensely improved and developed. Attention had been recalled to such questions by events of the previous war and after, and this interest became intense amongst economists with the occurrence of the great depression. Turning for guidance to the past, they found that in Wicksell's work one of the feats of unmistakable genius in the building of economic theory had already provided them with the basic conception which they needed. It was rudimentary and imperfect in many respects, but it was Copernican in its importance, for it combined into a single whole the theory of money and the theory of relative prices, and it described for the first time a self-reinforcing, disequilibrium process. New and fundamental ideas have been added to the basic conception of Wicksell by some of his Swedish exponents. Two of these authors in particular, Professor Lindahl and Professor Myrdal, have done more than merely incorporate some Wicksellian ideas in theories of their own. They have explicitly devoted much of their work to correcting, improving and developing the basic Wicksellian scheme as an entity in itself. It is with Myrdal's results in this work that I propose to deal.

There were to be found in Myrdal's essay,† which appeared in 1933, a number of new ideas, forming parts of a precise and coherent whole, which have become part of the most essential and characteristic frame of modern economic dynamics, but which have become associated, in the minds of English economists at least, with names other than their true author's. It is not too much, in my opinion, to claim for Myrdal's essay an originality and path-breaking importance equal to anything which appeared in economics in the period between the two wars; and my first purpose in putting together this essay is to claim for it a more just recognition. The fact that the essay appeared in German made it inaccessible to many, and it was a crowning misfortune that, when at last the book was produced in English, this

---

* *Oxford Economic Papers*, old series, no. 7 (1945), pp. 47–66.
† *Der Gleichgewichtsbegriff als Instrument der Geldtheoretischen Analyse* (included in *Beiträge zur Geldtheorie*, ed. Hayek).

version* was published on the very eve of the war. In spite of the excellence in style and language of the English version, Myrdal's theoretical conceptions may still, I think, be found unfamiliar and difficult by some readers. Believing that this book, for reasons deeper than the actual conclusions which it reaches, deserves to become a classic, I have ventured to write the following notes in the hope of making Myrdal's thought easier to follow. They are confined exclusively to his basic constructions, and are in no sense an epitome or comprehensive review. Besides attempting to substitute easier forms of statement for Myrdal's own, I have ventured to consider whether the concept of monetary equilibrium at which he arrives is satisfactory, not from the practical standpoint, regarding which his suggestions are of the utmost interest, but from that of pure theory. Here I have been led to the conclusion that, in the last resort, the idea of monetary equilibrium is merely a special application of that completely general concept of equilibrium in human affairs which Professor Hayek has advanced in an article† which thus becomes in a sense the coping-stone of the Wicksell–Lindahl–Myrdal theoretical structure.

The relationships in time which we encounter in economic dynamics can be rather complicated. For the sake of precision, without which such discussions are worthless, and also for the sake of that compactness which is essential for lucidity and easy reading, I have elsewhere introduced certain terms of my own. While in a purely theoretical argument there is little danger of confusion in the reader's mind between his own 'present moment' at which he is reading the article, the author's 'present moment' at which he was writing it, and the 'present moment' of the imaginary person whose decisions and mental processes are the subject of the argument, this confusion might arise in a discussion of topical questions against a theoretical background. I have, therefore, introduced the term *viewpoint* to mean the 'present moment' of the imaginary person with whose actions our argument is concerned. The other special term which I shall use is 'identified' date or period. The expression 'specific period' seems to me ambiguous, for it might mean simply that the length of the period was given, but not its location in historic time. By an *identified interval*, therefore, I shall mean such an interval as the month of January 1944, or the hour beginning at noon on 1 August 1943. Lastly, *accessions to capital equipment* will mean newly bought or newly constructed items which become part of a person's

---

* Gunnar Myrdal, *Monetary Equilibrium* (Hodge and Co., 1939).
† 'Economics and Knowledge', *Economica*, vol. IV (1937), p. 33.

capital equipment, *regardless of whether their advent effects an improvement or growth of his equipment, or whether it merely serves to make good concurrent wastage.* Thus, the outlay on accessions to capital equipment in any unit interval is the gross investment of that interval.

We shall be concerned with a closed system, and one in which the distinction between entrepreneurs and other individuals will rarely be needed. In seeking the meaning of *income*, Lindahl has given us a concept of great formal beauty and brilliance, by which all incomes, whether derived from the ownership of property and instruments or from personal powers of work or mental creation, can be regarded as 'capital' incomes. We can consider a schedule in which identified future dates are associated with specific quantities of money which the individual now expects that he will then receive, these being quantities which are clear of any deduction on account of direct outlay incurred in earning them. Income, conceived as something which proceeds at any moment at some particular time-rate, is then derived from this schedule by the consideration that as the individual's viewpoint advances through time it brings nearer and nearer each date at which an instalment of receipts is due. The discounted value of each instalment is thereby increased (provided that there has not been meantime any reason to revise the belief as to the rate of interest to be used in discounting), and the total of these increments, one for each future instalment, which arise from the transit of the viewpoint through any identified unit interval, is the individual's income for that interval.*

When such instalments are expected by an owner of capital equipment to be obtained by feeding to the latter an input of materials and services, the expected expense of such input must be subtracted from the expected sale-proceeds of the goods which will have absorbed this input. The difference, for any identified short interval of time, will then be such an instalment as we have in mind, and we shall call it an expected instalment of *net receipts*. The sale-proceeds themselves obtained in any specified interval from selling the output of this entrepreneur's plant, when these proceeds are a gross amount from which no deduction has yet been made for the outlay on materials and services, we shall call his *gross receipts* of the interval in question. Gross receipts and net receipts ought, of course, to be expressed as a time-rate. That is to say, either the time-interval used should be a unit interval or the quantity of money received should be divided by the length of the interval. Those individuals who do not own

* *The Concept of Income, Essays in Honour of Gustav Cassel.* George Allen and Unwin, 1933.

equipment, but expect to obtain instalments of receipts by their work, will usually have no deduction to make on account of input, and their gross and net receipts will be identical. We shall not need to make any distinction between instalments of receipts expected to be earned by persons and those which are expected to be earned by equipment, but shall represent the time-rate of such receipts by the same pair of letters in each case, g for gross receipts and f for net receipts, and h for the input-expense which is the difference between g and f.

The natural starting-point for an attempt to make Myrdal's thought easier to follow is, I think, his explanation of the concepts of net return, yield of real capital, and investment-profit.* As an alternative to Myrdal's explanation in words, we will present some of these concepts in symbols. We shall give letters the following meanings:

x the distance of a variable point of time from some fixed earlier point.

t the distance of the individual's viewpoint from the fixed date $x = 0$.

g the gross receipts in unit time at date x from operating the plant.

h the expense in unit time at date x for co-operating factors (labour, materials, etc.) needed to run the plant.

$f(x) = g - h$ the net receipts at date x from operating the plant.

ρ rate of interest for continuous compounding.†

v value of the plant, on given assumptions as to g and h for every date x, at the viewpoint.

Then

$$v = \int_{t}^{\infty} f(x)\, e^{-\rho(x-t)}\, dx,$$

and

$$\frac{dv}{dt} = \rho \int_{t}^{\infty} f(x)\, e^{-\rho(x-t)}\, dx - f(t)$$

$$= \rho v - f(t).$$

---

* Myrdal, op. cit. pp. 54 ff.

† For the sake of simplicity in presenting essentials, I assume in this article that according to the expectations held by an individual at any one location of his viewpoint, ρ will have the same value for all values of $x - t$. That is, in any one expression for v with specific values of the variables, such expression being the accepted hypothesis in the person's mind at some one location of his viewpoint, ρ will be a constant.

Beyond some identified date, $f(x)$ will be zero, and we could if we liked insert this date as the upper limit of integration. No difference would be made to our expression for dv/dt.

dv/dt or $\Delta v/\Delta t$ is what Myrdal refers to as the *value-change*. Reckoned *ex ante* Δv is the difference $v_1 - v_2$ between v_1 the total discounted value of the series of net receipts $f(x)$ when each instalment is discounted to the viewpoint and the latter is located at the *beginning* of some identified short interval Δx and v_2 the total discounted value, according to the individual's expectations held at the same location of the viewpoint, of that part of the series $f(x)$ which is subsequent to the end of the identified interval Δx, when each instalment, is discounted to this *end-point* of Δx. We see that this value-change is the sum of two terms, one of which, $-f(t)$, represents the removal from the value of the plant, during the passage of the 'present moment' from the beginning to the end of the short interval Δx, of the instalment of net receipts which is received by the owner, in the form of cash, in this interval. Clearly, if the owner's expectations when his viewpoint was at the initial point of Δx were correct, then the value of his plant as he then reckoned it included the amount of this instalment. When, at the final point of the interval, he has actually received this instalment in the form of cash, the new value of his plant, valued *as at* the final point of the interval, will no longer include this instalment. Therefore in reckoning the value-change which will occur during the interval, this instalment must come in as a negative item, and we have the term $-f(t)$. The other term of dv/dt is seen to be simply the rate of interest multiplied by the value, as at the viewpoint, of the plant. This term represents the fact that, as the point of time to which instalments are discounted moves through the interval, each of the instalments remaining in the future is brought nearer to this discounting-point, and is thus discounted over a shorter period. This shortening of the period of discounting for each remaining instalment of course increases the discounted value of each. Thus the term ρv has a positive sign. Indeed, it is easy to see why this term has the particular shape which it has. For if instead of thinking in terms of continuous compounding or discounting we break up any period, over which a sum of money, say k, has to be discounted, into a finite number n of equal time-intervals, then the discounted value of k will be

$$K_1 = \frac{k}{(1+r)^n},$$

where r is a percentage rather larger than ρ the equivalent rate for continuous compounding. Now when the individual's viewpoint to which the sum is being discounted advances through one interval, the new discounted value becomes

$$K_2 = \frac{k}{(1+r)^{n-1}} = (1+r)K_1.$$

Hence the value-change for this future sum of money is

$$(1+r)K_1 - K_1 = rK_1.$$

A similar statement is true for *every* such future instalment, and, no matter what is the number of intervals over which it is to be discounted, the change which its discounted value undergoes as the viewpoint advances through one interval will be its initial discounted value multiplied by the rate of interest. Consequently the value-change for the sum of a whole series of such discounted future instalments, such a series as constitutes the value of a capital-good, will be this value multiplied by the rate of interest, minus the instalment belonging to that time-interval which has slipped into the past. Now Myrdal's definition of the *ex ante* net return at some specified date requires us to subtract, from the gross receipts of some short interval beginning at that date, both the operating expense or cost of co-operating means of production in that interval, and also the net reduction which occurs in that interval in the value of the capital-good. This latter subtraction means that we must *add* the anticipated value-change of that interval. Thus the net return at date t is

$$g - h + \frac{dv}{dt} = f(t) + \frac{dv}{dt}$$
$$= f(t) + [\rho v - f(t)]$$
$$= \rho v,$$

and 'The yield, y, is obtained by dividing the net return by the capital value of the capital goods at the time of calculation'. This capital value being $v(t)$ we have

$$y = \frac{\rho v}{v}$$
$$= \rho.$$

We thus obtain the result stated by Myrdal: 'This means ... that there is always and necessarily a conformity between the yield thus defined and the interest rate in the market; for capital value and net return are defined in such a way that they must constantly fulfil this equation.'* And: 'The result of our analysis so far is that, if the yield of real capital is to fit into Wicksell's monetary theory, it has to be

* Myrdal, op. cit. p. 63.

defined in such a way that it always by definition equals the market rate of interest.'*

But what is now going to become of Wicksell's first equilibrium condition? This says that there is monetary equilibrium when the 'natural rate' is equal to the market rate of interest for loans of money. Myrdal has shown† that the natural rate, conceived as the marginal physical productivity of the time-factor, must be replaced by the concept of the exchange-value yield of real capital. But if the latter is identically equal to the rate of interest, their equality cannot, of course, constitute a condition. Myrdal therefore explains that by the *yield of real capital* we mean, not the yield of equipment already existing, calculated as above by dividing the net return by the capital value of the equipment, but the yield of planned investments, calculated by dividing the net return of the projected equipment by what it will cost to construct. Now the net return of a projected plant will still be calculated in the way shown above, and will still turn out to be the rate of interest multiplied by the capital value. Writing u for the cost of construction, we have as the expression for the yield $y = \rho v/u$, and the equilibrium condition now comes out as $\rho v/u = \rho$ or $v = u$. This is a genuine *conditional* equation. There can be a difference between the capital value and the anticipated cost of construction of a projected plant, and the size of the difference $v - u$ between them, if positive, will largely determine the strength of the inducement to construct this particular plant.

In the next two paragraphs we shall briefly digress from the main argument, which is concerned with the part played by the difference $v - u$, in order to use our preceding discussion to clarify Myrdal's account‡ of the three kinds of gains and losses.

Even in obtaining the yield of existing capital goods, Myrdal ought perhaps to have divided ρv, not by v, the value of this plant to the entrepreneur whose decisions we are considering (i.e. its value according to his own expectations), but by what its supply price would be to him if he sought to buy in the market, or construct, a similar plant. This price, in the case of buying an already existing similar plant, would be the value of such a plant according to the expectations of the least sanguine owner of such a plant (or perhaps the one most hard pressed for ready cash). It by no means follows, and is indeed unlikely, that the valuations, say v_a and v_b, of the same plant by two different individuals a and b will be the same. For the individual with the higher valuation v_a, the yield is $\rho v_a/v_b$. Alternatively, if no similar plant exists, the entrepreneur should divide ρv by

* Myrdal, op. cit. p. 64.   † Ibid. pp. 49 ff.   ‡ Ibid. pp. 59 ff.

what such a plant would cost, at his viewpoint with the most economical technique under the current circumstances, to construct. Here again, supposing this cost is u, there is no reason why v should equal u.

In reading Myrdal's discussion of the consequences (1) of changes of expectation regarding what is still in the future, and (2) of the occurrence of actual results which differ from what was expected, we must of course have in mind Myrdal's own definition of the yield of existing capital goods. He says: 'If these changes of anticipation relate only to the revenues and costs which accrue after the period under consideration, the resulting capital gains and losses do not indicate a difference between the yields *ex post* and *ex ante*. For although the capital value at the moment of the change in the anticipations increases or decreases with the amount of the gain or the loss, the rate of anticipated value-change, and consequently the net return, rises or falls correspondingly. The *ratio* between the net return and capital value is therefore the same *ex post* and *ex ante*.'* The introduction here of the anticipated value-change is an unnecessary complication, for the conclusion follows at once from our result $y = \rho v/v = \rho$. Myrdal proceeds: 'Even if the anticipations of future revenues and costs remain the same, capital gains and losses can...arise if the expectations of future interest-rates—which are the discount factors—change. Then the rate of value-change alters too, and consequently the capital value, the anticipations of future yields being adapted to the new expectations of the future rate of interest.' Here also we could simply say that capital value is a function of the rate of interest, while the yield in Myrdal's sense is the rate of interest itself.

A failure of revenues or costs *ex post* to turn out the same as their amounts *ex ante* is the source of a different kind of gain or loss: 'The gain or loss consists then in the fact that the capital value at the time of the realization of the expected revenue or cost elements did not fall or rise in proportion to the revenue or the cost, as naturally would have been the case if the revenue or cost element had corresponded exactly to the value of the expectations in the *ex ante* calculation.' Any sum of cash which is expected to be received or paid out during an interval lying immediately ahead of the viewpoint, in connection with the operation of the capital equipment, is an item to be added or subtracted in reckoning the capital value, as at the beginning of the interval, of this equipment. Suppose that the net difference between such revenue and cost is a positive amount of net receipts. Then this expected amount of net receipts will, when the viewpoint

* Myrdal, op. cit. p. 60.

is at the beginning of the interval, be part of the capital value attributed by the owner to the equipment. As the viewpoint passes from the beginning to the end of the interval, some actual quantity of net receipts (positive or negative) will be received. Suppose this is a larger positive amount than was expected. Then the excess of the *ex post* over the *ex ante* net receipts is an item of gain to the entrepreneur, and nothing in the way of extra capital-value change, corresponding to this item of gain, need be subtracted from the capital value; for this item of gain did not form part of the initially reckoned capital value. Thus the actual net receipts of the interval are larger, in this case, than the deduction from the initially reckoned capital value which has to be made on account of the sliding of this interval into the past, and the consequent erasure, from the fresh calculation of the capital value made when the viewpoint reached the end of the interval, of all the potentialities of this interval.

Of the three kinds of gains and losses which Myrdal distinguishes, it is, however, the third kind, which he calls *investment-gains* and *investment-losses*, which is important for Wicksell's theory. Myrdal says of them: 'These arise if the capital goods just *being constructed* have, at the moment when they are ready for use, a capital value which is larger or smaller than the total cost of construction. The expectations of such investment gains or losses by the entrepreneurs form the profit motive in the course of Wicksell's dynamic process.'* This kind of gain or loss is the difference $v - u$, whose role we have now to consider.

The essence of Wicksell's conception of a cumulative process, as interpreted by Myrdal, is, I think, a state of affairs where action induced by expectations of profit will lead to revised expectations of still higher profit, and thus to action of the same kinds as before but on a greater scale, and so forth. Putting Myrdal's constructions out of mind for a time, let us see how such a process could occur. We will lay aside entirely, in the following paragraph, the direct consideration of the book, and develop an independent notion of the nature of a cumulative process and of the state of affairs, namely, 'monetary equilibrium', which consists in the absence of such a process. The result will give us our bearings for considering Myrdal's and Wicksell's constructions. In the argument which now follows we shall not need to make any distinction between those individuals who do and those who do not finance and direct production at their own risk, nor between those who do and those who do not own capital equipment or install it at their own hazard. Some individuals have never been

* Myrdal, op. cit. p. 61.

entrepreneurs in this sense of having ordered capital equipment on their own account. All are 'potential' entrepreneurs; but for some of them, past or intended investment is zero. We shall therefore speak indifferently of 'entrepreneurs' or of 'individuals'. Nor shall we need to distinguish between those who sell material objects, or services rendered by equipment (e.g. transportation), and those who sell services rendered by themselves, whether manual or mental. Each of the three categories of expenditure which we shall be considering, on accessions to the purchaser's capital equipment, on the input of materials and services needed for running his existing equipment in order to produce goods for sale, and on consumption, will consist of payments for either or both kinds of goods, and we shall not be concerned with the proportions in which any given expenditure is divided between the two. We shall, however, be concerned with the proportions in which the total expenditure, in any given short interval, of all the persons composing the closed system, is directed to the purchase of the respective outputs, of whatever composition, sold by different individuals.

$v - u$ (if positive) is a belief or working assumption in an individual's mind as to the profit he can make, expressed as a capital value at a point of time, by laying out money on accessions to his capital equipment according to a certain time-schedule which appears, by balancing the advantage of earlier completion against the extra cost of accelerated construction, to be optimal, i.e. to maximize $\dfrac{v - u}{u}$, in the circumstances. The sum of the discounted outlays in this schedule will be u. This time-schedule specifies, for each of a number of consecutive short intervals extending forward from the identified date, say $x = \xi$, at which the viewpoint is located, the outlay on accessions to his capital equipment which, according to the expectations and provisional intentions in his mind at date ξ, the individual will make during this interval. We will therefore call it his *investment-schedule of date* ξ. Amongst these intervals will be the identified interval, say Δx_1, on which his viewpoint is about to enter. Let z_1 stand for his intended investment-outlay for the interval Δx_1. At the instant $x = \xi$ the individual will also have in mind a schedule specifying for each future short interval the expenditure which, according to the expectations and provisional intentions in his mind at ξ, he will make in that interval on materials and services needed to operate the equipment, which altogether he will then possess, in order to produce goods for sale. This we can call his production-outlay schedule of date ξ. For such outlays we have already used the letter h, and we will write h_1

for his intended production-outlay for the interval Δx_1. Lastly, the individual will have in mind at ξ a schedule of intended consumption-expenditure similar in purpose to his investment and production-outlay schedules, and based like the latter on the expectations he holds at date ξ. This consumption schedule of date ξ will specify the amount, say c_1, which he intends at date ξ to spend on consumption during Δx_1. The decisions he has reached at date ξ will also specify or imply the proportions in which the total expenditure $z_1 + h_1 + c_1$ which he intends to make during Δx_1 will be distributed over the products of the different individuals composing the system. Similar decisions as to the amount and distribution of their total expenditure, in their capacities both as entrepreneurs and as consumers, will have been reached at date ξ by all the other individuals. Now we shall choose Δx_1 so short that there is no time for news received by an individual subsequently to the instant ξ to affect his decisions concerning his own action in Δx_1. These decisions, so far as they concern actions such as expenditure, which, we can assume, lie entirely within the power of the individual, can therefore be treated as certain to be performed. Thus the combined effect of the entire set of expenditure-decisions of all the individuals at date ξ will determine for each of them, in our closed system, the actual gross receipts *ex post* which he will find, when the viewpoint reaches the end of Δx_1, that he has received during this interval. Subtracting from these gross receipts g the production-outlay h which he has made during Δx_1 (and which by our assumption is the same *ex post* as *ex ante*) he will obtain his actual net receipts *ex post* for the interval Δx_1. For each individual, his *ex post* net receipts f_p thus determined.may or may not be the amount he expected, that is, the amount which formed an element of the system of expectations he held at date ξ. If it is not, his system of expectations, in a given setting of other circumstances, will have to be altered, and this alteration, occurring at date $\xi + \Delta x_1$, will require a departure from the intentions he held at date ξ concerning his expenditures on equipment, production and consumption during a *new* short interval Δx_2 starting at $\xi + \Delta x_1$. Now if, when we consider together all the individuals composing the system, the net effect of such departures is to make the total expenditure* which will occur

---

* This total of the expenditures of individuals is of course not equal to the total of the net incomes of the individuals; the former contains, besides net income, all the payments involved in the passage of intermediate products from one individual to another in the course of production. But since we assume the number of individuals to be constant, the total net income will be an increasing function (approximately linear) of the total expenditure.

in Δx_2, on equipment, production and consumption combined, obtained by summing the revised individual intentions, greater than the sum of the old individual intentions, and also greater than the actual total expenditure which occurred in Δx_1, then we shall say that during the identified interval Δx_1 an upward cumulative process was in being, or that at ξ an upward cumulative process was implicit in the systems of expectations then respectively held by individuals. We define similarly, *mutatis mutandis*, a cumulative process downwards. These two criteria are called for because, first, we clearly cannot say that a 'runaway' or self-reinforcing process is in being if the whole of the excess of expenditure *ex post* in Δx_2 over that in Δx_1 (or vice versa) is already implied in the schedules existing at ξ; and secondly, we cannot say that such a process is occurring if the revision of expenditure-intentions merely serves to slow down a change in the time-rate of expenditure when this change is implicit in the schedules* existing at ξ. If, however, an actual reversal of the direction of change occurs, so that the sign of the difference between expenditure in Δx_2 and in Δx_1 becomes, say, negative instead of positive, we shall regard this as initiating a cumulative process. If no cumulative process, in the sense we have just defined, is implicit in the state of expectation at ξ, then we shall say that at ξ there is monetary equilibrium.

Monetary equilibrium in this meaning is a means of classifying the set, considered as a whole, of systems of expectations which are entertained, one system by each individual, at some one point of time. This classification begins by dividing all such sets into two kinds: those which by their own character must inevitably be altered when the consequences of the decisions based on them begin to emerge, and those which do not thus contain the seeds of their own dissolution. It then further subdivides the former kind into those which intensify or reverse the change, implied by the initial set of plans, of the aggregate time-rate of expenditure, and those which slow down this change without reversing it. The particular conception of monetary equilibrium which emerges from this classification is, in so far as the first dichotomy is concerned, a special application of a completely general concept of equilibrium applicable to any field of human action, which has been proposed by Professor Hayek. He says:

All propositions of equilibrium analysis, such as...that a person will equalize the marginal returns of any factor in its different uses, are

---

* That is, if more than the whole of the excess of expenditure *ex post* in Δx_2 over that in Δx_1 is already implied in the schedules existing at ξ.

propositions about the relations between actions. Actions of a person can be said to be in equilibrium in so far as they can be understood as part of one plan.... Since equilibrium relations exist between the successive actions of a person only in so far as they are part of the execution of the same plan, any change in the relevant knowledge of the person, that is, any change which leads him to alter his plan, disrupts the equilibrium relation between his actions taken before and those taken after the change in his knowledge. In other words, the equilibrium relationship comprises only his actions during the period during which his anticipations prove correct.

...In a society based on exchange the plans determined upon simultaneously but independently by a number of persons will, to a considerable extent, refer to actions which require corresponding actions on the part of other individuals.... Since some of the 'data' on which any one person will base his plans will be the expectation that other people will act in a particular way, it is essential for the compatibility of the different plans that the plans of the one contain exactly those actions which form the data for the plans of the other.

...For a society then we can speak of a state of equilibrium at a point of time—but it means only that compatibility exists between the different plans which the individuals composing it have made for action in time.

...It appears that the concept of equilibrium merely means that the foresight of the different members of the society is in a special sense correct. It must be correct in the sense that every person's plan is based on the expectation of just those actions of other people which those other people intend to perform, and that all these plans are based on the expectation of the same set of external facts, so that under certain conditions nobody will have any reason to change his plans.*

We turn back now to Myrdal's discussion of Wicksell's conceptions.

The first of the three conditions of monetary equilibrium, fulfilment of any one of which, Wicksell says, will ensure that no cumulative process is occurring, is equality between the natural and the money rate of interest. Myrdal's interpretation of this first condition is equality between the capital value of planned investments and their cost of production. Any entrepreneur who considers that, so far as possibilities open to himself are concerned, this equality is true, will, according to Wicksell's belief as Myrdal interprets it, decide to lay out such an amount in the next unit interval on accessions to his capital equipment as will exactly make good what this equipment will lose in this interval through its use in production and through natural decay and obsolescence; he will, that is to say, set the time-rate of his intended net investment at zero. Wicksell's conception of monetary equilibrium, so far as this first condition is concerned, is

* 'Economics and knowledge', *Economica*, vol. IV (1937), pp. 36 ff.

a state, existing at a point of time, where $v = u$ for every individual, and where, therefore, in his view, net investment decided on for the next unit interval will be zero for every individual and hence for the system as a whole. Myrdal rejects this idea on two grounds: first, that entrepreneurs will never, in fact, take identical views at any instant of the profit to be made by laying out given sums of money on equipment; and secondly, that zero net investment for the system as a whole is not a necessary condition for the absence of a self-reinforcing process. He proposes to overcome the first of these difficulties by combining the differences $v - u$, one for each individual, in a weighted sum where the weight for each person would be his *coefficient of investment-reaction*, of which Myrdal says: 'We define a firm's coefficient of investment-reaction as the ratio between the amount of net *new* investment—i.e. investment over and above the replacement of outworn old real capital—which it decides to undertake during a unit period and the amount of prospective investment-profit* $v - u$ necessary to induce this investment.'† In regard to his second objection Myrdal concludes that Wicksell's first condition of monetary equilibrium leaves indeterminate the level of investment-profit and the time-rate of investment for the system as a whole which will ensure the absence of a cumulative process. Determinateness, he says, can only be obtained by starting with Wicksell's second equilibrium condition.

Myrdal says: 'One can formulate the second equilibrium condition as follows: The money rate of interest is normal if it brings about an equality between gross real investment on the one side and saving plus total anticipated value-change of the real capital ... on the other side.... In this equation gross real investment, R_2, is compared with a magnitude, which I will call "waiting" or "free capital disposal", W, and which contains besides saving proper, S, the term anticipated value-change, i.e. depreciation minus appreciation, D.'‡ He has explained: 'We ... define saving as a part of *income*, namely that part which is not used in the demand for consumption goods. The term "income" is here and in what follows defined synonymously with "net return".'§

Let $c(t)$ stand for the intended spending of an individual on consumption in a short interval Δx measured forward from his viewpoint $x = t$, and $s(t)$ for his intending saving in this short interval. The net return as we saw is ρv, so we have

$$s(t) = \rho v - c(t).$$

* In this quotation I have replaced Myrdal's symbols by those adopted above (pp. 179, 182).

† Myrdal, op. cit. p. 78.   ‡ Ibid. pp. 96, 97.   § Ibid. p. 90.

The other component of 'waiting' is the *negative* of the anticipated value-change; for we have defined the anticipated value-change in such a way that the part of their capital value which will be shed or parted with by the capital goods during the short interval (a net reduction of value) is given a negative sign; but this part is for us, in reckoning the total of *ex ante* waiting, a positive item. Thus we have for the second component of waiting the quantity

$$-\frac{dv}{dt} = -\{\rho v - f(t)\},$$

and for *ex ante* waiting itself

$$w(t) = s(t) - \frac{dv}{dt}$$
$$= \rho v - c(t) - \rho v + f(t)$$
$$= f(t) - c(t). \tag{1}$$

In reckoning 'waiting', therefore, we can disregard altogether the net return. The latter will mainly determine, no doubt, the individual's decision how much to spend during Δx on consumption. But given his intended consumption and his expected net receipts, we can obtain his *ex ante* waiting without knowing his assumed net return. And it has now become clear that whenever saving increases through an increase of ρv which is not accompanied by any change in $c(t)$, then the negative of anticipated value-change decreases by the amount by which saving increases.

The quantities $f(t)$, $c(t)$ and $w(t)$ which we have been discussing represent the expectations and intentions of an individual concerning some short interval Δx measured forward from his viewpoint. That is, they are *ex ante* magnitudes. When the individual's viewpoint will have reached the end of the interval a set of *ex post* magnitudes will appear which are conceptually distinct from the *ex ante* magnitudes and show what his net receipts, expenditure on consumption, and waiting have actually been during the interval. To distinguish between *ex ante* and *ex post* magnitudes we will write the individual's consumption *ex ante* as c_A and his consumption *ex post* as c_P; and similarly f_A and f_P for net receipts, w_A and w_P for waiting. We will also write z_A for the quantity of money which the individual decides to lay out during Δx on accessions to his capital equipment, to maintain or improve it, and z_P for the corresponding *ex post* quantity; and similarly h_A and h_P for his production-outlay, that is, his expenditure during Δx on input to run his equipment; and finally g_A for his expected, and g_P for his actually recorded, gross receipts in Δx, that is, the whole takings or proceeds of the interval from selling his output, before deduction of any expenses. Myrdal does not consider the question whether the intentions, which occupy a person's mind at the instant when the interval for which they prescribe the action is about to begin, are to be regarded as certain to be executed provided they are possible: and I shall here introduce an argument of my own. The decisions which a man has reached concerning his action in some identified interval Δx on which his viewpoint is about to enter must, if we take Δx sufficiently short, be considered irrevocable: for some determinate time is required to digest fresh news and revise decisions, and we can take Δx shorter than this time. And if we do not wish to take Δx so short, still a person's intentions are in general less fluid according as they refer to a point of time nearer to his viewpoint; and so there is a schedule of compromise from which we can choose, between greater length of Δx and greater realism of the assumption we shall make, that the expenditure which a person decides on for a short interval extending forward from his viewpoint will in fact be performed. We can assume that the decisions represented by C_A and Z_A will always be possible and we shall treat these *ex ante* magnitudes as certain to be realized. g_A, f_A, and w_A on the other hand are beliefs or working assumptions about the outcome of other people's future actions, and cannot of course be treated as certain to be realized (i.e. certain to have been correctly assessed by an individual). If then we write $G_A = \Sigma g_A$ for the sum of the individual amounts g_A over all the individuals composing the system, calling it aggregate gross receipts *ex ante*, and similarly use capital letters for the other aggregate magnitudes $F_A = \Sigma f_A$, $F_P = \Sigma f_P$, $C_A = \Sigma c_A$, and so forth, we have in our closed system, in virtue of the meaning we attach to decisions,

$$G_P = C_A + H_A + Z_A, \tag{2}$$

and subtracting H_A from both sides

$$F_P = C_A + Z_A, \tag{3}$$

while from equation (1) we have

$$F_A = C_A + W_A. \tag{4}$$

Subtracting (4) from (3) we have

$$F_P - F_A = Z_A - W_A, \tag{5}$$

that is to say, any difference which emerges, when the viewpoint reaches the end of the interval, between the actually recorded aggregate net receipts *ex post* and the sum of the individual expectations of net receipts *ex ante* appears to be due to a discrepancy between the sum of the individual intended expenditures on accessions to capital equipment (intended gross investment) and the sum of the individual intentions to perform 'waiting'. Myrdal's second equilibrium condition, expressed in our symbols, would be $Z_A = W_A$, and our equation (5) shows that this is also the condition for equality between F_A the aggregate of individual expectations of net receipts and F_P the aggregate of realized net receipts.

$Z_A = W_A$ expresses that state of affairs at the moment when the viewpoint is at the beginning of Δx, which is necessary and sufficient to ensure that when the viewpoint reaches the end of Δx and F_P becomes known, the latter will turn out to be the same total amount as F_A. It is therefore also a necessary condition for the fulfilment of the expectation of each individual concerning his net receipts in Δx, but it is not a sufficient condition for this; for if the net receipts of some people are greater, and of others less, than they expected, the aggregates can still be equal. By adding C_A to both sides of $Z_A = W_A$ we have the equivalent

$$F_A = C_A + Z_A$$

which like the former is not an identity such as (1), (2) and (3) above, but an equation which not all sets of values of F_A, C_A and Z_A will satisfy. It seems possible that all three of these variables will be altered, *ceteris paribus*, if the rate of interest is altered. But there is nothing to ensure, so far as we can tell *a priori*, that in any given circumstances it will be possible, by manipulating the rate of interest, to attain a set of values which satisfies the equation. The fact that there may be no rate of interest or specific change of rate which will bring about equality between F_A and $C_A + Z_A$ does not prevent us from taking this equality as a condition of equilibrium: the criterion of equilibrium is independent of the question whether equilibrium is attainable or not. But the fact that equality between F_A and $C_A + Z_A$ does not ensure the fulfilment of individual expectations of net receipts does mean that it cannot be a true equilibrium condition. This we must briefly examine.

Let us again consider two consecutive short intervals Δx_1 and Δx_2, the earlier of which starts at a point of time $x = \xi$. And suppose that F_A, C_A and Z_A are sums of individual expectations or intentions entertained by individuals at date ξ and concerned with their actions or receipts in Δx_1. If the set of their individual expenditure intentions is such that $F_A = C_A + Z_A$, but is *not* such that all *individual* expectations of net receipts in Δx_1 will be fulfilled, then there will be one group of persons for each of whom actual net receipts in Δx_1, say f_P, will be more than the amount, say f_A, which at ξ he expected to receive in Δx_1, and another group for each of whom his f_P will be less than his f_A. It is reasonable to assume that at date $\xi + \Delta x_1$ members of the first group will revise upwards the expenditure-intentions for the second interval, Δx_2, which they entertained at ξ, while members of the second group will revise such intentions downwards. But clearly there is nothing to *ensure* that the total revisions made by the two groups will exactly cancel each other out, so that the sum of the expenditure-intentions for Δx_2 of all individuals in the system remains as it would have been had f_P and f_A been equal for every individual. Thus equality of F_A and $C_A + Z_A$ does not ensure the absence of a cumulative process in the sense which we adopted above.* But nevertheless, taking into account the large numbers of individuals which will usually be involved, there is clearly a strong presumption that when $F_A = C_A + Z_A$ the departure of the sum of the revised expenditure-intentions for Δx_2 from the sum of the old expenditure-intentions for the same interval will be small. In a closely similar line of thought Professor Hayek says: 'It is an interesting question... whether in order that we can speak of equilibrium, every single individual must be right, or whether it would not be sufficient if, in consequence of a compensation of errors in different directions, quantities of the different commodities coming on the market were the same as if every individual had been right. It seems to me as if equilibrium in the strict sense would require the first condition to be satisfied, but I can conceive that a wider concept, requiring only the second condition, might occasionally be useful. A fuller discussion of this problem would have to consider the whole question of the significance which some economists (including Pareto) attach to the law of great numbers in this connexion.'†

In the foregoing I have tried only to clarify some of the main structural members of the theory, not so much for the sake of these conceptions themselves, as for the sake of clearing the reader's way so that he may have more attention to spare, in reading the book, for those tools of thought which are its most interesting contribution.

* See pp. 184 ff above.
† 'Economics and knowledge', *Economica*, vol. IV (1937), p. 43, n. 1.

XV

THE DEFLATIVE OR INFLATIVE TENDENCY
OF GOVERNMENT RECEIPTS
AND DISBURSEMENTS*

The Exchequer, in deciding the size, method and timing of its levies and disbursements, must nowadays be guided by two quite distinct sets of considerations. There is first its original task of raising just enough revenue to pay for those goods and services needed by the government for the discharge of its functions and to meet the current claims of those to whom the Exchequer owes money from the past. If this were all, the criteria of good taxes would be that they must not cause obvious and great inequalities of hardship, that they must be unobtrusive, and that they must be cheap and easy to collect. And as regards disbursements, prompt payment of claims would best sustain the credit and dignity of the government. In these aspects of its work the Exchequer is simply the Accounts Branch of a very large business, procuring certain services for the citizens and seeing that the citizens pay their bills. But during the last 10 years† a revolution of thought has come about. It is seen that the government's demand for goods and services is a very important part of the aggregate demand for goods and services; and it is now understood that so long as this aggregate demand can be kept large enough, there will be no heavy general unemployment. Thus the problem of avoiding massive general unemployment can be solved if the quantity of goods and services bought per unit of time by the government can be increased by some means which does not entail an equal decrease of the quantity bought by private persons and firms; and provided the gap, measured in absolute terms, between the government's increase and the public's consequential decrease (if any) of demand can be made large enough. And it is seen that, correspondingly, if at some particular date the aggregate demand for goods and services, at the prices then prevailing, is greater than the supply, so that prices tend to rise, this pressure can be relieved in so far as extra money, taken by the government in taxes, will be found by the taxpayers out of what they would otherwise have spent on goods and services rather

* *Oxford Economic Papers*, old series, no. 8 (1947), pp. 46–64.
† This was written in 1946.

than out of what they would otherwise have added to their liquid savings; provided that the government does not itself lay out this extra revenue on goods nor hand it, e.g. as repayment of debt (so long as the shortage of goods continues), to those who would spend it themselves.

A decision of high policy that under-employment shall be attacked by government spending in excess of revenue, and that over-employment shall be attacked by taxation in excess of government spending, does not by itself guarantee the desired results. Knowledge is needed of the public's reaction to increases, or decreases, of the time-rate of flow of individual types of tax revenue and of individual types of Exchequer disbursement, in order that the *net* effect on the combined demand for goods and services, by government and public together, of these fiscal measures may be determined. The first step in obtaining such knowledge is to define a measure of the tendency of an increase or decrease in the time-rate of some specific stream of government receipts or disbursements to raise or lower prices.

By a person's *nominal income* I mean his wages, dividends, etc. (but not any part of undistributed profits of firms), net of expenses incurred in obtaining them but before deduction of personal direct taxes. By a person's *disposable income* I mean his nominal income less personal direct taxes. By a firm's *nominal profit* I mean its profit after meeting all obligations for resources but before any direct tax is paid in respect of this profit, whether on its distributed or undistributed portions. By a firm's *disposable profit* I mean its nominal profit less direct taxes on the undistributed part of this nominal profit.

A person who expects to have to pay in taxes x pounds per annum more than hitherto out of an unchanged nominal income must plan to reduce by x pounds per annum either his consumption or his saving, or else to reduce his consumption by px pounds per annum and his saving by $(1-p)x$ pounds per annum. A firm can cause extra tax out of an unchanged nominal profit to cut into dividends, net growth of equipment, or net growth of liquid assets, or divide the burden in any proportions between them. A person who expects to receive from the government for his free disposal (i.e. net of tax and of obligations, such as wage payments, incurred in earning it) x pounds per annum more than hitherto, can likewise add any proportion of this to his intended consumption and the rest to his intended saving; and a firm can divide such an increment of its time-rate of disposable receipts from the government into increments of its dividends, time-rate of growth of equipment, and time-rate of growth of liquid assets. In the simplest cases the measures of deflative or inflative tendency that we require will be weighted averages of the proportions of changes in their disposable revenues which individuals or firms meet by changes of their time-rates of expenditure on goods.

Let A_i be the extra number of pounds per annum which some one person or firm, labelled i, expects, in view of a given expected nominal income or profit, to have to pay to the government under some one head of taxation in a new or hypothetical alternative situation as compared with an initial situation; and let $A_i p_i$ be the number of pounds by which this person or firm, in consequence of this change in taxation, will decide to reduce his or its annual expenditure on goods not for resale.* Then the weighted average

$$P = \frac{\Sigma A_i p_i}{\Sigma A_i}$$

taken over all persons and firms in the system can be called the *deflative index*, in the initial situation, of the given increase of yield ΣA_i of the particular tax; provided, however, that the intended output per annum, in the system as a whole, of every good is the same in both situations. The concept of a deflative index can be applied to any flow of Exchequer receipts from the public, and not only to taxation. Likewise, let B_i be the extra number of pounds per annum that a person or firm labelled i expects to receive from the government, under some one head of Exchequer account, as nominal income or profit, all other expectations remaining unchanged; let T_i be the number of pounds per annum of direct tax which, at the rates in force when the expectation of B_i arises, will be paid by this person, or by this firm and its shareholders, out of B_i; and let $(B_i - T_i) q_i$ be the number of pounds by which this person, or this firm and its shareholders, in consequence of the increment $B_i - T_i$ of expected disposable income or of the disposable part of dividends plus disposable undistributed profit, will decide to increase his or their annual expenditure on goods not for resale.* Then the ratio

$$Q = \frac{\Sigma (B_i - T_i) q_i}{\Sigma B_i}$$

of sums taken over all persons and firms in the system can be called the *inflative index*, in the initial situation, of the given increase ΣB_i in the annual amount disbursed by the government under the particular head of account. It will sometimes be appropriate, however, to suppose that the extra receipts from the government are expected to

---

* 'Goods not for resale' comprises here the consumption of a private person or the owner or shareholders of a firm, and the net investment performed by the firm.

be substituted for receipts from elsewhere; and sometimes that the output, in the system as a whole, of certain goods is expected to be changed in consequence of the change in government disbursements; and to modify accordingly the assumption that all other expectations, except those of government disbursements, remain unchanged.

It is plain that when the estimated yield of some particular tax or other levy is reduced (as by a change, e.g. in the standard rate of income tax), this is a change for which an inflative index can be sought just as for an increase of positive disbursements; and similarly, a deflative index will apply to decreases of disbursements.

It might be thought at first sight that p and q must lie in every case between o and 1. But plainly q can sometimes be greater than unity, and even, conceivably, less than zero. Thus a firm with an insufficient total of free capital and borrowing power to embark on a large extension may be enabled to do so by a tax refund or war-damage payment, and may thereupon lay out more than the amount of such refund, in whose absence it would have laid out nothing. And conceivably a man to whom the attempt to save would seem hopeless and futile if he started from nothing might be induced to begin saving by coming into possession, say, of a post-war credit, for which q would thus be less than zero. It is harder, but still possible, to imagine cases in which p also would go outside the limits o and 1.

The purpose intended to be served by the concepts of deflative and inflative index can now be stated more exactly. To trace throughout the system, and through a period of years, the consequences of a change, e.g. in method or rate of taxation, would require us to know not only how each person reacts to this change before he knows how others are going to react, but also to consider the effects of these immediate reactions of individuals when they are observed by other individuals, and so on in an endless, even if convergent, series of terms. (And we cannot assume that it would be convergent in any short-period sense.) However, a change in the relative sizes of the flow into the market of goods for sale, and the flow into the market of money for the purchase of goods, may perhaps have broadly similar effects, no matter how, in detail, it arises. If so, some useful knowledge will be gained if we can say that the initial and immediate effect, e.g. of an announced change in the rate of some tax, or the intention to make certain disbursements, as, for example, post-war tax credits to old-age pensioners, will be such-and-such an increase in the time-rate at which money seeks to buy goods, the flows of goods remaining unchanged, or changing in some way 'mechanically', arithmetically, and logically necessitated by the particular change in disbursements. A deflative or inflative index seeks, accordingly, to present the 'state of intentions' of the persons and firms composing the system, when a change in the time-rate of some government levy or disbursement has been announced, before these intentions have begun to be acted upon and thus had the opportunity to influence each other. We begin by framing a suitable classification of streams of government receipts and disbursements.

By a disbursement I mean a stream of payments made by the government, under some one head of account, to private persons or firms; and by an imbursement I mean a stream of payments received by the government, under some one head of account, from private persons or firms. A change in the time-rate of any such stream will have a different significance according as the situation in which it occurs is one of full employment or more or less heavy under-employment; that is to say, the significance of such a change will vary according to the position which this situation occupies along a scale from zero to infinite elasticity of supply of productive resources. The following analysis deals first with disbursements and then with imbursements. Under each of these heads it first considers conditions of heavy under-employment or infinite elasticity of supply of productive resources; then conditions of full employment or zero elasticity; and lastly touches on the more difficult case of an intermediate condition.

In considering disbursements in conditions of extremely elastic supply of physical means of production, an important distinction must be made between those streams of government out-payments which are the purchase-money of extra flows of production, and those streams of out-payments (e.g. extra pensions, tax refunds, some war-damage payments) which are *not* directly linked with any increase of output of goods; and a further and equally important distinction must be made between those disbursements by which the government buys extra flows of goods intended to be resold to the public* (whether consumers or net investors) and those by which goods are bought for the State as such. And still another distinction is needed between disbursements to persons and disbursements to firms.

In a case where an extra disbursement is received by private persons otherwise than as earnings of extra production (e.g. an increase of old-age pensions), the inflative index is simply

$$Q = \frac{\Sigma(B_i - T_i)\, q_i}{\Sigma B_i},$$

---

* This category may become as important in internal trade as it has recently become, with State purchasing of raw materials, food, etc., in external trade.

where B_i is the time-rate of extra payments received by individual i, T_i is the time-rate of yield of direct tax on these extra receipts, and q_i is his marginal propensity to consume out of disposable income.

If, in conditions of heavy unemployment, the State calls into being extra outputs of goods and services (e.g. government office furniture or services of policemen) for its own use, things which serve the needs of the State as such and are not passed on by sale to private persons or firms, and if, means of production being in extremely elastic supply, these extra outputs are additional to all the flows of production initially proceeding, and do not have to be substituted for any of them, then the consequences fall into two phases: the first of these we can ignore, since it consists in two extra flows which exactly cancel each other, the extra output of goods and the extra outflow of government purchase money which buys them. But the tax-free part of this purchase money goes into the pockets of wage-earners, shareholders, etc., to be freely disposed of by them. Thus, in this second phase, the extra flow of out-payments is exactly like an extra flow of old-age pensions or tax refunds: there is more money to spend, but no more to spend it on; the inflative index of this extra flow of out-payments, in the simplest case where it goes direct to government employees, will again be simply

$$Q = \frac{\Sigma(B_i - T_i)q_i}{\Sigma B_i},$$

where symbols have the same meanings as in the preceding case.

In both the foregoing types of case the extra disbursement ΣB_i does not provide the government with extra goods to sell to the public, and the government may in consequence decide that the amount $\Sigma(B_i - T_i)$ by which a given extra disbursement ΣB_i exceeds the direct tax ΣT_i assessed, at given tax rates, on this extra disbursement, shall be matched by extra tax revenue secured by a change of tax rates. The extra disbursement ΣB_i will in that case be covered by extra tax yield made up of two components, one of these being the extra number of pounds per annum which the receivers of ΣB_i must pay in direct taxes at *given rates* in consequence of receiving ΣB_i and the other being extra yield obtained from the public at large by means of some change in tax rates. The first component we may call the *inherent tax yield at existing rates of tax* of a given disbursement, the second may be called *extraneous reimbursing taxation*. In calculating the inflative index of a given extra disbursement it will be natural to take into account such automatic consequences as the inherent tax yield or, in cases where this occurs, the creation of goods saleable to the public. But whereas, when goods or services are ordered by the government in order to be sold to the public, the two parts of the transaction form a unity, of a character which would be entirely altered if one part were performed without the other, so that it will be convenient to consider both parts together and obtain an inflative index which covers them both, we shall not follow this course in regard to extraneous reimbursing taxation. A disbursement and its extraneous reimbursing taxation are considered separately and separate indices obtained, because we have (in general; that is, save in such cases as the Road Fund) no reason to link any particular part of the total tax revenue (other than the inherent yield) with the government disbursement which buys any particular goods.

If a given increment in the time-rate of some government disbursement is the purchase money of an equal increment in the output, measured by market value, of some good or service intended to be resold to private persons or firms, and if this extra output is produced by resources hitherto idle (e.g. if the engagement by the Post Office of extra telephonists, hitherto unemployed, provides for and secures increased telephone traffic), it is plain that there will be no tendency (apart from a failure of the goods to be sold) for prices in general to be raised by this increase in the pace of disbursement. The measure of net inflationary or deflationary tendency appropriate to such a case is

$$R = \frac{r(u-y)-v}{u},$$

where v is the time-rate of government receipts from the sale of certain goods to the public, u is the increment, due to the production of these goods, in the time-rate of government outlay, y is the increment, due to the receipt of u, in the time-rate of direct tax payments by those who receive this extra government outlay, and r is the proportion of $(u-y)$ which is spent by them on goods, whether for consumption or investment. If $r < 1$ or $y > 0$ or both, R will be negative, that is, it will be a deflative index, since for every extra pound laid out in any year by the government in producing more of the goods in question, R pounds will be drawn off from the public's purchases in that year (supposing that its aggregate income is simply increased by u and not otherwise changed) of other goods.

The formula above raises two questions: First, what difference of treatment is called for according as the extra flow of out-payments u goes to government employees or, in the first instance, to a government contractor? The latter will usually, of course, hand on part of u

to his sub-contractors and they perhaps to still another rank of subsidiary firms, but with this we are not concerned. When the extra flow of production has been fully established, the whole of u will be finding its way into the pockets of ultimate income receivers, viz. private persons or else firms in their capacity as retainers and reinvestors or hoarders of net income. It is this situation, wherein all the flows of net income which together add up to u can be supposed to be proceeding smoothly, to which the government must look forward in determining the appropriate inflative index. Thus, whether u goes to one firm or to a pyramid of firms, it will be divided into two components, namely expenses of production, viz. wages, salaries, interest, etc., on one hand, and nominal profit on the other. The second of these components will itself be divided into dividends and undistributed nominal profit; and the latter again into its own contribution to the inherent tax yield of u, and a disposable portion dividing itself between net improvement or extension of equipment, and increase of liquid assets such as cash and gilt-edged securities. Let us call the first component u_1; write y_1 for the inherent tax yield of u_1, that is, the extra number of pounds per annum of direct tax paid out of the extra nominal income u_1 by the receivers of the wages, salaries, etc., which compose it; and write q_1 for the marginal propensity to consume of the receivers of these wages and salaries. Let us write u_2 for the dividends paid out of the second component, y_2 for the inherent tax yield of these dividends, and q_2 for the marginal propensity to consume of those who receive them. And let the undistributed portion of nominal profit be u_3 and its inherent tax yield y_3; and let the ratio of net investment (expenditure on net improvement of capital equipment) to disposable undistributed profit be q_3, so that $(1 - q_3)(u_3 - y_3)$ is the net contribution to liquid assets. Then our formula* will become

$$R = \frac{q_1(u_1 - y_1) + q_2(u_2 - y_2) + q_3(u_3 - y_3) - v}{u},$$

* We could instead write u_A for that part of u which goes in wages and salaries, ξ_1 for the proportion of u_A that those who receive these wages and salaries will hand back to the government as direct tax, and q_1 for their marginal propensity to consume out of disposable income; u_B for that part of u which is nominal profit of firms, h for that proportion of u_B which is distributed as dividends, ξ_2 for that proportion of dividend receivers' marginal nominal income which they hand back to the government as direct tax, and q_2 for their marginal propensity to consume out of disposable income; ξ_3 for the proportion of firms' undistributed nominal profit which will return to the government as direct tax, and q_3 for the proportion of the firms' disposable (i.e. tax-free) undistributed profit which is allocated to net invest-

where $u_1 + u_2 + u_3 = u$. Usually q_1, q_2 and q_3 will each be less than unity, y_1, y_2 and y_3 will each be greater than zero, and v will not be less than u. Thus R will usually be negative, that is (since we propose to form the product of R with a positive quantity u standing for an incremental government disbursement, and to regard this product as an incremental (if positive) or a decremental (if negative) flow of spending on goods) R will usually be a deflative index. It will be the deflative index appropriate, for example, to a government order (given in conditions of extremely elastic supply of resources in general to the system as a whole) for an extra output of aluminium ingots intended to be resold to private firms making kitchen equipment for sale to the public. An incremental government disbursement of this kind, in these circumstances, will, however, be deflative in a rather special and unusual sense. It will definitely *worsen* the market for the output of private firms other than those who receive the extra government order; but these firms themselves will be enabled to take on extra employees. But again, since the extra output has to be sold on the market, it is unlikely that the government will be able to cover its costs in the transaction: v is likely to be less than u. The explanation of the apparent conflict between these aspects of such government action will be seen when we consider the second of the two questions we spoke of.

The second question is: What difference of treatment is called for according as the goods ordered by the government for resale are consumers' goods, on one hand, or producers' equipment, on the other? Or let us ask instead: What would have to be the composition of goods ordered by the government from a contractor, in order that the government might plausibly assume, in the presence of abundant idle resources, that R will be zero? The extra demand, created by the extra outflow of government payments, falls into two parts, viz.

$$q_1(u_1 - y_1) + q_2(u_2 - y_2),$$

which is a demand for consumers' goods, and

$$q_3(u_3 - y_3),$$

which is a demand for capital equipment; and for the difference

$$u - \{q_1(u_1 - y_1) + q_2(u_2 - y_2) + q_3(u_3 - y_3)\}$$

ment. We should then have the useful concept: propensity of firms to distribute (nominal) profit, this propensity being measured by h, and could write our formula:

$$R = \frac{u_A(1 - \xi_1)\,q_1 + u_B\{h(1 - \xi_2)\,q_2 + (1 - h)\,(1 - \xi_3)\,q_3\} - v}{u}.$$

the extra flow of government out-payments does not generate any extra demand from private persons or firms at all. Thus the condition which, better than any other expressible in terms of broad categories, will give plausibility to the hypothesis that $R = 0$ is that the extra output should consist of three parts in determinate proportions, measured by market value, thus:

$J = q_1(u_1 - y_1) + q_2(u_2 - y_2)$ to be consumers' goods for resale (directly or after further processing) to private persons,

$K = q_3(u_3 - y_3)$ to be producers' equipment for resale to private firms,

$L = u - (J + K)$ to be goods for the State's own use.

The deflative aspect of such government action as we are here considering can now be understood. The amount by which incremental demand (from private persons and private firms) created by the government's incremental disbursement falls short of the incremental supply called into being by that disbursement is made up of two components: first, part of the disbursement is short-circuited back to the Exchequer as tax: this part is $y_1 + y_2 + y_3$. Secondly, the flow of saving, which the private persons and private firms wish to make out of the disposable incomes of the persons and the disposable undistributed profits of the firms, may be only partly covered by the net investment which these firms wish to make in consequence of the increment $u_2 + u_3$ in their nominal profit.*

If, instead of seeking to make $v = u$, the government aimed at a net profit for itself, but still wished to make $R = 0$, extra goods for the State's own use, of a cost equal to this expected net profit, should be ordered in addition to those required to fill the gap between the public's demand generated by the flow of out-payments u, and this flow of out-payments itself.

* Using the notation of the previous footnote, this incremental net investment will be

$$u_B(1 - h)(1 - \xi_3) q_3,$$

while the saving will be

$$u_A(1 - \xi_1)(1 - q_1) + u_B h(1 - \xi_2)(1 - q_2) + u_B(1 - h)(1 - \xi_3).$$

If q_3 were unity, the third term of this expression for saving would be equal to the sole term of the expression for net investment. But q_3 may be less than unity, and each of the first two terms in the expression for saving may be greater than zero. If either of them is greater than zero, the saving due to u will exceed the net investment due to u unless q_3 sufficiently exceeds unity.

The results of our analysis so far as it has gone can perhaps be presented more vividly as follows:

Let 'pensioners' typify all recipients of extra money from the government for which no return is required in extra output.

Let 'policemen' typify those who, being directly employed by the government, produce goods or services for the State's own use and not for re-sale to the public.

Let 'postmen' typify those who, being directly employed by the government, receive extra money from the government in exchange for extra output intended to be sold to the public.

Let 'palace-builders' typify those private firms which receive government contracts for goods (e.g. office buildings) for the use of the State as such.

Let 'paper-makers' typify those private firms which receive government contracts for goods (e.g. paper for White Papers, Ordnance Maps, publications of the Central Office of Information, etc.) intended for re-sale to the public.

Then 'pensioners', 'policemen', and 'palace-builders' are alike in that any extra money received by them in so far as it is not saved in liquid form is an extra flow of money into the goods market to which there corresponds no extra flow of goods. 'Postmen' and 'paper-makers' are alike in that extra money received by them and saved in liquid form will leave an extra stream of goods flowing into the market to which there corresponds no extra flow of money. Thus there is a prima facie presumption that extra payments to 'pensioners', 'policemen', and 'palace-builders' are inflative in tendency, while extra payments to 'postmen' and 'paper-makers', *ceteris paribus*, are deflative.

Let us now turn to the other extreme of the range over which the elasticity of supply of physical resources to the productive system as a whole, private and governmental taken together (as distinct from their elasticity of supply to individual sectors, industries or businesses), can vary, and, taking each of the five types of government disbursements in turn, suppose its time-rate to be increased in conditions of full employment.

For the inflative index of disbursements of the kind typified by pensions, the state of employment is irrelevant.

When, in conditions of already full employment, the government seeks to engage extra workers in its own service, whether as 'policemen' or as 'postmen', it may proceed by offering to some of the workers employed in private businesses (this being, *ex hypothesi*, the only source of supply) a higher wage-rate than they are there receiving. This will probably lead all workers of the occupation and grade in question to demand higher wages from their employers. Then if, for workers typified by 'postmen',

N is the total number of workers of a given kind in the system.

s is the proportion of these initially in government service.

Δs is the desired increase of s.

w is the initial wage-rate.

Δw is the increment of the wage-rate necessary to effect an increase Δs in s, so that

$$\epsilon = \frac{\Delta s}{s} \bigg/ \frac{\Delta w}{w} = \frac{\Delta s}{\Delta w} \frac{w}{s} \text{ is the elasticity of } s \text{ with respect to } w.$$

ξ is the ratio of the extra direct tax paid by such workers, on account of the extra earnings they receive when their wage-rate rises from w to $w + \Delta w$, to these extra earnings, and q is the workers' marginal propensity to consume, we have:

Increment of aggregate wage-bill for such workers for the whole system $N\Delta w$.

Increment of the government's wage-bill* $sN\Delta w + Nw\Delta s$.

Increment of real output   nil.

Increment of spending on goods $N\Delta w(1 - \xi)q$.

Inflative index $Q = \dfrac{N\Delta w(1 - \xi)q}{sN\Delta w + Nw\Delta s} = \dfrac{(1 - \xi)q}{s(1 + \epsilon)}.$

From this formula it appears that an increment of the wage-bill for workers employed by the State to produce goods or services for sale to the public (typified in our scheme by 'postmen') arising from the need to attract workers away from private businesses, will have an inflative index which will be higher, the higher is the marginal propensity to consume of workers of this grade, and will be lower, the higher is the elasticity of the government's proportion of the available workers with respect to the wage-rate which the government offers. It also appears that the inflative index will be lower, the larger the government's initial proportion of the total available number of workers of the grade or quality in question. This is not at first sight so easy to understand. The reason is that the larger the government's initial proportion S of the total number N, the larger will be the ratio, say, λ, of the increment of the government's wage-bill to the increment of the total wage-bill; but the inflative index is simply the

* We neglect the term $N\Delta s\,\Delta w$.

marginal propensity to consume of the kind of workers in question, multiplied by the ratio of the disposable to the nominal increment of their earnings, and multiplied again by the inverse of the ratio λ. Thus our formula yields conclusions agreeable to common sense. Moreover, it is evident, when we insert plausible (i.e. non-absurd) numerical values in this expression, how large it is likely to be in comparison with those appropriate to conditions of heavy unemployment, which indeed are often negative so that their numerical values measure a deflative instead of an inflative tendency. For example, let us assume the following values:

Marginal propensity to consume .   .   .   .   . $q = 0 \cdot 60$
Proportion employed by the government of all workers
of a given grade* .   .   .   . $s = 0 \cdot 05$
Elasticity of s with respect to the wage-rate offered by the
government .   .   .   . $\epsilon = 2 \cdot 00$
Proportion of increment of workers' earnings which
must be paid in direct tax .   .   .   .   . $\xi = 0 \cdot 10$
Then $Q = +3 \cdot 6$.

When the extra workers are wanted by the government as 'policemen' instead of as 'postmen', the only difference this will make to the inflative index is that, whereas up to the moment of their transfer to government service the whole of their output was helping to satisfy consumers' or investors' demand for goods, this contribution towards the public's purchasable needs will entirely cease when the extra workers become 'policemen'. It seems reasonable to regard this reduction of the flow of goods into the market as equivalent to an increase in the flow into the market of money seeking goods. If we take the market value of the output which the transferred workers used to produce when they were employed in private businesses as equal to their wage-bill in that employment, then the numerator of the inflative index must be increased, as compared with that for 'postmen', by this wage-bill, so that we shall have for 'policemen', in conditions of full employment, an inflative index

$$Q = \frac{(1 - \xi)\, q + N(1 - s)\, w}{s(1 + \epsilon)}.$$

Next, what will happen if, in conditions of full employment, the government increases its demands on private businesses for goods for re-sale to the public? Let us assume that the output of some particular

---

* A *given grade* of workers comprises all those whose wages will rise, as a direct consequence, if the wages of certain government employees rise.

good in the system as a whole is at such a level G that (in the short period) it cannot by any means be increased, so that G is completely inelastic to the price offered for the good. The share of this output which the government takes can nevertheless be increased by reducing the share going directly to the public, but this will presumably require the offer of an increased price to compensate the firms for the loss of goodwill. Then if

G is the aggregate output from all firms in the system of the good in question, measured in physical units,

z is the proportion of G initially going to the government,

Δz is the desired increment of z,

x is the initial price of the good,

Δx is the increment of x necessary to induce firms to transfer output away from private customers to the government to the extent Δz desired by the government,

w is the initial wages per unit of output,

Δw is the increment of w obtained by the workers on account of the intensified competition between firms for their services which arises from the firms' higher profits,

$\eta = \dfrac{\Delta z}{\Delta x} \dfrac{x}{z}$ is the elasticity of z with respect to x,

ξ_w is the proportion of their incremental earnings that wage-earners must pay as direct tax,

ξ_e is the proportion of their incremental nominal profit that profit receivers (firms and their shareholders) must pay as direct tax,

q_w is the wage-earners' marginal propensity to consume out of disposable income,

q_e is the profit-receivers' marginal propensity to spend out of the disposable part of dividends, or disposable undistributed profit, on consumption or net investment

we have:

Increment of the firms' aggregate nominal profit $G(\Delta x - \Delta w)$.

Increment of the firms' aggregate wage-bill $G\Delta w$.

Increment of the public's spending on goods

$$G\Delta w(1 - \xi_w) q_w + G(\Delta x - \Delta w) (1 - \xi_e) q_e.$$

Increment of government expenditure $G\{z\Delta x + x\Delta z\}$.

Inflative index

$$Q = \frac{G\{\Delta w(\mathrm{I} - \xi_w)\, q_w + (\Delta x - \Delta w)\, (\mathrm{I} - \xi_e)\, q_e\}}{G\{z\Delta x + x\Delta z\}}$$
$$= \frac{\Delta w\{q_w(\mathrm{I} - \xi_w) - q_e(\mathrm{I} - \xi_e)\} + \Delta x q_e(\mathrm{I} - \xi_e)}{z\Delta x + x\Delta z}.$$

However, if $q_w = q_e = q$ and $\xi_w = \xi_e = \xi$, we can write

$$Q = \frac{q(\mathrm{I} - \xi)}{z(\mathrm{I} + \eta)},$$

a formula for the inflative index in conditions of full employment, of an incremental disbursement to firms, for the purchase of extra output for re-sale to the public, which is formally the exact counterpart of that for an extra disbursement to 'postmen' in the same conditions: the only difference being that η, which replaces ϵ, is the elasticity of the government's share of output bought instead of its share of the labour force.

Lastly, we come to the case of 'palace-builders'. The inflative index of an incremental disbursement in conditions of full employment, for the purchase from private firms of goods for the State's own use, will differ from the one appropriate to 'paper-makers' which we have just obtained, in the same way as that for 'policemen' differed from that for 'postmen': we have to add to the numerator the annual value by which the public's purchasable supply of goods is reduced when some of it is transferred to the State; e.g. when the production of chairs and cupboards for the home gives place to that of chairs and desks for government offices. This annual value may be taken to be $\Delta z G x$, so that we have, for 'palace-builders'

$$Q = \frac{q(\mathrm{I} - \xi) + \Delta z G x}{z(\mathrm{I} + \eta)}.$$

We shall not consider in detail the inflative indices appropriate to intermediate states of employment. We have seen that for 'postmen' in conditions of full employment, Q might, in easily conceivable circumstances, be, for example, 4. In conditions of heavy unemployment it might be, perhaps, -0.4. A similar comparison holds for our other categories, between conditions of 'full general bottleneck' and perfect elasticity of supply of productive resources. It is evident that in any intermediate condition of 'fairly low' unemployment, the inflative indices will lie between the two extremes we have suggested.

We turn now to consider government receipts or imbursements, a category which comprises:

(1) Taxes: (i) direct taxes, e.g. income tax and surtax, excess profits tax;

        (ii) commodity taxes, e.g. purchase tax, excise, customs;

        (iii) licence revenue, e.g. receipts from motor-car and wireless licences.

(2) 'National Insurance' contributions.

(3) Receipts from the sale of government property, e.g. disposal of surplus war stores; and permanent State trading in raw or semi-finished materials.

We shall not try to deal with imbursements comprehensively, but shall select one or two of the more interesting types of direct tax for treatment by way of illustration of this side of the matter.

The numerical values of deflative (respectively, inflative) indices appropriate to various incremental (respectively, decremental) imbursements may differ in different conditions of employment: but their formal expression will retain the same structural elements at all levels of the elasticity of supply of productive resources: for they are not mechanically linked with production. For the sake of uniformity of treatment we shall consider decrements in the time-rate of government imbursements, so that we can in general expect to get inflative indices such as we can compare with those obtained above for increments of government disbursements.

The algebraic sign of an index belonging to a decremental imbursement, whose own algebraic sign will naturally be negative, will be negative if the index is inflative, positive if it is deflative. For a decremental imbursement which is associated with an increment of spending-on-goods is inflative in tendency, and the index of this effect is simply the ratio of the two differences, one negative, the other positive, and this ratio is evidently negative.

We shall again need the concept of inherent tax yield. But when the imbursement which we are studying is itself a direct tax on incomes or profits, the concept will only be needed if there is a second or third, etc., distinct direct tax on the same incomes or profits, whose yield will be changed by the decrement, whose effects we are studying, in the time-rate of the first imbursement. Thus, for example, a change in the rate or basis of an excess profits tax would affect the yield of income tax from firms and their shareholders.

The inflative index of a given decrement in the yield (expressed

H

in £ million per annum) of direct taxes on personal nominal* income of the members of a given income-bracket, expected incomes being *given*, will be simply the weighted average of their marginal propensities to consume out of disposable income.

The effect of reducing the yield of an excess profits tax will depend on the proportion of the extra amount allowed to be retained by firms, out of given expected nominal profits, that will be added to dividends. Thus if

$-\Delta g$ is the decrement of yield of excess profits tax, and

Δg is therefore the increment of: nominal profits less excess profits tax:

h is the proportion of Δg which will be added to dividends,

ξ_2 is the proportion of an increment of dividends that will have to be paid in direct taxes,

ξ_3 is the proportion of an increment of undistributed: nominal profit less excess profits tax: that will have to be paid as direct tax,†

q_2 is dividend receivers' marginal propensity to consume out of disposable income,

q_3 is firms' marginal propensity to expend an increment of disposable undistributed profit on equipment,

we have for the inflative index of a decrement of excess profits tax

$$Q = \frac{\Delta g\{h(1-\xi_2)\,q_2 + (1-h)\,(1-\xi_3)\,q_3\}}{-\Delta g}$$

$$= -\{h(1-\xi_2)\,q_2 + (1-h)\,(1-\xi_3)\,q_3\}.$$

A proposal sometimes made is an *excess dividends tax*, that is to say, a tax 'falling upon dividends either beyond a given percentage on capital or beyond the amount distributed by each company in a given base period'.‡ If

t is the number of pounds per annum that must be paid as excess dividends tax for every £1 per annum distributed as excess dividends, however defined, the tax being paid by the firms and not by the dividend receivers,

---

* I.e. income assigned to individuals, as contrasted with additions to the capital assets of firms of which they are shareholders.

† Pairs of colons are here twice used for the purpose served in algebra by pairs of brackets. Some convention of this kind is an indispensable addition to our resources of punctuation if ambiguity is to be avoided without clumsiness.

‡ *The Economist*, 6 April 1946, p. 546. See especially also the budget speech, *Hansard*, 9 April 1946, p. 1838.

$E(t)$ is the number of pounds per annum that will be paid out as excess dividends, in the whole system, the nominal profit of each firm being given, when the rate of excess dividends tax is t,

$Y = tE$ is the yield of the excess dividends tax,

$\theta = \dfrac{dE}{dt} \dfrac{t}{E}$ is the elasticity of excess dividends with respect to the rate of tax,

$\mu = \dfrac{dY}{dt} \dfrac{t}{Y}$ is the elasticity of the yield of the tax with respect to its rate,

ξ_2 is the proportion of an increment of dividends that will go to the Exchequer as direct tax (e.g. income tax, *not* excess dividends tax, which we are supposing to be paid by firms, not by dividend receivers),

ξ_3 is the proportion of an increment of the undistributed part of nominal profit that will go to the Exchequer as direct tax *other than* excess dividends tax, ξ_3 being *independent* of the amount of excess dividends tax that has to be paid,

q_2 is dividend receivers' marginal propensity to consume out of disposable income,

q_3 is firms' marginal propensity to expend disposable undistributed profit on equipment,

we have, for the differences associated with an increment Δt in the rate of tax,

decrement of excess dividends	ΔE
difference of yield of excess dividends tax*	$\Delta Y = t\Delta E + E\Delta t$
decrement of disposable income of dividend receivers	$\Delta E(1 - \xi_2)$
increment of disposable undistributed profit	$-\Delta E(1 - \xi_3) - \Delta Y$
decrement of dividend receivers' consumption	$\Delta C = \Delta E(1 - \xi_2)\, q_2$
increment of firms' net investment	$\Delta J = -\{\Delta E(1 - \xi_3) + \Delta Y\}\, q_3$
difference of spending-on-goods by private persons and firms	$\Delta S = \Delta C + \Delta J$

$$= \Delta E\{(1 - \xi_2)\, q_2 - (1 - \xi_3)\, q_3\} - (t\Delta E + E\Delta t)\, q_3.$$

* We neglect the term $\Delta t\Delta E$.

Thus for the inflative or deflative index of a difference ΔY in the yield of the tax, other expectations remaining unchanged, we have

$$R = \frac{\Delta S}{\Delta Y} = \frac{\Delta E\{(1 - \xi_2) q_2 - (1 - \xi_3) q_3\} - (t\Delta E + E\Delta t) q_3}{t\Delta E + E\Delta t}. \quad (1)$$

Also

$$\frac{dY}{dt} = \frac{d(tE)}{dt} = E + t\frac{dE}{dt} = E(1 + \theta),$$

whence

$$\mu = \frac{dY}{dt}\frac{t}{Y} = 1 + \theta,$$

so that we can alternatively write

$$R = \frac{\Delta E[(1 - \xi_2) q_2 - \{(1 - \xi_3) + (\mu t/\theta)\} q_3]}{\Delta Y}, \quad (2)$$

or

$$R = \frac{\theta\{(1 - \xi_2) q_2 - (1 - \xi_3) q_3\}}{\mu t} - q_3. \quad (3)$$

Again the index will be inflative if its algebraic sign is the same as that of the incremental (positive) or decremental (negative) government disbursement whose effect we are studying; deflative if different. For formula (1) above is the result of simply writing down the net difference made, by a change in the rate of excess dividends tax from t to $t + \Delta t$, to the time-rate of non-governmental spending-on-goods, and writing down underneath it as divisor the difference made to the yield of the tax by this same change in its rate. If the difference made to spending-on-goods is an increment the expression for it will be positive; moreover, the index will be inflative. If our 'causal' change is a decremental imbursement, its sign will be negative, and so also, if the difference made to spending is positive and inflative, will be that of the index itself. And so on. There are evidently four cases all told:

ΔS positive, R inflative, ΔY and R have like signs		ΔS negative, R deflative, ΔY and R have opposite signs	
(1) ΔY positive, R positive $= \dfrac{\Delta S}{\Delta Y}$		(3) ΔY negative, R positive $= \dfrac{\Delta S}{\Delta Y}$	
(2) ΔY negative, R negative $= \dfrac{\Delta S}{\Delta Y}$		(4) ΔY positive, R negative $= \dfrac{\Delta S}{\Delta Y}$	

Some insight into the values that R will take in various circumstances can be got from general considerations. It is plain that θ will be always negative. It cannot be doubted that at some finite level the rate of tax (the ratio of the amount which must be paid in tax to the amount of the excess dividends) would be sufficiently high to reduce 'excess dividends' to zero and with them, the government's revenue from the tax. It follows that there is some level at which, when the rate of tax rises above it, the elasticity μ of yield to rate of tax becomes negative. Let us look at formula (3). Evidently q_3 will virtually never be negative, for this would imply a net movement to exchange equipment for liquid assets on the part of the firms, all taken together, affected by the excess dividends tax. When q_3 is greater than zero, the second term, viz. $-q_3$, of formula (3) will be negative. Thus R will be negative, that is, will be an inflative index when applied to a decrement of yield, so long as the first term of formula (3) is not positive and numerically greater than q_3. At negative values of μ this first term will be positive when the expression inside { } is positive. Let us suppose that the effective rates, ξ_2 and ξ_3, of direct tax other than excess dividends tax, are the same on both the distributed and the undistributed parts of nominal profit. Then (with negative μ) the first term of formula (3) will be positive when q_3, firms' marginal propensity to expend undistributed profits on equipment, is less than q_2, dividend receivers' marginal propensity to consume. Now q_2 is likely to be high and q_3 is likely to be low in a depression; moreover, while ξ_3 in most schemes of taxation will be constant at all levels of activity of the system (since it will be, for example, simply the standard rate of income tax), ξ_2 is likely to be low in a depression because of the reductions then suffered by large incomes. It is therefore in a depression that R will, if at all, be positive and thus deflative when μ is negative, that is, when the rate of excess dividend tax is high. The conclusion is that the rate of such a tax should be kept very low in a depression. For there is likely to be some level at which, when the rate of tax falls below it, the influence of the tax on dividend policy becomes small or negligible, so that θ rises, algebraically, above -1 and $\mu = 1 + \theta$ thus becomes positive.

Some notion of a plausible value of R can be gained by assigning numerical values, judged to be themselves plausible or non-absurd, to the various quantities appearing in formula (3). If we put

$$\left. \begin{array}{l} \theta = -2 \\ \mu = -1 \\ t = 0 \cdot 1 \\ \xi_2 = 0 \cdot 45 \\ \xi_3 = 0 \cdot 45 \\ q_2 = 0 \cdot 9 \\ q_3 = 0 \cdot 5 \end{array} \right\} \text{ we have } R = +4 \text{ approximately.}$$

Sufficient illustrations have now been given, perhaps, of how the notion of inflative and deflative indices might be developed in detail to fit various types of case. These indices do not, it is plain, measure the ultimate effect of each action of the Exchequer upon prices. To attempt that would call for a distinct formula, or at least for one with different values of its parameters, for each different length of time supposed to elapse between the causal event and the measurement of its effect. Our scheme is intended only for judging the direction of the initial thrust given to affairs by a newly started or newly augmented stream of government disbursements or imbursements: that is, for judging whether it increases or reduces monetary demand in relation to the supply of goods.

PART IV

ON THE PHILOSOPHY OF ECONOMICS

XVI

A CHART OF ECONOMIC THEORY*

A list of the topics which have engaged economic theorists since 1870 would include many that are no longer part of the essential equipment of the analyst of today. Such tools as the period of production in the theory of capital, and the quantity theory of money, have been widely discarded. But the transformation which economic theory has undergone since 1931 or thereabouts has involved far more than a mere relegation of old-fashioned doctrines. In these last two decades, it is hardly too much to say, the whole conception of the character of the main economic forces has altered, the emphasis has been shifted from the idea of an inherent tendency in the economic system towards perfect and stable adjustment to the idea of an inherently erratic system where uncertainty alternately inhibits action or gives scope for self-regenerative explosions whose collapse leads back to temporary stagnation. The seeds of this change were sown by Wicksell before the beginning of the century, and in Sweden it had already in the later 1920's gained great momentum, but in the rest of the world it had to wait for the Great Slump and Keynes's *General Theory of Employment, Interest and Money*. The climate of frustration and crisis of the years since the First World War, together with their outgrowth in the change of theory, and then the needs of the Second World War, have led to an immense extension of the scope of the theory of Government economic intervention and the development of new doctrines to cover new fields of policy. Concurrently with this sudden emergence of whole new departments of economic theory, eclipsing for a time the old pre-eminence of value theory, there was, rather accidentally perhaps as to its coincidence in time, a great breakout from the bounds of perfect competition in value theory itself. The theories of imperfect or monopolistic competition were cast in the static mould, but those of oligopoly have moved from the form of traditional value theory to become the chief locus in economics of Neumann and Morgenstern's Theory of Games.

Thus if our purpose is to bring a university syllabus in economics into line with to-day's conception amongst research theorists of the shape and content of economic theory, more is needed than a mere purging of the collection of topics to be found in the literature. Some

* *Metroeconomica*, vol. v (1953), pp. 1-10.

principle of classification seems to be needed in order to make an intelligible pattern of those topics that are retained. One such possible principle is to consider for each topic to what degree time and its implications are of the essence of the matter.

There seem to me to be, for economists, at least three sorts of time. There is the time in which sequences of events, successive transformations of the situation, actually unroll themselves. This evolutionary or dynamic time is what we have in mind in looking at the 'present moment' whatever view we may take of its nature. Things *actually* happen in dynamic time. But *imagined* transformations of the situation are also arranged by our minds in quasi-temporal sequences: our expectations form a vista of events in perspective (or a whole set of such vistas in rivalry with each other), and this time-dimension of expectations we can call expectational time. There is thirdly the recorded pattern of history. So far as the traces and consequences of past events are wrapped up in and carried forward by the present, helping to shape it, this aspect of things can conveniently be embodied in our reasoning by assimilating historic and dynamic time, so that actual events, whether past or conceptually 'present', all fit into one framework. Imagined future events still form an entirely distinct category, since they do not constitute a unique series.

The accompanying chart, Fig. XVI 1, gives, on the right-hand side, a table of the suggested contents of a modern course in economic theory. The topics are here given their traditional or accepted names, and are grouped under 'subject' headings also according to accepted convention. The left-hand side of the Chart suggests a new classification of theories according to the degree to which each essentially involves (*a*) dynamic time and (*b*) expectational time and uncertainty. In what follows I have attempted three things: first, to explain what the terms:

A. Economics of Perfect Adjustment
B. Calculable Dynamics
C. Aggregative Comparative Statics
D. Economics of Uncertain Expectation

are intended to mean. Secondly, to give reasons for the particular decisions made in assigning each of the subjects α, β, ..., θ or parts of them to the types of theory A, B, C, D. Thirdly, to suggest in some detail a scheme of lecture courses based on the following considerations:

(1) That economic theory is valuable as a vehicle for teaching logical quantitative methods of thinking, that is, for giving a glimpse of the use and power of mathematics.

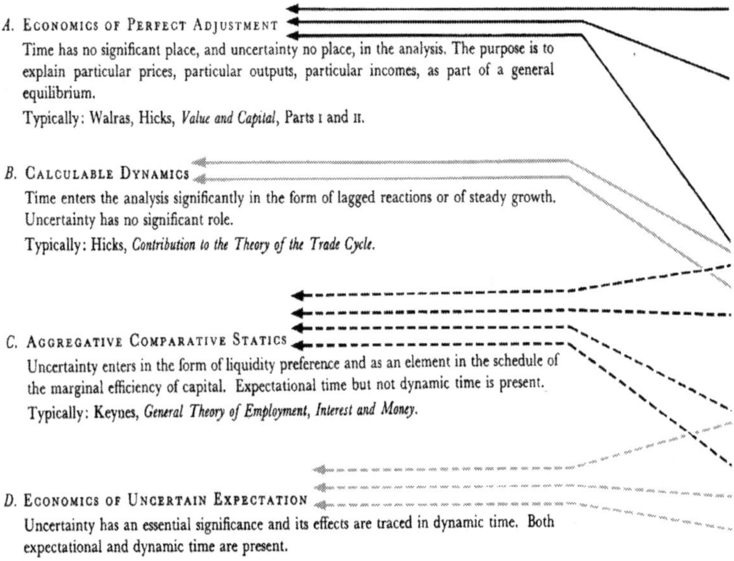

A. Economics of Perfect Adjustment

Time has no significant place, and uncertainty no place, in the analysis. The purpose is to explain particular prices, particular outputs, particular incomes, as part of a general equilibrium.

Typically: Walras, Hicks, *Value and Capital*, Parts I and II.

B. Calculable Dynamics

Time enters the analysis significantly in the form of lagged reactions or of steady growth. Uncertainty has no significant role.

Typically: Hicks, *Contribution to the Theory of the Trade Cycle*.

C. Aggregative Comparative Statics

Uncertainty enters in the form of liquidity preference and as an element in the schedule of the marginal efficiency of capital. Expectational time but not dynamic time is present.

Typically: Keynes, *General Theory of Employment, Interest and Money*.

D. Economics of Uncertain Expectation

Uncertainty has an essential significance and its effects are traced in dynamic time. Both expectational and dynamic time are present.

Fig. XVI 1. A chart of economic theory.

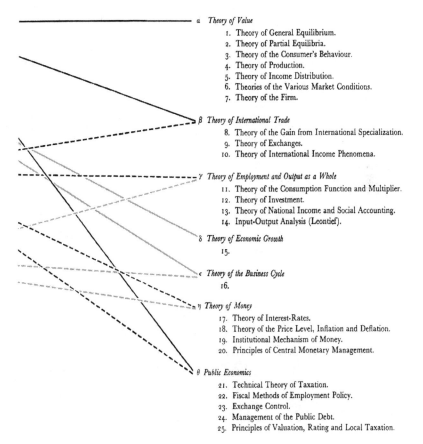

α *Theory of Value*
   1. Theory of General Equilibrium.
   2. Theory of Partial Equilibria.
   3. Theory of the Consumer's Behaviour.
   4. Theory of Production.
   5. Theory of Income Distribution.
   6. Theories of the Various Market Conditions.
   7. Theory of the Firm.

β *Theory of International Trade*
   8. Theory of the Gain from International Specialization.
   9. Theory of Exchanges.
   10. Theory of International Income Phenomena.

γ *Theory of Employment and Output as a Whole*
   11. Theory of the Consumption Function and Multiplier.
   12. Theory of Investment.
   13. Theory of National Income and Social Accounting.
   14. Input-Output Analysis (Leontief).

δ *Theory of Economic Growth*
   15.

ε *Theory of the Business Cycle*
   16.

η *Theory of Money*
   17. Theory of Interest-Rates.
   18. Theory of the Price Level, Inflation and Deflation.
   19. Institutional Mechanism of Money.
   20. Principles of Central Monetary Management.

θ *Public Economics*
   21. Technical Theory of Taxation.
   22. Fiscal Methods of Employment Policy.
   23. Exchange Control.
   24. Management of the Public Debt.
   25. Principles of Valuation, Rating and Local Taxation.

(2) That it helps to satisfy the desire to make sense of real situations and events.

(3) That when used with caution and sceptical alertness it can give the statesman some bearings in his navigational task and guide an empirical and experimental policy.

(4) That of his second and third university years (in a three-year stay at the university) a student may wish to devote only one to economics. Thus if the lecture-scheme covers two years, the earlier of these should be in some degree self-contained and should survey the greater part of the whole field by the easier routes, some of the ground being viewed again in the second of the two years from less accessible but more commanding viewpoints.

When economics is concerned with describing an ultimate pattern of perfect adjustment, and not with any path or process by which this equilibrium is approached, time enters only in the sense that some of the quantities are flows rather than stocks. The reasoning and solution are unaffected by the recognition of this character of the quantities. The form of the reasoning is essentially that of a system of simultaneous equations in which moreover all quantities relate to one and the same instant. The two statements, that the equations are simultaneous and that the quantities all refer to one date, mean of course entirely different things, the former meaning that all the equations are true within one and the same context of reasoning, a logical simultaneity, the other having its plain meaning.

When this type of system is generalized by including amongst its entries some referring to earlier and some to later dates, the power and scope of the analysis are immensely increased. With given parameters and a given initial pattern of values of the system of variables we can now deduce the behaviour of each variable through time. Time here means evidently the dynamic time referred to above, and this is so whether we attend principally to the movement of each variable, the difference between its values at two 'neighbouring' points of time, or whether we consider the pattern of its behaviour recorded over some interval. Moreover, we are not bound, in referring to this pattern, to speak of what has been recorded, for the system is as determinate as the static equilibrium, and there is here no meaningful or effective distinction between past and future. This 'calculable dynamics' is, however, in one important respect a less universal tool than equilibrium analysis. The answers it will give will differ enormously from each other according to the precise numerical values chosen for the parameters (the *coefficients of reaction* which state the degree of response of one variable to given behaviour of another,

or of itself at an earlier date). According to the choice of these parameters, the solution may be a non-oscillating path towards equilibrium,
a damped oscillation, an oscillation of ever-growing amplitude, or a
plain 'explosion'. The system is, in a sense, too precise and mechanical.
Of precise knowledge it offers too much and requires too much.

If we are bold enough to suppose that by resolute trial and error
Government monetary and fiscal policy can eventually work the
system to a desired state of affairs and stabilize it there, the important
question is what states of affairs are 'equilibrium' ones in the sense
that they can be stabilized by this set of measures or that. The kind
of equilibrium which can be achieved and preserved by vigilant,
flexible, and resourceful Government handling of the 'climatic'
controls such as the supply conditions of money and the tax structure
(as distinct from direct rationing, allocation and price dictation) is
remote from that in which we conceive of every individual 'micro-
economic' unit, every person or family and every firm, being
perfectly adjusted in its relations with all the others. Government
policy can at best achieve only an aggregative or macro-economic
equilibrium, subject to disturbance both by shocks from non-
economic sources and by the working-out of micro-economic mal-
adjustments which have been merely concealed by the superficial
balance amongst the broad aggregative categories. A *calculable
dynamics* assumes in the system a wholly unrealistic degree of simplicity and mechanical precision, and no elaboration of measurement could ever enable us to discern such a model, and meaningfully
determine its parameters, and its phase at any given instant, amongst
the data of the real world. For calculations about the effects of
policy measures we must be content with *comparative statics*, that is,
with the comparison of equilibrium states, for the attainment of
which states we should have to trust to trial and error. By eschewing
the attempt to forecast a path of the economy through time, with its
impossible requirements of definiteness and exactness in the data, we
are enabled to bring in that element which above all others divorces
reality from static models, namely, uncertainty. Though the formal
framework of the *General Theory* is that of Aggregative Comparative
Statics, its essence depends wholly on the effects in the economy of
uncertainty. Within these effects are embraced the source of liquidity
preference and the peculiar character of the inducement to invest,
and within them would be found also certain features of the consumption function, features which in fact the *General Theory* fails to
recognize, but which make the consumption function a potential
source of cyclical movements.

One further step may perhaps be possible. The utmost that we are likely to be able to do by way of predicting at any moment the economy's behaviour is to answer the two questions:

(1) What tensions exist at the moment within the economy tending to alter its state, and what is the general character and direction, and perhaps the speed, of such change in its immediate stages?

(2) How would the economy react, at first, to such-and-such type of political or other shock? Such a type of analysis, designed to make possible a sensitive empirical 'climatic' control with a near 'horizon', would be far less ambitious than a calculable dynamics but less restricted than a mere comparative statics.

The accompanying scheme is an attempt to relate the traditional topics of economic theory to the four main types of theory which, above, have been distinguished according to the part played in each by time and uncertainty.

The traditional core of economics, the analysis of adaptation to scarcity, where it is assumed that scarcity is actual and present and not merely potential as in a deep depression, embraces under the heading Theory of Value and Distribution the answers to the questions: Why is just so-and-so much of this good and of that produced and offered for sale in each unit time interval, why does so-and-so much of this exchange for so-and-so much of that, why are the services of so-and-so many workers, acres, flocks and herds, mines and machines offered for use and why are their rewards at such rates per unit? The underlying assumption of the central parts of this theory is *perfect knowledge* which gives meaning to the ideas of rationality in choice and perfect adjustment. It is perhaps not strictly true that time has no place here, for the Partial or Particular Equilibrium of one firm or industry or sector of the economy can be studied on the assumption that, although something has happened amongst the governing conditions to which the whole economy will eventually, if given time, seek to adjust itself, this adjustment takes place in distinguishable stages, so that what happens in the 'first round' of adaptation of that part of the system most directly and earliest affected can be studied separately. But the study is nonetheless one of a *state* and not a process. All topics of the Theory of Value and Distribution are accordingly assigned to the Economics of Perfect Adjustment. (Topics *1* through *7* → *A*.)

The Theory of International Trade belonged formerly in part to the Theory of Value, where it dealt with international specialization, and in part to the other great traditional department of economics, the Theories of Money and of Monetary Management, to which belonged the Theory of Currency Exchanges. But the Theory of Employment which since 1936 has escaped from the joint tutelage of Monetary Theory and Business Cycle Theory, and has tended even to swallow its tutors, has also important international aspects. Thus a topic called here the Theory of International Income Phenomena, concerned with the 'multiplier' effects of changes in a country's export or import surplus and the further consequences of these effects, has been added to the other two. The Theory of International Specialization belongs to the Economics of Perfect Adjustment. The other two topics, since they concern Money and Employment, are assigned to Aggregative Comparative Statics. (Topics $8 \rightarrow A$; 9, $10 \rightarrow C$.)

In the *General Theory* Lord Keynes and one or two associates virtually created a new department of economics. The book is a paradox, for its central concern is with uncertainty, decisions based on conjecture, and situations altogether lacking in objective stability, yet it uses an equilibrium method. Here as elsewhere, the irresistible fascination of assuming a tendency to equilibrium, or of discussing only the state and not the means of attaining it, is that thus the insoluble problem of the sequence in which events will occur, of the amplified effects of trivial accidents, and the whole Gordian knot which 'period analysis' and like methods can only fiddle at, is cleanly cut. The simplicity thus achieved is illusory and dangerous, but in the book it has served to illumine brilliantly the character of the structural members of the Theory of Employment and Output as a Whole. For any such theory must use, in however formally different an argument, the ideas of consumption function, liquidity preference and inducement to invest. Because of the mould into which Keynes cast his ideas the Theory of Employment must be assigned to Aggregative Comparative Statics, but because of the essential nature of these ideas, which perhaps did not fully appear to Keynes himself until he came to summarize his theory in an article published just a year after the book,* it belongs also to the Economics of Uncertain Expectations. (Topics *11*, *12* $\rightarrow$ *C, D*.)

The special accounting techniques, by which the life process of the economy is seen reflected in its money transactions (National Income Accounting) or in the pattern of 'real' inputs and outputs of the different industries and sectors of the economy, fall naturally under Aggregative Comparative Statics. (Topics *13*, *14* $\rightarrow$ *C*.)

The Theory of Economic Growth comprises two types of theory.

* 'The general theory of employment', *Quarterly Journal of Economics*, vol. LI (1937), pp. 209–23.

One of these deals with the secular growth of population, the secular accumulation of wealth, the movement of the 'frontier' across virgin territories, and the progress of knowledge and its exploitation in new technology. The incidents of this march are not the concern of what Professor Baumol has called 'The Magnificent Dynamics'. The other Theory of Growth is concerned with the precise conditions, imposed by the consumption function and the acceleration principle, under which the movement of the economy at any moment towards higher levels of income, consumption, and net investment can proceed exponentially in such a way as to maintain in every successive unit interval some particular percentage rate of employment. This is Mr Harrod's theory. Both in its own right and because it underlies Professor Hicks's highly interesting business cycle theory, Mr Harrod's theory belongs to Calculable Dynamics. (Topic *15 → B*.)

A necessary feature of all 'self-sufficient' business cycle theories is some sort of delayed action. This may take the form of simple time-lags between associated changes of variables. Or the delay may consist in the time required for some process of accumulation, 'real' or monetary, to build up sufficient weight to break some resistance or overcome some friction. Or the time-consuming process may be psychological and consist in the accumulation of items of evidence whose total effect becomes suddenly convincing and releases action, or in the fermenting, as it were, of evidence already factually present in the minds of those concerned. Despite this common element, self-sufficient theories (those which do not have to invoke a non-economic event, special to each separate occasion, to explain the breakdown of each boom and the recovery from each slump) fall into two groups: the machine-like theories where those who give orders for augmentation of equipment are not enterprisers or decision-makers properly so-called but passive reactors to circumstances who learn nothing, true or false, from experience; and the theories where operations of the mind and its states play an explicit part. Theories of the former type belong to Calculable Dynamics, those of the latter type belong to the Economics of Uncertain Expectation. (Topic *16 → B, D*.)

With whatever intentions it may have been begun, Keynes's *Treatise on Money* of 1930 emerged as an attempted Monetary Theory of Employment and Output as a Whole. The attempt failed and was abandoned in favour of the radically different *General Theory*. Had the *Treatise* succeeded, the Theory of Money would have engulfed the Theory of Employment and staked a large claim in the field of Business Cycle Theory. A special conception of the nature of money is one of the ideas at the core of the *General Theory*, but this special conception is part of the wider context of uncertainty and human reactions to it, and it seems better nowadays to restrict Monetary Theory to its own more technical concerns. These show a fairly continuous spectrum from the esoteric extreme of the theory of the determination of interest rates to the opposite pole of the practical rules of banking. It is only in the framework of Aggregative Comparative Statics that the Theory of Money can give any reliable guidance about the effects of policy measures. But the question of the nature of money and of interest belongs essentially to the Economics of Uncertain Expectations. Thus the Theory of Money is assigned to C and D. (Topics *17*, *18* → C, D; Topics *19*, *20* → C.)

All the effects of budgetary policy, except the inflationary effects of a policy requiring large creations of money, would until twenty years ago have been thought to come within the Theory of Value. Particular taxes or tariffs affected particular types of income or particular prices, but the possible effect of large deliberate deficits or surpluses on the level of employment as a whole were not considered. It was assumed that the Budget ought always to be balanced as nearly as possible, and the question of the effect on the nation's consumption-function of income redistribution within a balanced Budget lay outside the available apparatus of analysis. The employment-effects and inflationary or deflationary effects of Government finance belong to Aggregative Comparative Statics, the effects on particular prices and incomes to the Economics of Perfect Adjustment. (Topics *21*, *23*, *25* → A; *22*, *24* → C.)

Has the foregoing any relevance for the organisation of lecture-courses in Economic Theory? It seems to me that if all the topics, under their traditional names as used in the right-hand side of the accompanying scheme, that are still acceptable in a modern course, are simply presented as parts of a unified body of doctrine, the student who tries to form a picture of the whole will be puzzled and confused by the apparent contradictions. The left-hand side of the scheme seeks to provide a double *ordering principle*, according to which each topic would find a place on each of two scales, on one according to the degree to which it involves dynamic time, and on the other according to the degree to which it involves expectational time. These scales could be arranged as rectangular axes (Fig. XVI 2).

When a student asks: Is such and such a theory *true*? we have to inquire whether he means: (*a*) Are the stated assumptions of this theory mutually consistent and are they sufficient to entail as logical consequences the inferences which the theory purports to draw from them? or (*b*) Do the stated assumptions of this theory conform with observed reality? A careful separation of different types of theory according to one or more characteristics of their assumptions may help to make clear that while the answer to (*a*) is a matter of fact, the answer to (*b*) is a matter of individual judgement and may even be said to involve some element of aesthetics.

The scheme described above is concerned with the epistemological relations of the topics (numbered *1* to *25*) and the subjects (lettered α to θ) with each other. The temporal sequence and grouping of these topics in a teaching syllabus is a separate question.

What purposes are served by teaching economic theory? One of them is to illustrate the idea of deductive argument. We ought perhaps to say that the purpose is to teach people to argue rather than to teach them to think, for genuine creative thinking and the solving of essentially new problems proceeds by a blind groping or threshing about with unexplainable kaleidoscopic flashes of insight. In this aspect economic theory is a substitute for mathematics, able to appeal to types of mind for whom a logical process is elusive in the abstract but be-

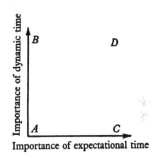

A   Economics of Perfect Adjustment
B   Calculable Dynamics
C   Aggregative Comparative Statics
D   Economics of Uncertain Expectations

Fig. XVI 2.

comes seizable when given content and concreteness. It is for this reason that the proposal to require students of economic theory to have a previous mathematical preparation must be judged entirely misguided. Economic theory should be a vehicle of mathematical habits of thought, the capsule enclosing and disguising what would otherwise be distasteful. If a student has a taste and aptitude for mathematics, he will either study mathematics for its own sake without ulterior motive, or he will be led naturally to study it by seeing the need and use of it in his study of economic theory. There are no unwilling mathematicians, and the attempt to manufacture them is foredoomed to failure. Now the most clear-cut, precise and elegant propositions in economic theory, capable of being presented with the brevity and cogency of a geometrical proof, are no doubt those of the Theory of Value and Distribution, and it seems accordingly proper to begin the student's serious study of economic theory with this.

The second main purpose of teaching economic theory is to provide the student with a means of making sense of what happens in the real world. If he can find some resemblance between the circumstances of a real situation and the assumptions of some theory whose structure he has grasped, he will have the satisfaction of being able to impose, in his mind, some structure on the unfolding of real events. He will be able to 'explain' them to himself. Thus if his specialized study of economic theory is to occupy two years, the first of these years should perhaps be in some degree self-sufficient and provide means of understanding the main aspects of a closed economic system. To the Theory of Value it might add a not too sophisticated treatment of the Theory of Employment (the Keynesian topics *11* and *12*), the Theory of Money (in the more institutional sense), and the Theory of Taxation. This group of subjects constituting the student's second year (the first year of specialized study) could be labelled 'Statics'.

Upon the foundation thus laid in the second year, the third year could build the more intricate subjects and a more sophisticated and conceptually difficult treatment of those already begun. The Theory of International Trade involves no fundamental notions which the student will not have already encountered, but it involves very complicated patterns of interdependent quantities, which do not lend themselves easily or safely to the 'bit at a time' method. Business Cycle Theory requires some use and understanding of difference equations, the mathematical tool for dealing with time-lagged functional connections, and is founded on Employment Theory and Monetary Theory. The third year is plainly the right place for these subjects β and ϵ. The Theory of Public Finance, where theory marches with Applied Economics, is a subject mainly for the third year. And at the very end of that year certain esoteric matters, such as the Theory of Investment Decisions, Social Accounting, the Leontief matrix, and the Theory of Games can be broached so far as time allows.

XVII

ECONOMICS AND SINCERITY*

What does an economist mean when he says, regarding such-and-such a theory, 'I believe it' or 'I do not believe it'? Can he formulate a single, precise, and unambiguous test which will confer on any theory that passes it the right to be used without misgiving for all and every one of the professional duties laid on the economist? Ought he to impose on himself a code which, if there is some theory that he disbelieves, would forbid him to base policy recommendations on it, to teach it, or even to use it in his own thinking? What are the particular kinds of temptation to which the economist is exposed, and in what, precisely, does the successful rejection of these temptations consist, and what kinds of self-denial does it involve?

When all life's questions are answered for any one of us, life itself will surely have ceased to hold for him any interest or purpose. Are we then to say that so long as a man finds a theory interesting he does not yet believe in it? And if we constrict the notion of belief to this extreme degree, are we therefore to forbid him to act upon, teach, or think with any theory that he still finds interesting? An absurd and artificial dilemma, perhaps you will say. But if it be once admitted that a theory which we take invariably, absolutely, and unquestionably for granted, and which we regard ourselves as having explored to the uttermost so that all its implications, and the consequences of acting on it, are known, could have no power of stimulating thought and indeed would be incapable of being any longer the object of thought, it follows of necessity that all the theories which have any active role in an economist's mental life and in his work must be ones that he can still cast doubt upon, can question and suspect, can feel to be incompletely worked out, and to hold unknown possibilities for good or evil when used as the basis of policy. To use only what we perfectly believe is therefore practically and essentially impossible. If to base advice upon, to teach, and to spend time in thinking about, things that we do not perfectly believe is morally wrong, the economist must shut up shop, must resign from his life-work and cease, as such, to exist. In what sense and in what degree, then, are we justified in using theories that we do not fully believe?

* *Oxford Economic Papers*, new series, vol. v (1953), pp. 1–12.

The very attempt to define an ideal and perfect degree of belief, in the sense of a willingness to commit ourselves wholly and unreservedly to some theory, to accept the consequences of applying it in any and every set of circumstances, shows that the concept is useless as a test of a theory's fitness to be used and taught. Perfect belief in this sense would require the perfect theory, able to interpret every situation, to predict the consequences of every course of action, to fit perfectly as a component mechanism into the great engine of human knowledge and link up economics with psychology, technology, anthropology, history, politics, ethics, and philosophy without loose ends. To call such a conception a theory is almost a contradiction in terms. Let us then ask what are the essential and inevitable limitations of theories in general; what is their true nature and proper purpose; in what respects they can be superior or inferior; and whether there are any absolute tests, or any tests adapted to circumstances, which will tell us whether or when a given theory may be honourably invoked or must be repudiated.

In making a theory we begin by selecting some features from amongst all those that the world seems to present. Deliberate rejection and neglect of a part of reality is, then, part of the process of theory-making, and at the very start we have an immense disparity between the simple and poor pile of materials out of which the theory will be built, and the measureless wealth and complexity of detail afforded by whatever part of the field of phenomena we may have marked out for our operations. Now our chief guide in making this basic and all-important selection is tradition and historical accident, or, at best, the intuitive genius of one or two men living in a remote time when, superficially, human circumstances were vastly different. Why does the economist repudiate any suggestion that he should become an engineer, a chemist, or an expert in agriculture? Why does he say that technology is none of his business? Does not the wealth of nations intimately depend on these very kinds of knowledge, and the growth of that wealth upon advances in them? Who drew this frontier where it stands today? Economics is not a natural science, pure or applied, but a human science, you will say. Why then does the economist say that psychology is none of his business? Do we say that economics is concerned with men's preferences, choices, hopes, fears, beliefs, decisions, imaginings, motives, behaviour, and yet say that the inner truths about the working of their minds are none of our business? When a man chooses in the market-place, he is a fit object of study by the economist, but not when he chooses in the polling-booth. Ethics is not for the economist: economic man must play his queer game according to the rules, not presume to discuss them. The rules, indeed, are changed for him from time to time; sometimes he is rationed, sometimes not; sometimes he is exhorted to exercise patriotic restraint, at other times to exercise patriotic abandon; sometimes to save, sometimes to spend; it is very confusing for him when the rules are changed in the middle of the game, and all the good habits carefully conditioned into him from his youth turn out to be bad habits, and then perhaps good habits again, just when he has conquered them. But the economist must only allow himself a side-glance at the springs of that history-in-the-making which necessitates all this. Who drew these frontiers where they stand today?

But does it matter if the materials for the theory are chosen according to an ancient and an arbitrary canon? Indeed it does, for these materials have got to be built up into a machine that will work, a pattern that will make sense. We may remember the disaster that overtook the Sleeping Princess in the fairy-tale, simply because her parents had forgotten to invite to the christening party one of the most powerful fairies. If our selection of materials for a theory leaves out of account some powerful factor, all our plans based on that theory are liable at any moment to go astray. Sooner or later the princess will prick her finger; the trifling accident, unnoticed at the time of its occurrence, will set off a train of consequences which our inadequate theory has not warned us to be on the look-out for.

Let us sum up this first stage of our argument. Economics is a field of study enclosed within arbitrary boundaries. These boundaries are not part of the nature of things. No doubt after 175 years we can say that they correspond to a consensus of powerful minds. If the physiocrats failed to set economics off on a different path it was, perhaps, because its actual path was the true highway. Nevertheless these boundaries are artificial. Is there any natural discontinuity between a man's economic motives and conduct on the one hand, and, on the other, his conduct as politician, scientist, philosopher, poet, lover, or mystic? It is fair to ask, I think, whether the builders of economic theories are not in these days unduly conservative and somewhat tradition-bound in their choice of materials.

Having chosen his materials, the theorist proceeds to fashion from them a variety of structural members, a collection of ideas or concepts with which to build his theory. The economist has thus carved out such things as perfect competition, general equilibrium, the stationary state, marginal productivity, liquidity preference, the enterpriser or taker of decisions in face of uncertainty, and so forth.

Each of these is designed to reflect some feature of what the economist observes, and does reflect it more or less faithfully. But now there is a second process of selection to be gone through. Like the misguided amateur of horology who has taken his watch to pieces, the economist finds that even in his restricted box of tricks there are far more pieces than he can contrive any use for in any one attempt at reconstruction. Some of the concepts are mutually incompatible and some are seeming duplicates with recondite but essential differences. Must we then admit that we can construct a number of entirely different models to explain one and the same world? Like a small boy who has thrown his cricket ball through a window, the economic theorist offers a variety of mutually contradictory explanations. I think it can justly be contended that modern economic theory does not show one picture but many highly contrasted ones, maintaining none the less that they are all likenesses of the same reality.

If, when he button-holed the Wedding Guest, the Ancient Mariner had propounded the question 'What is a theory?' perhaps his harassed victim might have answered, 'Well, it's something that tells you what to expect in the circumstances; when things happen that weren't happening before, a theory makes you feel you are still in a familiar world; a theory tells you what to do to get desired results.' And I think this answer, considering the adverse conditions in which the *viva* was conducted, might at least have earned a pass mark. Seen in this light, a theory looks extremely practical. It is plainly the most essential of all tools for dealing successfully with one's environment in space and time. Yet in another light a theory has nothing to do with reality. It is an abstract deductive system, perfectly exemplified by a modern version of Euclid. Here we start with some words or other symbols which we do not define. We then make a number of statements about the ways in which these un-defined things can be related to each other, taking care that these postulates are not mutually contradictory. Then we proceed to draw out the logical implications of this set of postulates, we work out, that is, what the postulates say *in effect*, beyond what they say patently and explicitly. Now suppose we can find amongst the phenomena we observe in the external world some that seem to be related to each other in the ways that the undefined entities are assumed in our abstract deductive system to be related to each other, and suppose we assume that this structure of relations between phenomena is invariant. Then we must conclude that all the theorems which are true of the undefined entities in our abstract system are also true of the observed phenomena of reality. What we have done is to assume a structural identity between the two patterns: the logical pattern of ideas in our abstract system, and the association, concurrent or in temporal sequence, of certain selected types of events in the external world. Now it is a common experience to find that amongst our friends Harry resembles John, and John resembles Alfred, but Alfred does not seem at all to resemble Harry. The reason is evidently that while, for example, Harry and John are alike in features and colouring, John and Alfred are alike in voice and manner. We cannot hope to find an abstract structure simple enough to give us a feeling of imaginative grasp and familiarity, and yet comprehensive and subtle enough to account for the limitless variety of detailed pattern in the unrolling tapestry of historical events. We have to choose between theories each of which accounts for some features and not others. To see what sort of consequences this has, let us consider some of the types into which economic theories fall.

There are many different cabinets each with its own set of pigeon-holes amongst which we can distribute economic theories. There is the cabinet which divides them into *general* theories and *particular* theories. But we must be careful. The word 'general' can here mean either of two quite different things. It may mean that, within some context of thought (perhaps very limited), all possible types of situation have been provided for. This is what it means in the title 'The General Theory of Employment, Interest, and Money'. Or it can mean that the theory to which it is applied is one where everything in the whole economic world is explicitly admitted, and shown, to depend on everything else. This is how we are using the word when we say that Walras constructed a theory of 'general equilibrium'. It is in this second sense that 'general' theories stand over against 'particular' theories. Each kind has its own dangers. A particular theory builds an insulating wall round a small piece of the economic system and declares that nothing which happens inside that wall shall be deemed able to set up waves which can pass outwards through that wall and, being reflected or even amplified by contact with what lies outside, to come back through the wall and affect what is going on inside it. Thus, for example, we often regard the supply conditions and the demand-conditions for a particular commodity as independent of each other. We justify this in either of two ways. We may say: 'Only a very minute percentage of those who demand this commodity are also those whose services help to supply it, and whose incomes, in consequence, depend partly on how much of it is sold in unit time, and at what price.' Or we may say: 'Those who are demanding this commodity *today* will not, by offering higher prices and buying larger quantities of it, be able thus to affect their own incomes until *tomorrow*. Thus *today* demand and supply in this market are independent of each other.' Now the former argument is very well for such particular commodities as do not bulk large in any one person's budget. For them clearly the incomes of its suppliers will be in total only a small fraction of that total of incomes whose variations could shift the demand curve for the commodity. But it will never do to apply it to the market for labour, as those theorists used to do who thought that a fall in money wages would cause more people to be given employment. When we are tempted (often with ample justification) to use a particular theory, we ought to make sure that the insulating wall does not enclose so large an area that jangling and disturbing echoes will come back from what lies within the wall. General theories, on the other hand, may make the solution of special problems so difficult that thought is paralysed and we are prevented from reaching some valid conclusions. It has been said that the economist, by too drastic use of simplifying assumptions, 'may fail to see the wood because he has cut down most of the trees'. General theories, by contrast, tell us too little about too much.

Another cabinet divides economic theories into static and dynamic. A static theory describes a state of affairs which, once attained, nobody would have any incentive to alter. It is a conception which owes much more to physical analogies than to psychological insight. Nobody, so far as I know, has yet written that chapter in the history of economic thought which would explain how 'equilibrium' came to be a technical term of our subject and would trace the part this word has played and the meanings it has borne in our literature. But perhaps it is not too fanciful to suppose that the immense prestige and ascendancy in men's minds which mechanics, and in particular celestial mechanics, came to possess during the seventeenth, eighteenth and nineteenth centuries must have suggested to economists the search for some simple and all-inclusive principle to explain the structure of their world. Impressed first of all by the physical constraints which nature and geography imposed on the satisfaction of men's abiding needs, they turned then to those needs themselves, and in the opposition between desire and scarcity they perceived the principle of *balance*, of the ultimate compromise which nobody could alter to his advantage. Implicit in the idea of equilibrium is that of stability, an inherent tendency of things to recover their 'balance of power' adjustment if any change in the governing conditions, the bounty or parsimony of nature and men's own desires and knowledge and institutional arrangements, disturbs it. Now to say that things have a tendency to recover an equilibrium is to say that they have a tendency to seek one: if the notion of stable equilibrium truly fits some aspect of reality, we have an explanation not only of rest but of movement. Economists have indeed sometimes come to believe that a tendency towards an equilibrium is part of the nature of every economic system, and that in seeking to explain movement, that is, why the system occupies a different situation at the end of each successive unit time-interval, we need only discover what shift in the governing conditions has made a movement necessary, and what it is that prevents the adaptation to this shift from being instantaneous. But once it is admitted that adaptation need not always be instantaneous, we have brought in the idea of time-lags between events and their consequences. And this idea is dynamite for the believers in a universal tendency to equilibrium.

Beginning, perhaps, with Wicksell and his rocking-horse analogy, some economists, most notably Professor Frisch, have sought inspiration in the behaviour of physical systems with quite different results from those of the equilibrium theorists. They have looked at mechanical and electrical systems whose natural and inherent response to an impulse is to *oscillate*. The time-lag is the key which unlocks this door and permits the economist to play with wave-motions of every kind. And what may well amaze him is the simplicity of the assumptions that suffice to provide us with damped, undamped, or anti-damped oscillations by a slight adjustment in the numerical value of one coefficient. Functional connexions of the simplest and most obvious kind are all we need assume, provided the connexion is between variables at different dates. But if small changes in the numerical values of parameters can so radically affect the behaviour of the system, is it not of prime importance to find out what are the actual values of such parameters in existing economic systems?

Economics in the older-fashioned sense finds itself nowadays rather in the position of a legitimate monarch of retiring disposition who finds his authority challenged by the dynamic personality and boundless ambitions of a young brother, newly grown up and of somewhat doubtful pedigree. Econometrics, if we date its birth from the founding of the Econometric Society in 1930, is now twenty-two years old, and claims the throne by its descent from economics, mathematics and statistics. To an avowed legitimist this seems an inflated claim. As for the application of mathematics to economics, what of Cournot, Marshall, Wicksell, Edgworth and Fisher, to say nothing of Walras and Pareto? As for statistics, what of Tooke, Newmarch, Stamp and Sir Arthur Bowley? What, we might ask, is there new in econometrics except its name, which attains, as it were, the second degree of portmanteaux-ism by eliminating one of its essential *m*'s: surely it should be ECO/*NOMO*/METRICS, or better, perhaps, metro-economics? However, this insinuation is not fair. There *is* something new in econometrics; something that is not to be found in mathematical economics in the sense of Marshall's Appendixes, nor in economic statistics as understood by the great compilers of the past. Mathematical economics is the expression, in rather general analytical forms, of hypotheses concerning the essential structure of the economic organism and the drawing of inferences from it. We are content to write $y = f(x)$ without specifying the precise sequence of operations denoted by the symbol $f(\ )$. But the econometrician is *not* content with this. He wishes to write out in full an equation, not merely with all its parameters explicitly represented by letters, but with actual numerical values assigned to them. And how right he is to want this. Professor Hicks has reminded us that if the numerical value of the coefficient which expresses the dependence of current net investment on a single earlier change of output is altered from a trifle less to a shade more than some critical value, the result will be altered from stability to explosion. In economics, quantitative as opposed to mere qualitative thinking is essential, and the econometrician is amply justified in seeking to test and to quantify the hypotheses of the qualitative economist (and this term includes the mathematical economist) by reference to recorded facts. Yet the econometrician has suffered painful shocks and disastrous disinflation of his claims. What did he tell us about unemployment in the post-war transition? Why does he speak pompously of 'incomplete information' when all he means is uncertainty, that familiar spirit who walks with us everywhere? Does the econometrician realize that his references to 'incomplete information' imply that there can come within human reach and ken something that could properly be called 'complete.information'? And does he realize that omniscience has not, traditionally, been claimed by mortal man, at any rate in his more sober moments of decent humility? Small wonder that this ὕβρις has sometimes fallen into the pit. For this phrase 'incomplete information' betrays a gross and cardinal error: the belief or supposition that, in real life, a man can ever know whether or not his information is complete. Does there not come to us, upon the echo of this phrase, a faint ripple of Homeric laughter rolling down from Mount Olympus?

The only problems where information can be known to be complete are those of the pure mathematician, the class of problems, that is to say, which we expressly define as being entirely unrelated to the world of external observation. The econometrician is an applied mathematician: for him there never will and never can be information known to be complete. The forms of the functions which he has fitted, with great labour and an ingenuity which we must all admire, to data supplied by observation, to data, that is to say, about the past, cannot be guaranteed to hold in the future. Economics is not physics, it is psychics, the study of men with all their capacity for learning and experimenting and inventing and imagining. We are bound to applaud the econometrician for seeking to put numbers in place of letters in the formulae supplied to him by the theoretical economist, but we must warn ourselves that these numbers are not eternal truths.

We have glanced at the nature of theories and considered its bearing on the ethics of employing them. Let us turn for a moment to their genesis. I have nothing to say of the unaccountable spark which fires new thoughts in a man's mind and gives him moments of almost painful excitement. I wish only to consider what happens to a theory when it becomes the common property of the colleagues and pupils of its originator to the third and fourth generation.

What are the merits and the dangers of an oral tradition? It is, I suppose, a sign of greatness in a university faculty or department, or at least a source and sign of prestige and evidence of time-honoured respectability, to be able to claim an oral tradition. The two great examples that spring to mind are those of Cambridge and Vienna. How does an oral tradition come into being? Surely it must be founded by some thinker of superlative achievement who is also an able and assiduous teacher. He must also, no doubt, be fortunate in his pupils, some of whom, if the tradition is to gain influence and momentum, must approach him in intellectual stature. This will assure the doctrine of a sufficiently prolonged vitality and widespread renown for it to become established and respectable, a staple of text-book diet and a yoke under which all future students will have to pass. But more is needed. If the master had no pupils, the doctrine would become part of the literature but would not hang in the sultry air of lecture rooms and impregnate the very furnishings of those where seminars are held. If he had only pupils of high originality the doctrine would be too rapidly transformed and developed to be properly called at any time a tradition. There must be a host of lesser men, able to receive and to impart the doctrine but not to improve it. These will give it stability of form, will make it gradually easier for pupils to understand, will rub off the rough edges of its original formulation, and polish it to become a presentable, civilized item of the teaching economist's stock-in-trade.

Which parts of this process are good and desirable, and which are bad? The bringing to bear on any doctrine of the searching light of able, leisured, well-informed common-room discussion, over many years and by a great number of perfectly disinterested men, must tend to discover weaknesses and elucidate assumptions, to ensure that the assumptions are mutually compatible, to elicit clear definitions and reveal ambiguities, to drive out infelicitous terminology, to refine, simplify and clarify verbal expression. So much for what happens in the evening. *In vino veritas*. But what of the morning? Then the teachers must teach. They must present the doctrine as something worthy of being studied, grasped, learnt, and acted upon. They are no longer impartial critics but purveyors of a commodity. Moreover, they may feel themselves to be guardians of a tradition. They can permit themselves to offer pious emendations of classical texts, but not to embark on wholesale heresy. Thus the doctrine will tend to become fossilized. Some of its assumptions will cease to be mere assumptions in the modern, formal, non-committal sense and become Euclidean 'self-evident truths'. Finally it may be asked: 'why have an oral tradition?' Are men too lazy, or too much afraid of criticism, to put their thoughts on paper? Economists ought to be a guild of craftsmen, not a priesthood with mysteries.

I have one more topic to broach concerning the genesis of theories, and it is this: ought those of us who embrace economics as a life-work to feel entitled to specialize to no matter what extreme degree, to concentrate all our powers and affections upon one narrow tract or upon one single kind of work? Is it right that those whose inborn urge and aptitude is teaching (I mean teaching in the strict sense, the art and practice of imparting and eliciting ideas, of sowing thoughts and garnering enthusiasms, of implanting skills and shaping minds) should be encouraged to devote themselves wholly to this, or (to see the matter in a harsher light) should be so burdened with teaching duties that they have no time nor reserves of strength for anything else? Is it right that those whose bent is the gathering, sifting and sorting of facts, and their compilation in orderly array, should never be compelled to lift their heads from their Holerith cards and let their minds run free upon the philosophy of what they are doing? Is it right that those whose strong magic is locked up in the hieroglyphs of confluence analysis and factor analysis should never be called upon to explain themselves to us others, so that in fact they would have to explain what they are doing to *themselves*? Ought theory to compartmentalize itself so that the grower of business-cycle roses never looks over the wall at the vegetable marrows of monetary theory with their vast inflations, or peers sourly at the grapes in that hot-house, the theory of value? I do not think these exclusivities (for this word I salute *The Times* fourth leader) can be good either morally or intellectually. Can it be good for our moral fibre to be always free to do just what we really enjoy doing? Ought not teachers sometimes to be given an enforced rest and made to research, and ought not researchers to have thrust upon them at intervals an unwanted holiday and be made to teach? But whether or not it is good for our characters and our self-respect to be faced sometimes with tasks that do not lie on our chosen track, with the unfamiliar and the formidable, I cannot doubt that it is good for the freshness and the richness of our minds. The professional expert tends to be a man who knows what cannot be done; the amateur, free from such inhibitions, sometimes just goes and does it.

May I turn finally to the question of how theory should be expressed? One aspect of this is the choice between literary, diagrammatic, and algebraic or analytical modes of thinking and of communication, but a frontal attack on this theme would require a book rather than a paragraph. I can only strike it a glancing blow in pursuing a rather different quarry.

It is the ambition of some economists to establish their subject's claim to be a science. However that may be, the *exposition* of an economic theory is an art, and in art, according to some experts, we are faced with a conflict and a competition between the claims of content and of form. How real is this opposition? Are form and content like guns and butter at present, the one needed to preserve the other but none the less compelled to elbow it out? What is the scarce resource for which they compete? Is it the writer's nervous energy and powers of concentration, or is it, more fundamentally, something to do with the structure of a sentence or the design of a chapter, which structure cannot (so it might be asserted) accommodate at one and the same time the thought in its purest essence and the adornment needed to give it grace and power of fascination? Let us seek light on this from some analogies. An architect drew attention recently to a surprising contrast, which I will express in my own words in the form of a question: Which was the more beautiful, the Victorian age's imitation gothic buildings encrusted with ornaments and turrets, or its utilitarian suspension-bridges with their cobweb strength? The content, so to speak, of a steel bridge is its strength. What gives it that strength is nothing other than its form. In pure mathematics is it not true that content and form are one?

Economics is essentially a mathematical subject, for it treats by logic of the relations between quantities. I am far from suggesting that its arguments can only be handled by means of a formal notation using the symbols of algebra or the calculus. Economic theory, mathematical by its very nature, can yet often be best expressed in words. But the verbal statements must then strive to compete, in exactness, lucidity and economy, with the symbolic statements that could replace them. For the verbal statements too (can we not argue?) meaning and form are inseparable.

I have listed exactness, lucidity and economy as the first essentials of expository prose. I do, indeed, think that these three qualities are the ones we ought most to strive for, seeking precision first of all since here in particular the oneness of form and content must reside. A thought can have no public existence save in virtue of the way it is expressed. Some of us may think primarily in mental images or form-phantasms, we may possess the power to make the arcs and ogives of our diagrams curl, shift and unbend, shrink and expand, in a verbal silence in the mind, arguing with ourselves purely by means of a visual imagination. But to convey these thoughts to others we must resort in part at least to words, and the shape of our sentences will be taken for the shape of our thoughts. To convey these thoughts at all, however, to get anything across, we must be lucid. People sometimes speak as though precision and clarity were one and the same. This is a mistake. The painful contortions of legal phraseology are necessary and justified because only thus can the framers of laws say exactly that which they mean. These strivings for exactness make the statute book unintelligible to any but a lawyer. Lawyers, however, are driven to these extremities because they are deprived of one powerful device which the theorist can call in aid: abstraction. The lawyer must expect to have his meanings 'twisted by knaves to make a trap for fools'. He cannot simplify and select the objects of his discourse by means of definitions. He cannot draw up the rules of his game before he consents to play it. For the theorist it is different. The things referred to in his theories are not men and women of flesh and blood, unsimplified, passionate, cunning, mercurial, devious, incalculable, but are mere chess-pieces, their possible moves and powers exactly known. To be both clear and precise at the same time is possible for the theorist, and to fall short in this is to be second-rate. Thirdly, there is economy. The good sentence contains not a wasted word. By this I do not mean that a word should be left out if *nearly* the same meaning could be expressed without it. The subtlest nuances, the most impalpable distinctions, are within the theorist's rights, and he must not be accused of prolixity merely because he has elected to bind elusive thoughts with many verbal strands. Nor need we think that economical prose is necessarily plodding and flat-footed. The athlete's leanness is one secret of his speed.

There is a well-known saying that 'knowledge is power'. It would be at least as true to say that 'language is power'. It is not only the professional spell-binders, the politicians and dictators, the leader-writers, the novelists, the poets, priests and prophets, for whom a silver tongue is the indispensable vehicle of their magic. We also, humble economists, working, as some think, in the mere kitchen of the palace of culture, are entirely dependent on the power to compress our thoughts into the mould of words.

Have I given the impression in all this that I think of the economist as a mere dabbler in ideas remote from the realities of life, a spinner of fine webs of thought that break at a touch, a player of meaningless games with symbols, a verbal juggler, and an oracle of more than Delphic ambivalence and obscurity? I did not mean to. The great economists have been moved as surely by a hunger for truth as any natural scientist. Pure curiosity, the desire to know for the sake of knowing, the sheer inner need to understand, is what has impelled them. Like the philosophers, they have been subject to their temptations. They have sometimes fallen in love like Pygmalion with the beauty of their own creations, and allowed elegance the ascendancy over realism. Sometimes they have succumbed to the lure of paradox and made things needlessly difficult in expression. Some economists, lesser than the greatest, have been dazzled by the flash and glitter of their own algebraic swords as they whirled them in the ritual dance of formal analysis. Yet on occasion these sharp tools alone could cleave the Gordian knot, and the list of the greatest economists includes a high proportion who have in some degree been also mathematicians: Cournot, Marshall, Wicksell, Pareto, Edgeworth, Keynes and Irving Fisher are enough to tell us this.

And finally, what of the economist's right or duty to offer counsel in the practical contingencies of the nation's life? Being sure that he does not know everything, being certain only that nothing is certain, ought he to be silent? The class of economists are like a ship's crew who have been wrecked in a swirling tide-race. Often a man will hear nothing but the roar of the waters in his ears, see nothing but the dim green light. But as he strikes out his head will come sometimes well above water, where for the moment he can see clear about him. At that moment he has the right to shout directions to his fellows, to point the way to safety, even though he may feel sure that next moment he will be again submerged and may then doubt whether after all he has his bearings.

XVIII

WHAT MAKES AN ECONOMIST?*

To be a complete economist, a man need only be a mathematician, a philosopher, a psychologist, an anthropologist, a historian, a geographer and a student of politics; a master of prose exposition; and a man of the world with experience of practical business and finance, an understanding of the problems of administration, and a good knowledge of four or five foreign languages. All this in addition, of course, to familiarity with the economic literature itself. This list should, I think, dispose at once of the idea that there are, or ever have been, any complete economists, and we can proceed to the practical question of what arrangements are likely to provide us with men who will feel not wholly confounded when an important economic decision confronts them.

Thoroughness in attacking this problem requires us, I think, to start by considering the nature of theoretical knowledge in general, then the character and the scope of economic theory in particular. Having seen what kind of intellectual tasks the economist is required to perform with what material, we can hope to discern the kind of aptitudes and attainments that will give a schoolboy or girl the promise of doing well in economics, and advise his schoolmaster about what the pupil should do with his years in the sixth form at school if he decides thus early to look forward to a university degree in economics. To the end of persuading some boys and girls of high ability to look at this possibility, we can show what claims economics can make as a cultivation of the mind and as a background for the administrator and the statesman. And at last we can ask what ingredients the university itself should pour into the mould thus provided by nature and the schoolmaster.

The business of creating theoretical knowledge consists in describing structures which repeat themselves. Here I use the word *structure* to name the very essence of all knowledge beyond the mere memory of direct impressions from our surroundings. It is our common experience that such impressions are classifiable. To each class we give a name, and then we arrange these names in patterns, linguistic, geometrical, pictorial and so on, to indicate that impressions belonging to certain classes occur, in some sense, 'together', in

* Liverpool University Press, 1953.

logical, spatial, or temporal-sequential association. The suggestion that some particular associations are repetitive or, we may say, invariant, is called a law or a theory. The palaeontologist finds a bone of a certain shape, and his theory tells him that search in the locality will reward him with other bones, of whose sizes and shapes he has a mental image. Here we have structure in a very concrete and obvious form, that of a skeleton. The chemist weighs the water displaced by a piece of some solid, then weighs this piece. The ratio of the two numbers he gets puts him in mind of a whole group of impressions of various classes, colour, softness, ease of melting and so on, suggested by a theory summed up in the word 'lead'. The medical man notes his own headache and the dryness of his skin, and decides that it will be five days before he can work again; influenza is his name for a structure of impressions involving duration. I need not give more examples. We manage our lives on the assumption that under the infinitely various and changeful combinations of particular sights, sounds, scents, savours and sensations there is a dependable repetitiveness. This kind of invariance of structure is the subject-matter and necessary presupposition of all theory.

If what I say is true, the materials which compose these structures are words, symbols or images, and not things which nature gives us direct and ready-made. Some of these words are the names of classes of our impressions of nature, such as length, weight, colour; or of crystallized patterns of such impressions, such as gold, flame, man. Some of them are the names not of patterns of receivable impressions but of ghosts or fictions which play a somewhat analogous part in our thinking; gravity and ether for the physicist, gene for the biologist and so on. Lastly, some words are names of different ways in which our impressions of nature, or our constructs from those impressions, can be related, the ideas of spatial or temporal relative location, of equality or of greater than or less than, of logical equivalence or definition, and perhaps, more hazardously and elusively, of cause and effect. The phenomena, the classes or the patterns of impressions, having been distinguished, and the possible relations between them conceived, how do we know what relations to postulate between given phenomena? How are the essential shapes of our theoretical structures determined? From the infinite variety of possible shapes the choosing of a few to be tried and used is an act of imaginative and even artistic commitment of a kind which is as near as mortal man can get to ultimate creation.

Some of us may recall the words with which Victorian children were admonished to tell the truth:

O what a tangled web we weave,
When first we practise to deceive!

Any statement, whether we believe it to be true or false, carries implications far beyond what it explicitly says. What it says in so many words may not obviously conflict with some other statement which we accept. But when one or other of these statements is unravelled and interpreted and allowed as it were to grow from the acorn to the oak, so that some of what is latent in it is displayed, then we may find that the two statements in fact contradict each other. When we draw consequences from a set of premises we add nothing to what is already in the premises but merely make what is there more visible and thus easier to compare with other statements. If the agreement is unsatisfactory, we may decide to modify our premises and see, by drawing out the fresh consequences that our new assumptions yield, whether the coherence of our whole system of statements is thereby improved. Thus we seek progressively to satisfy one criterion of a good theory. Now this work of spreading out the content of a statement, of drawing out inferences from a set of premises, is the whole business of logic or mathematics. It is, as we all know, in its higher flights a business demanding very special aptitudes and rare kinds of insight, as well as intensive practice and much knowledge of certain stylized or crystallized forms of thinking, the formal mathematical methods which relieve our memories of part of the weight of long concatenations of argument. This exploration and mutual confrontation of hypotheses is as much a part of theory-making as the invention of the explicit hypotheses themselves.

The building-up of a body of theoretical knowledge calls then for two kinds of intellectual capacity and effort. One of these is imaginative, or as we may say creatively selective, and thus creative in a primary and radical sense; the other is analytical or logical, and thus creative only in a secondary, a corrective or completive sense. There is no doubt in my mind that the majority of highly gifted men are specially endowed in one or other of these ways and not in both; when a man has both powers in superlative degree we have an Einstein or a Keynes. The only point I would make here is that we must not suppose analytical power alone is sufficient to make a great theorist. Many men have studied economics whose capacity for handling mathematical tools was by no means inferior to that of Keynes; but they did not produce the Keynesian revolution.

From this glance at the nature of theoretical knowledge in general let me pass to the character of economics in particular.

Explanation is the relating of the unfamiliar to the familiar. The essence and prime purpose of theory or explanation is to show that a large collection of seemingly diverse and unrelated appearances is in truth merely a large number of different views of the same thing, and that thing itself from some viewpoints familiar. Thus, explanation seeks in a sense to reduce the mysterious to the prosaic, and diversity to unity. Now science as a whole will never be able to start its explanations from nothing and carry them through the whole of human experience. A part of that experience must be treated as belonging so essentially to the very nature of human consciousness that men feel no need for any truth interior to these direct intuitions. Science as a unity must of course seek the minimum such basis and on it build up all else step by connected step into a coherent picture of the whole cosmos and of human life. But it would plainly defeat the whole purpose of the division of science into distinct disciplines, if each of these attempted to go right down to the minimum intuitional basis. The chemist assumes that you know what he means by weight and volume, and for an explanation of these refers you to the physicist. The biologist assumes that you know what he means by carbon, hydrogen and oxygen, and for an explanation of these refers you to the chemist. The economist assumes that you know what he means by hunger and by fertility, and for an explanation of these refers you to the biologist. So there arises the question of the best place for the frontier between one discipline and each of the others, and this is peculiarly troublesome in the case of economics.

Some of us may remember a verse by Edmund Clerihew Bentley which explains the difference between geography and biography:

> Geography is about maps
> But biography is about chaps.

I doubt whether a geographer would accept the suggestion here that geography is not a human science; it is very largely concerned with human activities. But far more so is economics. Economics is entirely concerned with men's doings and arrangements, their wants and their means of satisfying them, their hopes and fears, beliefs, ambitions, conflicts of interest, their valuations and decisions, their governments and their material well-being. Economics emphatically is about chaps.

Many men have attempted to say in a sentence or a paragraph what economics is about; it is better, in my view, to begin by saying that economics is about human nature, human conduct and human institutions, and then to say which parts of this huge field the economist is willing to leave to others. Nevertheless, he must set up his flag at some particular spot in order to show the kind of ground he wishes to regard as his own; and I think there is still good reason for saying that this spot must be the market-place. Men's conduct and decisions can be influenced in many ways; by threats of violence or duress, by the firing of their spirit and imagination by rhetoric or by example, by the preacher's eloquence and the teacher's toil, or by the blandishments of lovers; but the simplest and most reliable, the commonest and the easiest, is to offer them something *in exchange* for what they are required to give or do; and the market-place, in the wide and rather abstract sense in which, of course, I am now using this word, is where exchanges of all kinds take place.

It is by coming together in the market-place that men are able to be *economical*, in the ordinary sense of that word. For it is there that they can find out what other men are most keenly anxious to obtain. If by a given sacrifice of ease and leisure I can produce any one of half-a-dozen different things, I shall do best for myself by producing the one that other men most eagerly desire; for that thing, of all the half-dozen, will elicit from them the most effort and sacrifice on my behalf; and thus by studying their interest I shall serve my own, and get the most possible satisfaction in return for a specified amount of effort; and that is precisely what we mean by 'economy'.

If this market mechanism plays a less predominant part today than it did forty years ago in answering the questions: How much work of this kind and of that shall be done? How much shall be produced of this stuff and of that? and: In what proportions shall each of these products be shared out amongst those who contributed in one way or another to their making? yet even today in Western countries it does most of the work of answering those questions, which express between them the core of what is agreed to be the subject-matter of economics. If, then, the economist takes up his stand in the market-place, he is correctly indicating where his interests start from. But they will lead him far afield. What he is watching there is human conduct, and questions will arise in his mind about human motives and human nature. Economists have sometimes come to believe that they can get little help, in understanding the economic aspect of men's actions, from the psychologist. Such a feeling cries out for the most searching examination, since it is on the face of it absurd. This attitude has indeed, in my view, been rendered completely untenable by the development of economic theory itself in the past 20 years. I do not suggest that the fault is all on the side of the economist.

Whether the psychologists can meet our needs I am not yet sure, but that we have needs that they ought to meet I am quite certain. Economics is concerned, solely concerned, with some of the manifestations of human nature, and psychology is the science of human nature. Somewhere at the heart of this estrangement there is a mistake which we must try to find. At any rate it is plain that on one side economics has a frontier with psychology, or rather, that there lies between them a no-man's-land crying out to be explored and appropriated, that we might call economic psychics. Here, in my view, interest should centre on the workings of the individual mind rather than on the total behaviour of huge human aggregates. We need, for example, to understand the processes of forming expectations and making decisions. The famous question of the form of the Keynesian consumption function rests upon foundations of individual psychology which no one so far has seen fit to explore as a psychologist. By what kind of psychic test does a man detect just that stage in the day's work at which the fruits of a further half-hour's effort will not quite compensate him for that effort? What scheme of incentives would make him postpone that judgement? A long list of other such questions will occur to every economist. Here indeed is a ripe field for imaginative research, if only the economists will haul up their iron curtain out of sight and seek appropriate help.

I said a moment ago that the market mechanism is no longer the only means by which the practical questions are answered: How much of this and of that shall be produced, by what means, and for whom? But since the manner in which these matters are decided is still the prime concern of the economist, he must study whatever it is that has partly ousted the market from this function. In Western countries the individual, nominally and ultimately at least, can still make his contribution to the answering of those questions, but nowadays there is much that he can no longer influence by a continuous direct pressure in the market, where the smallest details of his preferences could be signalled to his suppliers and make themselves felt; there is much that he can only affect at long intervals, in an exceedingly crude and uncertain way, by means of the electoral vote that he can cast for one big bundle of ill-defined, ill-assorted and changeable policies or another. The whole question of government: its nature, purpose, justification and detailed working, the source of the authority exercised by statesmen, the basis of society's claim to the individual's acquiescence in its decrees, the justice and admissible scope of the administrator's interference in his life—all this, in a country where the central government takes away from the citizens some two-fifths of their income and spends it on their behalf, must loom large on the economist's horizon, and it is plain that just beyond another part of the boundary of his subject there lies political theory. But a very large part of the whole study of government activities is actually inside his province, and perhaps we are already well on the way to that situation where the government, rather than the consumer or the enterpriser, will be the economic agent to which the economist will direct most of his attention. The revolutionary change which has come about since 1939 in the relation between the importance, in the economic field, of those impersonal market forces of competition which were the main concern of economists until the 1930's, and the importance of those radically different mechanisms by which the inarticulate purposes of a people are channelled and rendered explicit stage by stage via the polling-booth, the parliament, the cabinet-room, and the Whitehall department, has not yet had time to revolutionize our text-books. Still less has there been any recognition in them of that other but closely related revolution whereby the international exchange of goods has become a game for governments, a field for all the arts of diplomacy, negotiation and bargaining, calling for a combination of the talents of the chess-master and the poker-player. It may surprise those of my audience who are not economists to be told that one of the most important and radically novel contributions to economic theory that appeared in the past ten years was called the *Theory of Games and Economic Behaviour*, by John von Neumann and Oskar Morgenstern (Princeton University Press, second edition, 1947). No longer can economic theory be called the pure logic of choice. It is many things besides, and this book has brought into it the pure logic of strategy in the widest sense of that term.

The study of government is the study of institutions, and there are other human institutions, in all three senses of organizations, of practices, and of social inventions or devices, which profoundly influence the character and largely govern the outward forms of the economic process. The most fundamentally important of these is perhaps the device of money, in all its manifold aspects. The history of the evolution of money, I could almost venture to suggest, is a strand in the history of the growth of civilization second in importance only to that of language. Money began as a commodity, and has ended as a system of recording transactions and bringing every act of purchase and sale, of borrowing and lending, of working and producing and consuming, that takes place anywhere in the whole world at any time, into some degree of relation with every other such act. In its tremendous power and radical simplicity this tool of human advancement, money in its basic meaning and role of an accounting system, ranks surely next to the alphabet itself. If, then, such things as money and monetary habits, and all the intricate machinery which has been built on them, are part of the very fibre of man's civilized existence and are things of gradual and painful growth from primitive beginnings, ought not the economist to call in the anthropologist, the student of cultures and social machinery in a general sense, to aid him to understand these things?

Economics is concerned with man; with man as a creature capable of thoughts and feelings, of likes and dislikes, of hopes and fears, of invention and imagination. But, perhaps you will say, all this, no doubt, is what makes him human and distinguishes him from the brute creation; yet he is an animal, and in the last resort his life is conditioned and his survival determined by biological factors; his needs are bodily needs. What has economics to say of hunger, of the body's need for warmth and shelter, of the capabilities of muscles, of the physiological basis of fatigue? Are not these things relevant? The economist will agree that they are, but he will enter a caveat. The sum of human happiness is not arrived at by adding up calories and kilowatts, nor reckoning working hours per week. There are people, I am told (I find it hard to believe) who can see nothing in the dancing flames upon the hearth, whose hearts, if they have any, are warmed as well by a hot-water pipe as by all Prometheus' magic. To them, no doubt, an open fire is so many therms per hour wastefully supplied. To the economist the question how most *heat* can be obtained from a given quantity of fuel is irrelevant. He is only concerned to know how most *happiness* can be obtained from it. This happiness may be derived from bodily warmth, or from spiritual comfort and inspiration. Man is the measure of all things. Every object and occurrence that has economic significance derives it wholly from the relation of this object or event to man's desires and beliefs and valuations. Thus although, beyond yet another frontier of economics, there lie engineering, chemistry, agricultural science and all the gamut of technology, these things are not in themselves the economist's concern. The frontier here is clear and definite. This does not mean, of course, that the economist can dispense with *facts* from the technologist; on the contrary, before he can make economic statements of fact about particular industries in particular places, or give practical advice, he will need such facts in great quantity and detail.

There are yet two more directions in which the economist can look out from his own territory over that of other specialists, and here the frontier is again in doubt. For here he sees geography and history, one partly and the other wholly concerned with man himself. Whenever the economist is asked to give practical advice in the affairs of a nation or an industry, his thoughts will turn at once to his friend the geographer, without whose help he himself, *qua* economist, can say little to the point. All the physical and many of the human factors which should guide the location of industry are matters for the geographer. As for the frontier with history, there is a whole province in dispute. I have the impression that in the past the historians neglected it to their loss, and that it is the economists who on the whole have shown themselves apt to become historians, rather than the historians who have readily put on the spectacles of the economist. But from whatever source, economic history in Britain has gathered to itself a learned and ardent band of specialists, who reckon nothing impossible in their effort to recreate our past manner of life, and who will soon, I think, establish this branch of knowledge as an autonomous discipline.

As a necessary background for my problem—What kind of man or woman, with what aptitudes, interests and training, is likely to find in some aspect of economics a congenial study, an equipment for a career, and perhaps a field for original work?—I have tried to survey very briefly the ground that economics calls its own and the ground of other disciplines whose aid the economist needs or whose findings he must treat as data. Against this background, let me try now to set the scene of the selection and training of an economist, as it seems to me that these things should be done.

If a schoolmaster, tossing one night on his sleepless bed, were suddenly to realize that his insomnia was due to the pangs of conscience arising from his never having tried to prepare any pupils to become economists, or even given the matter a moment's thought, what advice should we give him in his effort to repair this omission? What tests, actual or within his own mind, ought he to apply to those of his pupils who had just completed their fifth form studies and so were now free to specialize, to see if they were likely to do well in economics? What qualities or performances ought he to look for when scrutinizing their results in examinations? Above all, what ought he now to encourage them to do with their last year or two at school? Ought they to begin the actual study of economics? Or are familiar themes the best for practising with that master-tool of all our thinking, that greatest organ of intellectual expression ever yet evolved, the English tongue? Ought they to be still sharpening their mathematical tools, or already trying, in an unfamiliar, subtle and treacherous subject-matter, to apply them? And, finally, if his decision is that he himself will not open to them the books of economics, but will yet tell them that such a subject exists, what account of it ought he to give? Ought he to make it seem easy or difficult? Are some notions of it indispensable furniture of every cultivated person's mind, or is it decorative but useless embroidery on the practical man's knowledge of the world? Can it be a vehicle of intellectual excitement and beauty, like pure mathematics, or is it only something that will help you to get a job?

The economist, like the teacher of nearly all other subjects, must open his heart to two kinds of pupil. He will, of course, hope to find sometimes the quiet flame of an inquiring mind, the true contemplative, even the bold seeker of adventures of the spirit who one day will be able to say to himself

libera per vacuum posui vestigia princeps.

But for the most part he must be content with those who will accept an economics course as an interesting way of learning how to build and exhibit arguments of their own, to test and perhaps demolish those of others, to interpret and make sense of a complex mass of facts, to see through the casuistry of special pleaders and the verbiage of propagandists; and a means of practising these arts in that context of life in which their own professional careers as business executives, civil servants, administrators, accountants or lawyers will be laid. There are, I think, two things that he can reasonably ask the schoolmaster to do. First, to bear economics in mind as a possible eventual outlet for the outstanding intellectual all-rounder with some leaning towards the arts rather than the natural science side. The boy who finds mathematics fascinating without, perhaps, marching through the school course with that instinctive and professional certainty that would mark him as an out-and-out mathematician; who betrays a connoisseurship of words and a delight in language, a gift for expression in English and a sufficient pleasure in the classical languages to awaken thoughts of scholarships, without really promising to become a Porson's Prizeman; who can find in every chapter of the history book the universal and eternal problems of man's dependence on his fellow-men side by side with his rivalry and conflict with them, and can see with the historian's eye the age-long empirical struggle to reconcile self-interest and enlightened compassion; who delights in maps and finds them, perhaps, more interesting than test-tubes—this is the potential real economist. Secondly, I ask the schoolmaster to realize that today our economics classrooms are filled with some of the best brains amongst the university's whole student membership. Ours is not the department where he can find secluded corners for those who are all-rounders in a different sense, and who, having never shown the slightest aptitude for anything whatever, are equally well fitted for all professions, and (I suspect him of sometimes having thought) might just as well become economists as anything else. A few such did on rare occasions in the past infiltrate the economics classrooms by a process that you, schoolmaster, will easily understand. They had shown their distaste for all the subjects studied at school, plainly they must try something else. But what is there? 'Ah', you said to yourself 'economics; besides, I have heard that it's a soft option.' You left us to secure our good students for ourselves. All your more responsive pupils had been good at something in particular; at French, perhaps, and if they felt they had already spent enough years upon that, still it would be natural now to try Spanish or Italian; or it seemed the obvious thing to go on with the history or the geography which your own enthusiasm had rendered absorbing. Thus many of your better pupils came to the university already pre-empted, in their own minds, by one or other of the regular school subjects, or allied subjects. Today, when the practical questions on which economists are supposed to give advice are so prominent in our national life, economics has by the end of school-days already secured a footing in many of the most enterprising minds amongst school-leavers. Our duty is all the plainer, therefore, not to let our subject be looked on as one where exact and rigorous thinking is a pedantry. Send to us, then, schoolmaster, as in recent years you have done, a share of your best pupils. Send us those whom, fifty or sixty years ago, when the range of university subjects was so much narrower, you would have been in doubt whether to advise to read classics or mathematics, and whose minds have something of the fineness and urbanity that a joy in Greek and its philosophers implies.

So much for the question what kind of young man or woman has the best hope of shining in economics. Now, what is the best use for the specialist years at school, what should be done in the sixth form? This is, I think, only a question of expediency and not of principle. But to answer it we must consider a question that perhaps should have come earlier in this essay. It is all very well to ask ourselves what kind of person can give most to economics, but we ought also to ask what economics can give to those who devote to it one or five or six of the years of their youth. In short, why study economics?

First, because as an ocean on which to practise the art of intellectual navigation, economics has fathomless virtues. It presents every kind of difficulty which any scientific study can throw up; the area to be charted is so immense and covers so many mysterious deeps that there can be no end to the work, however many may engage in it. Once he is launched upon this sea, a man's life work, if he be of the true scholarly temper, spreads away before him to his life's horizon. Some have found their way across this ocean by a patient following of the coastline from one set of landmarks to another, never having to grapple with more than a small part of the whole problem at any one time. These were the Marshallians, working in the tradition of the great English empiricists who distrusted vast structures reared upon a single supposedly all-conquering idea, and preferred a construction in the English spirit of trial and error, of many supports and a variety of building methods. Others, if I may return to my metaphor of navigation, believed, like Walras, that they had found a star to guide them across the ocean in one swoop. In the equimarginal principle, embodied in a system of simultaneous equations, they believed they had found a key to unlock the whole economic universe and explain everything. Their system was very beautiful, as well it might be, since it made in effect the tremendous assumption that every economic decision is a choice between perfectly apprehended alternatives. In their world, man knows what he is doing. But though it may seem absurd to explain human conduct in abstraction from human ignorance and fallibility, the so-called General Equilibrium Theory invented by Walras and developed by Pareto is one of the greatest creations of economists. It made unmistakably clear once for all that the whole economic world is *interdependent*. The ocean to which I have been comparing our economic world is an apt metaphor in yet another sense. We may think of every individual, every firm, and every government as a boat upon the surface of this ocean. Every movement made by any boat will set up waves which, after a shorter or longer time-lag, will affect much or little every other boat on the ocean. This conception of complete and all-embracing human interdependence is not one, I think, which occurs naturally to an unsophisticated mind. Yet what understanding of man's lot in this world, and of his own personal situation in a deeper sense, can any human being claim who has not grasped it?

Thus I claim for the study of economics two chief merits: First, that it is difficult, not, however, in the way that some parts of mathematics are difficult, because their proofs involve a tremendous concatenation of logical steps, but in the sense that the subject-matter of economics is elusive, subtle and complex to an extreme degree, because it is, in the last resort, the unsearchable heart of man.

Mathematics, maybe, teaches men to scale intellectual crags, where each ledge or handhold can only serve if it is part of a chain or ladder of such ledges; but economics teaches men to walk upon quicksands or to find ways to overleap them. Now this call for resourceful and daring inventiveness in the manufacture of concepts to reason about is very well indeed for those who are already well-practised in reasoning about ready-made familiar things which, although just as truly fictive as the notions of the economist, appear to be drawn more directly from observation. But to pile this added difficulty of finding the straw on top of the more ordinary labour of intellectual brick-making is, I think, too much to ask of those who are still at school. And for the second merit of economics; this is, that it teaches men who are about to embrace some policy or course of action, to bear in the back of their minds the warning that this step will affect, much or little and sooner or later, everything in the economic universe; this again, I think, is an idea more acceptable and assimilable by somewhat mature minds. Thus it is my own feeling that the schoolmaster, having seen with all his care and energy to the sharpening of the tools of thought and expression, should be content to see them exercised upon the natural sciences, and, except for geography, should leave the human sciences to the student's university years with their better opportunities for free and leisured meditation and their, perhaps, more developed scepticism.

And so to the university course in economics. The first task of the university teacher of any liberal art is surely to persuade his students that the most important things he will put before them are questions and not answers. He is going to put up for them a scaffolding, and leave them to build within it. He has to persuade them that they have not come to the university to learn as it were by heart things which are already hard-and-fast and cut-and-dried, but to watch and perhaps to help in a process, the driving of a causeway which will be made gradually firmer by the traffic of many minds. The ordinary student can perhaps contribute little to this except by striving to say clearly what are, to him, the unsatisfactory things, the gaps and puzzles, and the incantations that hide some secret he does not share. But this he can only do by thinking, and once he has begun to do that with a feeling of freedom and a sense of independent experiment and exploration, he is already a worthy member of the class.

It may be wondered why I have undertaken this long discussion of what economics is about and what subjects lie next it in the great fabric of human knowledge. Economics is like a country of the plain, lacking sharp natural frontiers within which it could pursue a self-contained existence, and the greater versatility that this calls for in its citizens, who, because of the constant intellectual traffic with their neighbours, have to be able as it were to speak several languages, poses a serious problem for the designer of the syllabus. There is one problem in particular, which has been a cloud of steadily growing blackness upon our horizon for many years. This is the question of how far, and how, economists should become mathematically literate.

No one nowadays would deny that economics is an essentially mathematical subject, even in the old-fashioned sense of mathematics as a discipline concerned always in some way with quantities, for the business of economics also is to reason about quantities. But this is far from saying that all economists should equip themselves to use the formal notations of algebra, the differential and integral calculus, matrices, the theory of sets, and so on. There is much to be said for acquiring some mathematical insight and technical competence, for as 'he moves easiest who has learned to dance', the pedestrian tasks of the economist will be performed with all the more grace and efficiency if he has practised something demanding a formal elegance of procedure, while the ready-made tools of thought which mathematics provides will save him as much trouble as a vacuum cleaner saves the modern housewife. But let him beware of putting his vacuum cleaner on the mantelpiece as an ornament. The kinds of mathematics that economists use are humble and utilitarian, seldom of a sort to arouse the thrilled interest of the mathematician. However, the mathematically trained economist is exposed to a more subtle and far more serious danger than that of mere barbarity in the presentation of his argument. This arises from the domination of applied mathematics in the past by classical dynamics. The world which we explore in that well-known chapter on the dynamics of a particle is a wholly deterministic, predestinatory world, where, and this is the nub of the matter, there is no real or significant distinction between past and future. The astronomer feels as certain that a total eclipse of the sun will be visible in Cornwall in 1999 as he does that a total eclipse was visible in Birmingham in 1927. But the writer of the text-book of classical particle dynamics feels more certain even than the astronomer; he feels absolutely certain just where his particle will be at any given instant, for he has excluded by assumption every possible accident which could interfere with its career. Can the economist reasonably analyse the conduct of men and women, on the supposition that those men and women believe themselves to know for sure all the relevant consequences of their actions? It is a cardinal fact of human life that we do not know the future, we cannot calculate the consequences of our actions but only guess them. A world without uncertainty would be an utterly inhuman world, of a character which we cannot imagine, and which some have very plausibly suggested is actually logically impossible to conceive and self-contradictory. The assumption of perfect foresight makes nonsense of economics, and yet it is so natural and obvious an assumption for the economist trained in classical dynamics (as some great economists have been) that some have sometimes actually made it unconsciously. Now, of course, the physicist of today has greatly modified the views that his grandfather held in the nineteenth century, about the nature of determinism in the physical world. Let me quote to you a passage from a recent article in the *Times Literary Supplement*:*

Do not the 'social scientists'—the psychologists, political scientists, sociologists and *par excellence* the now almost completely symbolical, formal and econometrical economists—groan and travail for a nineteenth-century certainty of 'laws', two generations late, just when the most advanced physical scientists are rounding the bend towards chance, uncertainty and all fortuitousness?

I am delighted, as some of you will understand, to hear someone telling the economists, in effect, that they should regard uncertainty as the very nerve and essence of their subject, or great parts of it. I myself have been telling them so for a dozen years and more. My only doubt about the statement I have quoted is whether our friends the natural scientists are in truth as far round the bend as the anonymous writer says. The Heisenberg uncertainty principle, even as interpreted by Sir James Jeans, does not, I think, involve for physics anything which can be easily recognized to resemble the consequences that human ignorance of the future has for economics. Indeed, habits of thought derived from statistical procedures, or from the statistical interpetations of determinism to which the 'uncertainty principle' has driven the modern physicist, can be as dangerous for the economist as the outlook unconsciously induced by classical mechanics. Statistical methods are a means to increase knowledge, not a means for analysing or describing men's feelings and conduct in face of true, irreducible uncertainty, which can be ascribed in the last resort, if to nothing else, then to the ultimate impossibility of their ever knowing whether or not, in any particular case, they have all the relevant information. The econometricians

* 5 September 1952, p. 1.

have invited rebuke by publicly declaring that only the present crudity of their techniques (which they will improve) prevents them from telling us in advance what future months and years will bring. There are great scientific tasks for econometrics to perform, but to confound science with prophecy is an unworthy blunder.

Let me, then, try to state briefly my own faith in the matter. Mathematics must be the servant of economics and not its master. The kinds of mathematics required (statistics apart) are relatively workaday ones, and when the occasional cry is heard that some particular branch of economics calls for some new branch of mathematics to be invented, we must not think that even if this appeal is gloriously answered by the mathematicians, anything will be fundamentally changed. The important and practical questions are, first, whether the modest equipment of mathematical conceptions and methods which is all that most economists have time or good reason for aspiring to, should be taught to them by mathematics teachers quite separately from their course in economics, or whether this instruction should be infiltrated into the economics course itself so that mathematical notions and their economic applications and illustrations are inseparably interwoven; and, secondly, if we opt for a separate course in mathematics for economists, whether this should precede the main attack on economic theory, as a necessary preparation for it, or whether the need for mathematical equipment should be allowed to arise in the students' minds as they grapple with their economics course, and should be satisfied by a series of mathematics lectures very carefully dovetailed into those on economics so that each need is met as it arises.

To require students who abandoned algebra two or three or five years ago and have never heard of the calculus, to embark suddenly on an intensive year's cold-blooded instruction in these things, before they are allowed a glimpse of the need for them in economics, is, it seems to me, as though one should ask a man to swallow a table-spoonful of coffee-berries and then pour a cupful of hot water down on top of them in the hope that the two ingredients will somehow get appropriately mixed up in his inside. Half the difficulty in teaching the art of manipulating symbols to those who are not natural symbol-riggers is that it seems to them a purposeless game whose rules cannot be understood. If, in spite of your best efforts, you are always offside for no reason that is ever made clear in a game where the goal-posts are invisible, you are bound to lose interest in the affair. It is in order to make the goal-posts visible that I think we should interweave the two courses, letting the need for some mathematical notions arise in the economic context and satisfying it on the spot. We need a text-book, and it should be a book of economics which insinuates mathematics, not a book of mathematics illustrated from economics.

I have discussed the aptitudes and interests, the types of personality, the aims and objectives, the methods of selection and of training, the syllabuses and curricula, that contribute to the making of an economist, but there is one thing I have not mentioned. The good economist is like a bottle of wine. He must begin by having the luck to be laid down, as it were, in a vintage year, when he himself and his class companions are the high-quality stuff in which ideas and theories ferment and discourse sparkles in a glow of golden light. But this is not enough. He must mature.

INDEX

Made in the USA
San Bernardino, CA
27 January 2019